KIM IL SUNG
AND KOREA'S STRUGGLE

KIM IL SUNG AND KOREA'S STRUGGLE

An Unconventional Firsthand History

Won Tai Sohn, M.D.

Forewords by In Kwan Hwang *and* G. Cameron Hurst III;
Introduction by Samuel S. Song

McFarland & Company, Inc., Publishers
Jefferson, North Carolina, and London

LIBRARY OF CONGRESS CATALOGUING-IN-PUBLICATION DATA

Sohn, Won Tai, 1914–
  Kim Il Sung and Korea's struggle : an unconventional firsthand history / Won Tai Sohn ; forewords by In Kwan Hwang and G. Cameron Hurst III ; introduction by Samuel S. Song
    p.   cm.
  Includes index.

  ISBN 0-7864-1589-4 (softcover : 50# alkaline paper)

  1. Sohn, Won Tai, 1914–   2. Korea (South)—Biography.
3. Kim, Il-sæong, 1912–   4. Korea—History—20th century—
Biography.   I. Title.
CT1848.S585A3   2003
951.9504'092—dc21   2003007124

British Library cataloguing data are available

©2003 Won Tai Sohn. All rights reserved

No part of this book may be reproduced or transmitted in any form or by any means, electronic or mechanical, including photocopying or recording, or by any information storage and retrieval system, without permission in writing from the publisher.

Cover photograph (left to right): Dr. Won Tai Sohn, President Kim Il Sung, Mrs. Won Tai Sohn, May 7, 1992

Manufactured in the United States of America

McFarland & Company, Inc., Publishers
  Box 611, Jefferson, North Carolina 28640
    www.mcfarlandpub.com

To the memory of my loving father,
the Reverend Sohn Jong Do,
and my loving mother,
Park Shin Yil,
and to all those who dedicated their lives
to the liberation and independence
of Korea

Contents

Foreword by In Kwan Hwang   1
Foreword by G. Cameron Hurst III   5
Preface (by Won Tai Sohn)   11
Introduction by Samuel S. Song   15

Part I : My First Relationship with President Kim Il Sung

1. My Childhood   21
2. My Father, the Reverend Sohn Jong Do   28
3. Jilin, China   42
4. The Association of Korean Children in Jilin   51
5. My Thoughts on the Soul of the Nation   58
6. An Unfading Picture in My Mind   66
7. A Campaign to Get Ahn Chang Ho Released from Detention   71

Part II : Hearing the Legendary Tales of General Kim Il Sung

8. The Crossroads of Our Lives   81
9. An Article Carried in the Shanghai *Dagongbao*   89
10. In the Nagasaki Prison   97

11 Love Overcomes My Depression	103
12 To Testify to the Truth of History	110
13 The Road to Pyongyang	120

Part III : My Reunion with President Kim Il Sung

14 "Where Have You Been Only to Come Now?"	131
15 With the Mind of My Own Brother	138
16 A "White House" on the Mountain	152
17 For the Benefit of the People	159
18 Applying the Truth of Independence to Practice	165
19 Genuine Patriotism	174
20 A Noble and Clean Country	181
21 Unchanged Friendship	188
22 On the River Taedong	193

Part IV : President Kim Il Sung Is Immortal

23 Overcome with Shock by Unexpected News	205
24 My 80th Birthday Celebrated in Pyongyang	211
25 Leader Kim Jong Il	218
26 For Eternal Friendship	224
27 My Brother, Won Yil, Is Memorialized	232

Index	237

Foreword
by In Kwan Hwang

Today, despite the bitterness of the division, many extraordinary events are happening between the two Koreas, raising the hopes of genuine national reconciliation and of eventual reunification. It is inevitable that Korean reunification will be determined by the sentiment of the political leaders of the two Koreas. The late President Kim Il Sung was in many ways an epitome of much of the recent history of North Korea and his legacy will continue under the rule of his son, Chairman Kim Jong Il.

Viewed in that light, Won Tai Sohn's memoir *Kim Il Sung and Korea's Struggle* is a timely and important addition to the literature on the Korean struggle for independence. It gives a wealth of fascinating details of his long-lasting relationship with President Kim Il Sung. It is an epic that reads more like a novel than an investigative history. However, the book is not meant to be a sole memoir of Kim Il Sung, but rather a source for the various independent movement leaders under Kim Il Sung and others and their views on a variety of issues as well as political and military activities during the Japanese colonization of Korea between 1910 and 1945.

Beginning with his childhood in Jilin, China, with his inspiring father, the Reverend Sohn Jong Do, who was a Methodist minister and an uncompromising independence fighter against Japan, Dr. Sohn carries us forward to 1994 when President Kim Il Sung died. He portrays vividly an array of characters involved in the national liberation movement from his father Sohn Jong Do and his brother, Admiral Sohn Won Yil, founder of the South Korea Navy, later defense minister to Kim Hyong Jik (father of Kim Il Sung), to Ahn Chang Ho, Kim Ku, Yun Tong Ju, Oh Tong Jin, Kim Kyu Sik, Ri Jang, Ye Sun, Choe Tok Shin, Sin Chae Ho, Syngman Rhee, and Hong Tong Gun, along with many others.

Dr. Sohn reveals the close relationship between his father, the Rev. Sohn Jong Do, and President Kim Il Sung, who professed that "the Rev. Sohn Jong Do was the savior of my life." Dr. Sohn's own relation with President Kim Il Sung was that of elder brother, not merely a boyhood friend and teacher who shaped the course of his life until the last moment of President Kim's death on July 9, 1994. Thus, Dr. Sohn's rather subjective, emotion-laden but sincere and unswerving adoration for President Kim Il Sung is based on this lifelong brotherly relationship. It is no wonder that Dr. Sohn gives the same enthusiastic admiration to President Kim's son Chairman Kim Jong Il as "replica of his father."

Contrary to the unpopular sentiment in the South, Dr. Sohn repeatedly portrays President Kim Il Sung as "a sacred man carrying out politics through love and virtue and, as the father of the country would be, worrying and concerned about all sorts of affairs of his great family." Dr. Sohn thoroughly debunks the South Korean characterization of President Kim Il Sung as a Stalinist dictator and murderer by quoting Kim's statement that "the people are my God," which is undoubtedly drawn from the Juche ideology — the basic political philosophy of North Korean society.

Another striking feature running throughout this book of subjective and nostalgic memoirs is Dr. Sohn's unflinching determination and confidence in establishing once and for all the true identity of President Kim Il Sung as "the Tiger of Mt. Paektu," who fought against the Japanese army in Manchuria. He succeeds brilliantly in this effort by disproving the various theories of a false Kim Il Sung based on his own personal eyewitness accounts. On the other hand, any readers (especially South Koreans) looking for a more balanced and objective analysis of President Kim's long career may be somewhat disappointed for the incompleteness of the story and the blind faith–based interpretation. Nevertheless, if anyone wishes to learn more about the Korean struggle for national independence from Japan, this book contains many critical and useful activities and episodes of the independence movement that could be treated as primary sources for further research. This is no small feat.

Even though Dr. Sohn's book's original title *The Divided Korean Peninsula* seems to suggest that Korea must be unified soon, no major proposition for future reunification is discussed except for a few remarks about

Korea being influenced by the great powers and having to accept the inescapable geopolitical fate of a small country. A need for a strong Korea is emphasized repeatedly in order to ward off the great power intrusion through the use of Juche ideology, which is acclaimed by Dr. Sohn as the "Scriptures" of the nation of Korea and the "Gospels" for all mankind. This could be so.

However, the Juche ideology alone may not be sufficient to bring about national reunification, for it is a problem not only between the two Koreas, but also a problem between Korea and the four surrounding external powers—the United States, China, Russia, and Japan. Because of such multilateral interrelationships between Korea and the four powers, the best reunification formula will be the one that satisfies the needs of both Koreas and the four powers. In this connection an often used instrument of diplomacy known as "neutralization" would well serve as a maximum common denominator in achieving Korean reunification without producing winners and losers in the process. Current good examples of small countries which are surrounded by greater powers but enjoy national independence and prosperity are Switzerland and Austria. Korea has much to learn from those two countries.

The chief motive for a small country in being neutralized is to maintain its political independence and territorial integrity by preventing any neighboring state from interference, threat or aggression through the international framework of permanent neutrality. For the great powers, the neutralizing of small states is motivated by the desire to maintain peace among themselves through the erection of the protective wall of neutrality. The Korean adage "when whales [surrounding great powers] fight, the back of the shrimp [Korea] gets crushed" is the most fitting expression of the predicament of Korean geography, and the best way to guard the small shrimp against the big whales is to set up a huge protective stone wall (permanent neutrality guaranteed by the great powers as in Switzerland and Austria). A reunified Korea can fully exercise the Juche ideology and can transform the earlier practices of *sa dae ju i* (serving the great power China at one time) to *yong dae ju-i* (having the great powers serve the Korean interest).

An immediate question arises as to the methodology of achieving such a status for a reunified Korea. Since North Korea already in 1980 declared that the unified Democratic People's Republic of Korea (DPRK) should be a neutral country if not a permanent neutral country (which requires an international guarantee), it must have some understanding on the nature of permanent neutrality. However, there is a fundamental difference between the two Koreas. North Korea wants a neutral policy after reunification. Permanent neutrality implies a reunification process; that is to say, an adoption of permanent neutrality as a reunification tool to produce a neutralized and unified Korea simultaneously. In other words, the reunification process must be destined to produce a permanently neutral reunified Korea. It will be very difficult to achieve such a Korea, but it must be done in order to alter the course of Korean history. Korea cannot remain indefinitely the prisoner of its history of division.

There is another lacuna in Dr. Sohn's book with regard to the Korean War — the most cruel and devastating fratricidal event in the annals of the Korean people. There is little mention of it in this book, probably because he resided in the United States during the war and ever since. Also, it may be that the tragic topic is too sensitive, too painful, and too controversial to be brought out. In any event it should be remembered so as not to repeat it ever again.

One minor fault of the book is the lack of bibliographical references or footnotes, which would immensely enhance the quality of the content even though it is a personal, subjective memoir. This does not, however, lessen the appreciation of the laborious hard work undertaken by an elderly medical doctor.

Dr. Sohn concludes his memoirs of the close friendship with the late President Kim Il Sung by making a determined, solemn pledge to devote his remaining years to bridging the gap between the two Koreas by promoting mutual trust and by facilitating national reconciliation through his long years of life experience. This is indeed not only a patriotic, noble personal mission, but also a triumph of human spirit. Korea needs more people like Dr. Won Tai Sohn.

—I.K.H., September 2002

In Kwan Hwang, Ph.D., is professor emeritus of international studies at Bradley University, Peoria, Illinois.

Foreword
by G. Cameron Hurst III

The twentieth century wrought amazing changes in the lives of the people of Korea. We can get some sense of the scope of these changes by looking at three generations of an extended Korean middle class family. Consider, for example, the youngest generation, the grandchildren who may just be entering college. They have always lived in a stable democracy, and even the Kwangju Uprising occurred before they were born. For them, Korea has always been an affluent society, and they take for granted the nation's status as a global economic power whose products are household words around the world. They have always had the time and resources for international travel and leisure activities, and they are not fazed by the fact that currently four of the top ten money winners on the Ladies Professional Golf Association are Koreans.

Their parents know a different Korea altogether. Born just after the terrible destruction of the Korean War, these baby boomers know something of economic hardship, and they lived for years under harsh authoritarian rule. They don't take the affluent lifestyle of contemporary Seoul so casually because they know its costs. But it is the grandparents whose experiences are really mind-boggling. The well-dressed septuagenarian grandmother may outwardly seem fully at home window-shopping in Apkujung-dong, but she has seen much over her life. Her cohorts have experienced harsh Japanese colonial rule, occupation and division by two super powers, and a fratricidal civil war that developed into an international conflict and devastated their homeland; they have known long years of authoritarian rule and economic deprivation. In their youth, they could never have dreamed that they might one day live as they do now.

This unfortunate history for much of the twentieth century has given birth to a widespread diaspora movement, as Koreans have been moved, pushed or pulled by political and economic pressures to China, Japan, the United States, Europe, and Latin America. Ironically, the very circumstances that caused the diaspora have created millions of middle class Korean global citizens with bi- and tri-cultural social linguistics identities. It is common to find Korean or Korean-American students on American campuses whose families are located in Seoul, Honolulu, and Hong Kong, and find themselves at home in all those places.

Dr. Won Tai Sohn is the product of this Korean diaspora. Born in Seoul in 1914, just four years after the Japanese formally annexed Korea, he soon moved to Pyongyang with his family. He subsequently lived in Jilin, Beijing, Shanghai and elsewhere in China before returning to Seoul, only to leave for the United States in 1949 for medical training at Northwestern University. After that training, Dr. Sohn pursued a successful career as a pathologist in America. Now in his eighties and retired, he enjoys tending his garden in Omaha, Nebraska. His older brother, Won Yil, by comparison, spent most of his post-liberation in the Republic of Korea, where he served, among other posts, as the founder and first chief of staff of the South Korean Navy, Minister of Defense and ROK Ambassador to Germany. Dr. Sohn's extended family is now multi-national as well as multi-ethnic.

Dr. Sohn's new memoirs, published here for the first time, represent an important contribution to the growing body of Korean diasporic literature. His references deal mainly with the period of the 1920s and 30s, and thus his work joins a large body of works touching on the Korean experience under Japanese colonialism by such noted authors as Younghill Kang, San Kim, and others. Dr. Sohn's memoirs— he seems to remember clearly things that happened when he was only four or five years of age — are especially valuable for the light they seem to shed on the youthful background of Kim Il Sung, former head of state and Great Leader of the Democratic People's Republic of Korea (DPRK), or North Korea. Dr. Sohn also writes at length about the reunion of these two Korean youths some sixty years later in Pyongyang.

Kim Il Sung must surely be one of the most enigmatic figures of the twentieth century. Born in 1912 in Pyongyang long before it was the capital of the DPRK, Kim came to power very early in life. Already active in anti–Japanese activities as a youth, he became a noted guerrilla leader in his twenties. In fact, he was only thirty-three when he returned to Korea in the wake of the Japanese defeat in World War II. Soon he was swept into power under the Soviet occupation in the northern half of the peninsula, where he remained in firm control for a half-century until his death at eighty-two in 1994.

Kim Il Sung not only presided over the birth of a new nation in an old land, he was inextricably bound to the fate of North Korea. Perhaps to a greater degree than any other modern political leader, he may be seen as the full embodiment of the state. Indeed, Kim was more integral to state and society in North Korea than Stalin in the Soviet Union, or Mao in China. In Bruce Cummings' formulation, North Korea under the "Kim dynasty" is a form of socialist corporatism, with the Great Leader—"Great Sun"—at the core or nucleus of the state, from which everything emanates outward.* While many nations have created personality cults for their rulers, one is hard pressed to find a more enveloping one than that of the Great Leader. For North Korea, Kim was—and remains—a benevolent father figure, a genius, a sacred ruler who has, it seems, defied the theorists and managed to pass both his charisma and his genius along to his son Jong Il in the first communist dynastic transfer of power.

Yet what do we really know of the background of this man, who lived so long and held such sway over his society? Sadly, not very much. Several conditions have transpired to make this so. First, the isolationist stance of the regime has meant that Kim himself never traveled much beyond the borders of the DPRK, save for a few visits to Russia and China. And although Kim feted many foreigners in Pyongyang, few ever developed close enough relations to have learned much useful information about him. So non–Korean sources on Kim's background are virtually non-existent.

Second, most of the guerrilla comrades he fought with in the days of resistance against the Japanese are long dead, save the few that constituted the core leadership circle for so long. They are unlikely to share any information that would run counter to the official line. And finally, the intensive rivalry between the two severed halves of an old nation have conspired to work against the development of a fuller picture of Kim's past. The authoritarian nature of the Pyongyang regime has largely curtailed the development of a market of candid accounts of "My Life with the Great Leader" in the north, where the state has run a mini-industry in the careful cultivation of a personality cult. Official North Korean publications

---

*Brice Cummings, "The Corporate State in North Korea," in Hagen Koo, ed., State and Society in Contemporary Korea *(Honolulu: University of Hawaii Press, 1993), pp. 197–230.*

have concentrated on praising the path of North Korea's unique *juche* philosophy of self-reliance and honoring the genius of Kim Il Sung, while failing to credit anyone else with any significant contributions to the struggle against the Japanese or the building of the nation. There is really little "biography" in the acknowledged sense of the word, but hagiography abounds. Scholars outside of North Korea like Suh Dae-Sook have evaluated that body of work for what it is worth.*

And, in the south, the Republic of Korea, the creation and client of the United States during most of the Cold War era, adopted a strict anticommunism as a pillar of the educational system from the outset. Thus, for decades information coming out of Seoul regarding Kim Il Sung had to be as damning as the North's propaganda was effusive. Information on Kim given up by defectors from the north was also affected by the politics of polarity. For decades, it was impossible to say anything negative about Kim in Pyongyang or positive about him in Seoul.

The upshot is that very few people who have known Kim Il Sung well have ventured to put down in writing much about his past. Perhaps when and if we see a north-south rapprochement, let alone unification, and some liberalization of the political atmosphere occurs, there might be some chance at a more balanced view. But of course by that time, anyone who knew Kim well will long be dead, and the nature of the documents that might be "discovered" in North Korea will not likely shed a great deal of light on this man either.

In this context, Dr. Won Tai Sohn has come forth with this new memoir that purports to shed some new light on the life, or at least some phases of it, of Kim Il Sung. As teenagers—for much of the book they are thirteen and fifteen respectively—both the young men lived in Jilin, China. This area of Manchuria was a Mecca for Koreans fleeing the Japanese colony, and there they both attended school, Dr. Sohn primary and Kim Sung Ju, as he was then known, middle school. The two families shared ties before the boys developed their friendship in Jilin. Dr. Sohn was the second son of a well-known pastor and anti–Japanese resistance leader, the Rev. Sohn Jong Do. The elder Sohn was the minister and pastor of Jongdong Church, the largest Methodist church in Seoul, before moving to Pyongyang when Won Tai was just a very little boy. It was there in Pyongyang, according to Dr. Sohn, that the Sohn family became familiar with the parents of Kim Sung Ju, themselves Christian and active in the anti–Japanese movement.

---

*Suh Dae-Sook, Kim Il Sung: The North Korean Leader *(New York: Columbia University Press, 1988).*

In fact, Dr. Sohn attributes the decision of Kim Sung Ju to come to study in China to the efforts of his father, the Rev. Sohn, who seems to have taken a liking to the youth and developed an interest in furthering his education. According to Dr. Sohn some sixty years later when he met Kim Il Sung in Pyongyang, the Great Leader still recalled the kindness with which his father had treated him. As Sohn describes their conversation, Kim told him "the Reverend Sohn Jong Do is the savior of my life."

Most biographies of Kim contain little information about his youth, but Dr. Sohn's memoirs are vivid, and tinged still with a great deal of admiration for the young man. Hindsight, the old saying goes, is twenty-twenty, and Dr. Sohn, writing in his eighties, recalls being impressed with Kim Sung Ju from the beginning; and right down to their final meeting shortly before Kim's death, Dr. Sohn's admiration remains strong, as naïvely devoted to the man as though those sixty years had never passed. He seems to have seen the spark of leadership, the charisma that certainly goes a long way to explaining the incredible durability of the Kim legend, in the elder boy from the beginning. Speaking of Kim in their youthful days, Dr. Sohn wistfully recalls: "I cannot remember Kim Sung Ju merely as 'my boyhood friend.' He was my brother and senior ... the teacher who shaped the course of my life!"

China was of course an important staging point of the Korean independence movement, and the elder Sohn an important participant. Thus some of the most major figures in the movement move in and out of the lives of Sohn's in the 1920s and 1930s: Yi Kwang-su, Ahn Chang Ho, Sin Chae-ho, Kim Ku, and many others. But the hero of this memoir is really Kim Il Sung, to whom Dr. Sohn pays all tribute and praise, even going so far as to attribute to him the liberation of the Korean people from the yoke of Japanese colonialism: "It was President Kim Il Sung who had accomplished the national liberation for Japanese occupation which my father had aspired to achieve so earnestly all of his life...."

In fact, one of the more disappointing aspects of the memoir is that we really learn so little of the life of Dr. Sohn himself. How did a young Korean, raised in very difficult circumstances during the colonial period — his father died when he was quite young, having lost most of his money to support the independence movement, and his mother had to work hard to make ends meet — manage to get out of a poor and struggling South Korea right before the outbreak of the Korean War, come to the United States for a medical degree at a top school, and then make himself a career here in the United States as a pathologist. Sadly, this is not what Dr. Sohn has chosen to remember in his memoir, glossing over fascinating stories for which we long for more detail. Instead, he has determined to try and restore the image of Kim Il Sung in the Western world, where he has been the object of harsh criticism and his personality cult ridiculed in the press.

While Dr. Sohn has provided much very useful information about the early life of Kim Il Sung, what stands out is the extraordinary praise which he heaps on the Great Leader after their reunion when they were both in their eighties. Accustomed to Western and South Korean accounts of purported harsh and inept rule on the part of Kim Il Sung and his son, readers will likely shake their heads in disbelief at Dr. Sohn's assessment of the Great Leader and North Korean society. One reaction will surely be to question Dr. Sohn's critical abilities. Perhaps, however, we can read his text in a more positive light. Can we simply dismiss Dr. Sohn's glowing praise for Kim's leadership in the face of so much evidence to the contrary, or can we read these memoirs somewhat differently?

Outsiders have always tended to dismiss as incredulous the prose attributing everything that happens in North Korea, from victory in a ping-pong match to a rise in pig production, to the genius of the Great Leader, first Kim Il Sung and now his son. But behind the obvious fabrication and hagiographic prose which seems to be frozen in an early Cold War idiom we once associated with the cult of Mao, we surely underestimate the persuasive power of the charisma that Kim Il Sung seems to have projected. Dr. Sohn saw it and claims that so did his father. While it may be that the duration of Kim's rule owes more to coercion than persuasion, the degree to which the North Korean people felt deeply and personally attached to their leader is striking. Witness, for example, the incredible outpouring of love, affection and genuine grief at the state funeral following Kim's death in 1994. That a well-educated medical doctor, living in the United States for virtually all the time that Kim was building and administering North Korea, could maintain the same naïve childhood impression of his old comrade all these years—in the face of a half century of skeptical U.S. and South Korean writings—may tell us more about the man than we have been willing to admit.

—G.C.H., November 2002

G. Cameron Hurst III, Ph.D., is director of the Center for East Asian Studies and professor of Japanese and Korean at the University of Pennsylvania, Philadelphia.

Preface
(by Won Tai Sohn)

Having lived the life of an ordinary medical doctor, I remain unconvinced of my worthiness to leave memoirs to the world. However, as I have been advised by many people to write my memoirs, I resolved to do so.

It was when I was studying at a university in Shanghai that I first was advised to write an autobiography. One day while I was studying at the dormitory, I looked up at the sky listlessly and was unable to suppress nostalgia. My Chinese roommate, who had the surname of Zuo, touched me on the shoulder and asked what I was thinking about. Full of emotion, I told him about the deprivations besetting my motherland, how I had left my country at the tender age of seven, about the doubts surrounding the cause of the death of my father (an independence champion and Methodist minister), and the subsequent wandering life of my family. My roommate suggested that I should relate my life story as an autobiography, saying that it would be a history also of the suffering of my nation.

Unfortunately, I have witnessed, experienced and participated in the most trying periods of my nation's sad history. Because the life of a man can concurrently reflect the life of his nation, my memoirs might become valuable in communicating the true history of the national suffering. Until now, I did not attempt to write it because it was too excruciating for me to call back to memory those days full of wounds.

One evening, a short time after I had returned from North Korea where my meeting with President Kim Il Sung had ended our 60 years of separation, my wife and I went to a café frequented by intellectuals in Omaha, Nebraska. Korean compatriots of my acquaintance circled around our table and began to ask about my impressions of the North Korea of today. Some young people who were drinking at tables nearby soon joined with our group, apparently out of curiosity upon hearing mention of North Korea. One of my friends introduced me to them, saying, "This is Dr. Sohn Won Tai who has just returned from North Korea after meeting with President Kim Il Sung." They were students from South Korea who were pursuing their education in the United States. All of them seemed surprised by this information.

I told them briefly about my friendship with the president during our days in Jilin, about his long drawn-out struggle against the Japanese invaders in Manchuria, and how our relationship now had been resumed after a lapse of sixty years, both of us now being in our eighties.

Their comments indicated their confusion, their skepticism, and their realization that, strange as it might seem to be, they had grown up with the knowledge only of part of their country's history. "Is this true? It can't be a lie? We haven't been aware of it!"

My heart ached to realize that an entire generation of Koreans growing up in my homeland cannot distinguish between the true history and the false history of their country, or recognize true patriotism as opposed to the betrayal of their nation by collaborators with Japanese imperialists.

Some of those present earnestly urged me, "You must write your autobiography, come what may, Dr. Sohn. You are a witness of Korea's history and that of President Kim Il Sung. If you pass away, there will be no one who can tell the true history of Korea."

Thanks to the grace of Heaven, I have become an eyewitness to an unusual chapter in history, my life being linked to that of President Kim Il Sung from early youth until joined again when we were both in our eighties, a span of 60 years. In our reunion, the intimate feelings of yesteryears seemed even warmer and closer. In spite of the toll of so many years of wind and frost, President Kim Il Sung still was Kim Sung Ju, the boy who was so full of sentiment in his days in Jilin. I was particularly pleased to discover that this world-famous senior political leader still remained Kim Sung Ju, the great commoner, at heart.

It was not a waste of time for me to have been to Pyongyang in the closing years of my life. In an article about my visit to Pyongyang, the *Wall Street Journal* stated that "of the two friends, one had become a medical doctor and the other a dictator." The comment revealed the editor's lack of knowledge about North Korea and of President Kim Il Sung. The President Kim Il Sung whom I visited was not a dictator; he was a sacred man carrying out politics through love and virtue and, as the father of a country would be, was worrying and concerned about all sorts of affairs of his great family.

I saw with my own eyes how he had embarked on the road for national salvation in his early years. I am also aware how he had fought in the armed struggle against Japanese imperialism in the wilderness of Manchuria to win national independence for Korea. And I saw the nation he had built in the northern half of the liberated country. On that land were planted the seeds of true patriotism and the true history of the nation.

I placed my mind and body in the care of Pyongyang, as a man does on returning to his native home after a long and lonely journey full of agony. The behest my father, the Rev. Sohn Jong Do, had left for me, the cross I had carried steadfastly, from one end of the earth to its other end, was patriotism. It is a natural conclusion that my life, full of vicissitude, would find a place to rest in the land of President Kim Il Sung where true patriotism could be found. I have nothing to fear, even though I may be wrongly denounced as a sympathizer with or an ally of communism.

How can one think about Korea separately from President Kim Il Sung's struggle for national liberation? I believe that false politics may confuse people for a time but that false history will be eradicated sooner or later.

Thus I have come to realize that it is my duty to tell the true history to the rising generations. I think that by doing so I can live up to the affectionate feeling with which President Kim Il Sung regarded me as his own brother and as a true friend until the last moment of his life.

I hope you readers will understand the feelings of this old pathologist who cannot but speak and write the truth!

I am deeply indebted to Mr. Robert Lars Shannon for his expert assistance in preparing the manuscript. Special thanks are due to Dr. Samuel Song for his invaluable and detailed review of the manuscript, without which it might never have been published.

Won Tai Sohn, M.D.
Omaha, Nebraska
March 2003

Introduction
by Samuel S. Song

As a consequence of the Yalta Conference (February 4–11, 1945), Korea was divided by the United States and Soviet Union after World War II in August 1945. Prior to this division, Japan annexed Korea in 1910 by military and political power against the will of the Korean people and the Korean government. Japan's control over Korea was tightened after the First Sino-Japanese war (1894–95) and the Russo-Japanese war (1904–05). During the period Japanese troops moved through Korea to attack Manchuria. These troops were never withdrawn, and in 1905 Japan declared a virtual protectorate over Korea and in 1910 formally annexed the country. Taro Katsura served as war minister, then as prime minister (1901–06, 1908–11). During that administration, with the Anglo-Japanese Treaty (1902) and the defeat of Russia (1905), Japan emerged as the strongest power in the Far East and gained effective control over Korea. In the Anglo-Japanese Treaty (February 12, 1902), Taft-Katsura Agreement (July 29, 1905), and Portsmouth Treaty (September 5, 1905), Great Britain and the United States recognized that control. Katsura annexed Korea (August 22, 1910) during his term as prime minister (1908–11).

During the 20th century the most destructive, demoralizing wars and thirty-six years of inhumane Japanese military colonial rule over Korea claimed an estimated four to five million Korean victims that Japan has distorted and denied as if it had never happened. It has been almost sixty years since the end of Japan's occupation and colonization of Korea, and hence, the end of World War II in 1945. Japan declared unconditional surrender on August 15, 1945, only after the atomic bombing of Hiroshima on August 6, 1945, and again of Nagasaki on August 9, 1945. The anger among Asian people due to World War II crimes by Hirohito and many Japanese imperialists deepened with the deliberate exclusion of Hirohito from the death sentence list and other formal punitive terms by General Douglas MacArthur, the General Commander of the United States Occupation Army in Japan. Hirohito had commanded and led Japan into war, occupying the entire Asian region, other than Australia and New Zealand, until the end of World War II on August 15, 1945, and invaded these countries in the name of Dai Toh Ah Kyo Ei Ken (Greater Asian Co-Prosperity Sphere). Among colonized nations, Korea suffered immeasurably under harsh Japanese colonial rule over 35 years.

At the end of World War II, Korea was arbitrarily divided into North and South Korea as a temporary expedient; Soviet troops were in the north and American troops south of the line of lat. 38 N. The U.S.S.R. impeded all U.N. efforts to hold elections and reunify the country under one government. When cooperation between the U.S.S.R. and the United States deteriorated, trade between the North and South came to an end and severe economic hardship resulted, since the regions were economically interdependent, industry being concentrated in the north and agriculture in the south. The devastating Korean War (1950–1953) was the result.

Kim Il Sung and Korea's Struggle is a unique, remarkable autobiography of Dr. Sohn's frank description of his harsh life experiences and his humane, personal and family relationship with President Kim Il Sung from their early boyhood under autocratic military imperial Japanese colonial rule, perhaps the worst in human history. According to Dr. Sohn's personal knowledge of the late President Kim Il Sung and numerous newspapers, journals and published books, President Kim since his youth devoted his entire life to Korea's liberation, starting with fighting against the Japanese occupation army stationed in Northern Korea and China with outstanding strong patriotic leadership of the Korean People's Revolutionary Army. There has never been a book like this memoir of Dr. Sohn that describes the details of his intimate friendship since childhood, though interrupted, with the late President Kim Il Sung, the patriotic independence fighter against Japan. Previous biographical books of President Kim Il Sung describe only one aspect of his public life, based on collections of scattered data in the United States and Korea. This book contains invaluable and esoteric historical events such as Dr. Sohn's harsh life experiences as a son of the Reverend Sohn Jong Do, a leader of the Korean Provisional Government in Shanghai, and a patriotic independence fighter who saved the life of Kim Sung Ju, later to become President Kim Il Sung. Dr. Sohn also recounts the horrific memories of Japanese atrocities against Korean patriotic independence fighters, himself and humanity.

I have known Won Tai Sohn, M.D., very well since July 1992, during our meeting in New York City with two other members of the Christian Association for Medical Missions. We had passionate discussions about promoting medical assistance programs in the Democratic People's Republic of Korea (North Korea). All of our personal relations have primarily centered on our common interests of humanity and medical assistance programs to Pyongyang Third Hospital, with 500 inpatient beds and other medical facilities.

Throughout my life, I have rarely found a person with such a gentle heart as Dr. Sohn. I have always found him to be naïve, civil, affectionate, affable, humble, and courteous towards others. He is truly a man of integrity, humanity, courtesy, artlessness, simplicity, and purity. I believe those qualities were cultivated by his loving father, a Methodist church minister, the Reverend Sohn Jong Do. The Reverend Sohn devoted his entire life to philanthropy, patriotism and leadership of the independence movement. He also served the Great Commission in Korea and China for many years until his mysterious death in a hospital operated by Japanese on February 19, 1931, in Jilin, Manchuria, during a period of harsh imperial Japanese colonial rule. During that time, the Reverend Sohn saved the life of the young independence movement leader Kim Sung Ju from Japanese prison, leading him to eventually become President Kim Il Sung in 1948.

Unlike his late elder brother, Admiral Sohn Won Yil, the founder and the first chief of staff of the Republic of Korea Navy (South Korea) and later minister of the Department of Defense, Dr. Sohn spent his entire life as a devoted physician, primarily in the United States from 1949 until his retirement in 1986, after his cardiac bypass surgery. Dr. Sohn, now 88 years old, is a unique live eyewitness of contemporary Korean history in the 20th century. He details highlights in relation to the late President Kim Il Sung involving events of patriotic independence fighting — movements against brutally oppressive Japanese imperial military colonial rule over the people of Korea.

This book is the culmination of eleven years of Dr. Sohn's dedication to collecting and sharing the most prominent personal and historic events of the indescribably harsh Japanese treatment of Korean people in Korea, Manchuria, China and Japan. This memoir is not historic or political rhetoric, but a genuine account of an ordinary person, Won Tai Sohn, and his life experiences. For over 60 years, he had close personal relations with the late President Kim Il Sung, who had struggled from age 14 to his sudden death on July 9, 1994, to preserve Korean independence and leave a great legacy to his people through his great leadership and national sovereignty with self-reliance, the so-called Juche ideology.

At the request of Dr. Sohn, I have been privileged to have the opportunity to review his accounts and offer feedback for the final manuscript prior to publication. This book is essential reading for anyone interested in understanding true contemporary Korean history and the genuinely close relationship between Dr. Sohn and President Kim Il Sung, rooted in their harsh suffering and tribulations under Japanese colonial rule. Even more, this work will certainly shed light on real historical events and is a testament to the human struggle when a culture is in danger of losing its identity under the peril of another oppressive nation that brutally strips away the language, culture, heritage, customs, and traditions of its captive nation. I earnestly hope that this work will help promote understanding, reconciliation, confidence building, cooperation and prosperity between the Democratic People's Republic of Korea (North Korea) and the Republic of Korea (South Korea), leading to peaceful reunification of the two Koreas. This will also contribute to an easing of tensions and the process of peacekeeping in Northeast Asia and the rest of the world.

— S.S.S., March 2003

Suggested Reading:

Edward Behr, *Hirohito: Behind the Myth*, Villard, 1989; Edward Behr, *The Last Emperor*, Bantam Doubleday Dell, 1987; Herbert Bix, *Hirohito and the Making of Modern Japan*, Perennial, 2001; Eiji Takemae, et al. *Inside GHQ: The Allied Occupation of Japan and Its Legacy*, Continuum, 2002; Toshiaki Kawahara, *Hirohito and His Times*, Kodansha International, 1997; United Nations, General Assembly Fifty-fifth Session, Agenda Item 183, Peace, Security and Reunification on the Korean Peninsula, October 20, 2000.

Samuel S. Song, M.D., Ph.D., is a federal government retiree and is active in overseas medical missions and efforts for the peaceful reunification of Korea.

# PART I

My First Relationship with President Kim Il Sung

1

My Childhood

I was born in Tongdaemun hospital in Seoul, Korea, on August 11, 1914, as a son of a ruined nation. Korea already had been conquered by Japan and the sufferings of the nation were falling upon my family. In 1912 my father, the Reverend Sohn Jong Do, had been arrested on the implication that he had been involved in the attempted assassination of Katsura Taro. He served a term in prison and then was sent into exile on Jin Island.

Those days were rarely happy ones for my family, even after my mother, two elder sisters and an elder brother were able to live with my father after he was released from exile and had returned home. My father, the Rev. Sohn Jong Do, was the minister of the Jongdong Methodist Church in Seoul and our house was in the church compound.

The Jongdong Church was the parent and most authoritative Methodist church in Korea. The American missionary, the Rev. H.G. Appenzeller, had built it in the 1890s and served as its first minister. In those days all of the Methodist churches throughout the country were subordinate to the Jongdong Church. A considerable number of men of religious orders who were active in the missionary movement in Korea were linked to the Jongdong Church. The second minister, succeeding Appenzeller, was Choe Pyong Hon. The church's third minister, Hyon Sun, had participated in the Eastern People's Congress held in Moscow in 1922 as a representative of Christendom in Korea.

My father was the fourth minister of Jongdong Church and, as its leader, enjoyed the limelight in Seoul's activities. The church grew to more than 2,000 members and was the largest Methodist congregation in all of Korea. There was hardly room for the parishioners to stand at service, so eventually a building expansion project was undertaken to accommodate their numbers.

In his memoirs, my elder brother Won Yil recollects that he carried bricks during the building project, but I have no such memories because I was only three years old at the time. However, I do dimly recall that a tall, strange man came to our house and took a photograph of my family.

Many years later, when I was living with my children in Chicago, Illinois, I unexpectedly received a letter with a photograph enclosed. It was that family photograph of my father, my mother, my elder sister Jin Sil, my elder brother Won Yil, and me, a baby sitting in my mother's lap. Missing from the picture was my other elder sister, Song Sil, who was staying with my grandmother in the countryside at the time. My younger sister, In Sil, was yet to be born. This was a family photograph to be cherished. (This photograph can be seen in Chapter 2 along with other family photographs.)

The photograph had been sent to me by Dr. Youngho Choe, a postgraduate at Harvard University. He wrote that he had found it by chance while reading a type of "Who's Who" file of Korean people in the school library. There is no way of knowing how the photograph had been preserved in the Harvard University library over scores of years but without doubt it was truly a valuable discovery for my family. The photo showed me the house we had lived in and how my father and mother looked then. Time has taken away my beloved ones but the photo restored them to me in the world of memory. I surmise that the picture must have been taken just before my family left Seoul during one of the happiest, but rare, times for my mother when the whole family lived together.

Not long afterward, my father suddenly moved the family to Pyongyang on the eve of the March First Popular Uprising. Preparations for the uprising were growing to fruition. It was a bitter, biting winter cold spell. My father had been more engrossed in the campaign for independence from Japanese occupation than in his missionary work. In fact, he was one of the Korean patriots who drafted the Declaration of Independence. He did not appear in the public eye, however, because he was preparing to go to Shanghai with the Rev. Hyon Sun on an important freedom-related mission.

The Rev. Hyon Sun had been assigned to smuggle the Declaration of Independence out of Korea and convey it to United States President Woodrow Wilson. My father was going to Shanghai to expedite plans to send the Prince of Uichin, Ri Kang (the second son of King Kojong), to the Versailles Peace Conference where post–World War I decisions on freeing occupied nations would be made.

My brother, Won Yil, recalled in his memoirs that our family's move to Pyongyang was intended as deception related to that plan. We were able to leave for Pyongyang without difficulty except from the severe winter weather. My father had arranged to rent a house on the Taedong River but as soon as the family had unpacked our household possessions, he left for Shanghai, dressed in mourning clothes as a disguise. He kissed me and In Sil on our cheeks as we slept and, as he departed, told mother that he would be back soon. But it was a parting with no assurance that they would ever see each other again. In fact, it was the last time my father would see his motherland; he would never return again and would die and be buried in an alien, albeit friendly, country: Manchuria, China.

As part of the strategy, the Prince of Uichin had crossed the Amnok River disguised as a Chinese traveler. Riding in a third-class carriage, he made a successful crossing but then his subterfuge was discovered in Dandong, a Chinese town bordering upon Korea. Thus the plan to have the Prince go to the international peace conference from Shanghai was aborted.

Meanwhile, only my father was able to get across the border successfully, although his mourner's clothing was drenched with sweat, I learned some years later from stories told about the hazardous undertaking.

Following my father's self-imposed exile in Shanghai, my mother literally worked her fingers to the bone to eke out an existence for her family. She did sewing for a Christian hospital and was hired to wash clothes by other families. Still vivid in my mind's eye are memories of my mother, weighed down under a large burden of firewood, which she carried on her back, struggling through a narrow gate to get into our yard. She endured great troubles all of her life while supporting her husband when he was deeply engrossed in the independence movement. She never complained of the hardship as she raised her children with loving care and fostered their education.

After my father's departure, our house was placed under surveillance by the Japanese police. They often would summon mother to report for interrogation and the house would be searched time and again. Mother always remained composed despite this continuing harassment. She was really a courageous and high-minded person ... but how anxious she must have been for news about my father! Then one day, holding me closely to her bosom, she whispered, "I've had news from your daddy; he has arrived safely in Shanghai." Her eyes glistened with tears and she appeared to be very happy.

Without complaining, my mother trod that thorny road, seeking independence for Korea, shoulder to shoulder with her husband. Without her unwavering support, how could my father have devoted himself so completely to the independence movement? I still feel deep sorrow remembering how she struggled to provide for our family in spite of the mental agony and physical suffering she was enduring under the oppression by the Japanese.

Despite so many days filled with distress, my childhood somehow had some happy moments that I can recall. When my mother went to the hospital to work, she would leave two sweet potatoes in the cauldron as lunch for In Sil and me, and we would play happily together.

When I was young, I had a docile and retiring disposition and my mother would say that "several old men" were in my mind. In contrast, my elder brother, Won Yil, was more impetuous by nature and inclined to be mischievous. He and his playmates occasionally would raid the Rev. Mun's vineyard as well as the vegetable fields of Chinese farmers along the Pothong River, giggling as they nibbled away at their tasty loot. When they were stopped from getting into the theater by using discarded ticket stubs, they would attempt to get in by crawling through the ventilator window of the toilet room. Not all of their escapades left them unscathed; once, while chasing dragonflies and grasshoppers, they disturbed a colony of bees and received some painful stings for their antics.

We found pleasure in fishing from the banks of the Pothong River. One day I caught a silver carp which was larger than Won Yil's fish and he tried to snatch mine away from me. I eluded him, dashed home, and proudly gave it to our mother. She prepared a delicious silver carp soup for our dinner.

I took great delight in watching Won Yil and his teammates play soccer matches. How proudly I tagged after them with Won Yil's sports gear hanging from my neck, and what joy to eat cakes with them after his team had won a game! When Won Yil's Kwangsong Middle School soccer team emerged victorious in the West Korea tournament, I was as high-spirited as if I had won it myself. Actually, Won Yil was the star of the team. I was a first-year pupil at the school and apparently was as proficient in my studies as Won Yil was in sports. He told me some years later that I had won the first grade citation at the close of my first year in primary school.

The next move for our family was to a small straw-thatched house on Namsan Hill. A presbyter of a church in our new neighborhood would, in the future, become my father-in-law for he would beget a daughter, Lee Yoo Shin, who would become my wife.

Sungsil School, which I would attend, was only a short walk from our house. Mother, seeing the school building again, appeared to be troubled about something in her past. She said that my father had attended that school and, feeling a need to explain, added that she had experienced mental unhappiness while living in his family home, which my father had left after hearing about the doctrine of Christianity and becoming determined to learn more about it. I couldn't tell whether her sadness was caused by recalling those unhappy days or because she was missing father so much.

I later learned that Kim Hyong Jik, father of President Kim Il Sung, also had attended Sungsil School at the time my father did; apparently the relationship between my family and the president's had been established then. Indeed, that little school educated many independence fighters, patriots and progressive Christian leaders. Mr. Cha Ri Sok, once secretary-general of the Korean Provisional Government in Shanghai, and Yun Tong Ju, a patriotic poet who sang zealously about the soul of Korea, both were graduates of this school.

In addition to our modest dwelling, our neighborhood was graced by the imposing house of a wealthy family, which was surrounded by a high brick wall. We had laid out a flower garden in our front yard and we tended the flowers with utmost care. When the forget-me-nots, iris, rose moss and coxcomb were in full bloom and attracted swarms of bees and butterflies, our garden was a place of beauty for all to behold.

One day as I was returning home from kindergarten I saw that most of the flowers in my garden had been picked by someone. I climbed up the brick wall to discover that two girls were playing in the yard, pretending they were taking part in a wedding. They were festooned with garlands of flowers they had picked from my garden. I shouted at them, "You shameless robbers!" Startled and frightened, they tossed away the flowers and began to weep. Then I felt sorry to have spoiled their mood. I don't know why, but the image of the girls, silhouetted against the setting sun, the flowers adorning them, has remained in my mind's eye. It must have been one of the most beautiful and memorable impressions of my boyhood.

It would be correct to say that my boyhood actually had ended with the March First Popular Uprising. That morning my mother told me to lock the gate and keep the house secured. Then she hurried out of the house, carrying my baby sister on her back. Won Yil had left for somewhere soon after eating his breakfast.

Around noon a bell began ringing loudly at the Sungsil School. It had the sound of urgency and I rushed out of our gate and joined the people who were hurrying to the Pothong Gate. The Sungsil schoolyard was packed with people. A man was delivering a speech and, as he gesticulated to emphasize his words, he flung white sheets of paper into the air and they wafted over the heads of the people. The tracts were appeals to support the independence movement. Then the crowd marched toward the municipal building, shouting and cheering. Pinned among people, I was swept along with them.

The multitude was massed in front of the municipal building when, without warning, the fire department directed water cannons mercilessly into the throng. The people obstinately held their ground but then Japanese police suddenly opened fire into the crowd. A man in front of me fell to the ground, blood flowing from his throat. I was horrified at the sight of the man writhing in agony, his clothing drenched with his own blood. This, I came to realize as I grew older, was a typical picture of the fate of my motherland, my nation. His image appeared frequently in my dreams while my country writhed and groaned in agony under the brutal rule of Japanese imperialism.

My mother had participated in that demonstration and Won Yil also was among the marchers, waving the flag of Korea which he had prepared in advance.

I learned much later that Kim Sung Ju, who was born in a lowly straw-thatched hut, and grew up in Mangyongdae, had accompanied the demonstrators to the Pothong Gate, and that he and I actually had been within hailing distance then. Just as I had been horrified to see a human being shot down in cold blood, the youth who was destined to become President Kim Il Sung also experienced the shock of seeing, for the first time in his life, a fellow man bleeding to death on the ground beside him. He wrote later that it was the wanton cruelty he had witnessed in the village square that day which led him to his revolutionary decision that the brutes who fire at unarmed peaceful demonstrators must be defeated by force of arms because it would be fruitless to petition them to withdraw or to ask them to give Korea its independence peacefully.

I believe that destiny already had bound us together with the ties of kinship. From that time onward, the world appeared differently to me. No, the world had not changed; I had suddenly aged mentally without realizing it. Misfortune surely can hasten a child to maturity!

Mother would not dress Won Yil and me in the serge suits which were the Japanese school uniform. Instead, she made clothes for us, using homespun cotton cloth. We gladly wore those togs because we intensely disliked the serge suits the Japanese mandated as school outfits.

I had just started second grade in the Kwangsong Primary School when my family once more packed our meager belongings and moved to Jilin, China, in response to instructions in a letter from my father. It was delivered by messenger from Shanghai, where my two elder sisters, Jin Sil and Song Sil, already were enrolled in school. Won Yil and I were happy to accompany mother to Jilin because we would join our father there, but we also felt a tinge of sadness to be leaving our little town and the friends we had made.

I had planted the seeds from a melon I had eaten and now a few unripened melons, no bigger than a baby's fist, were hanging on the vines in our yard. Because we were about to move, I decided to eat them. I picked one and gave another to Won Yil. They were as bitter as quinine but I didn't want to throw them away. Was this because I had a premonition that it would be the last time I would be able to savor a melon grown on my native soil?

Probably not; I was too young to think that way. For instance, when In Sil asked where we were going, I said, "To Shanghai. We can sleep on a table; it will be interesting, won't it?" How else to describe the working of the mind of a young boy who would eat a bitter melon instead of throwing it away. Almost 70 years would pass, my hair turned gray, before I would walk on the soil of Pyongyang again.

2

My Father, the Reverend Sohn Jong Do

I went on a long journey by train for the first time in my life with my mother, Won Yil and In Sil. Mother cautiously packed our household goods to avoid being seen by the Japanese police and we boarded the train, being careful to evade their surveillance. The prospect of riding on the train was an exciting adventure for In Sil and me, two young and innocent children not fully aware of the intrigue, and part of our excitement was anticipating seeing our father again. I was not aware that I was leaving the motherland with no prospect of returning but, as the train rattled out of the station, I felt a pang of sadness to be leaving Pyongyang. Pyongyang was not far from Kangso, the home town of my ancestors for many generations; to me, Pyongyang was my home town. It was there, for the first time, that I saw the blood of my nation spilling onto the street and where I began to conceive a vague understanding of what my country meant to me.

As the train gained speed, I looked out of the window hoping to see the Pothong River, where I had gone swimming and caught that large silver carp, and the Kwangsong Primary School, where I had played, kicking a grass ball. Those childhood scenes fell quickly behind, leaving me only a few glimpses as I mentally said goodbye.

The train was buffeted by blizzards as it plodded through the mountains and the vast fields of an alien country, but the initial excitement gave way to boredom as we subsided into exhaustion. Then, at last, we arrived in Jilin, Manchuria.

The unfamiliar language of people dressed in unfamiliar clothing seemed threatening to our ears and eyes so In Sil and I clung tightly to our mother's skirt as we waited in the train station. Only a few minutes passed before a middle-aged man dressed in Chinese clothes approached us. He had a livid scar on his forehead which made a strong impression on us. He hugged Won Yil, In Sil and me in turn, and then tapped me on my forehead saying, "Oh, my! You've grown beyond recognition." He talked affectionately with mother who was shedding tears of relief and happiness.

We climbed into a carriage which the man had waiting for us. I felt comfortable and happy as we jolted and slewed along a road that was muddied from thawing snow. Soon the carriage stopped in front of a church in a suburban neighborhood and we were ushered into a house of Chinese architecture which adjoined the church. I fell down as I was trying to crawl up to the high Chinese floor but the man quickly lifted me to my feet and asked me if I was all right. I liked him immediately, finding him to be a kindly and obliging man.

I asked Won Yil in a whisper who the man was. Bursting into laughter, Won Yil replied, "That's Daddy, Won Tai!"

I looked searchingly at my father; he had gone into exile when I was very young and he appeared somewhat different from the image I carried in my mind from seeing him in a photograph which mother kept locked up out of the sight of others. The photo had captured the youthful appearance of his days as a Confucian scholar, a horsehair hat on his topknot. He was quite handsome, with thick eyebrows and glaring eyes. People who had heard his sermons would recall that they had been over-awed, feeling that those piercing eyes were reading their innermost thoughts.

My father was a man of fiery temper before he became a Christian, the son of a comparatively affluent Confucian scholar who lived in Ohung-ri, Jungsan subcounty of Kangso county, not far from Pyongyang. In 1902, at the age of 23, he was en route to Pyongyang to a take state examination when he happened to obtain lodging at a Christian pastor's house. There he learned about Western culture and the Christian doctrine.

Absorbed in learning the doctrine of Christianity, my father cut off his topknot and delivered himself from his nobleman's house. One can understand without difficulty that he could make such a decision, given his fiery temper and enterprising spirit. Unlike his ancestors, he was captivated by the new learning and plunged himself into studies of advanced social ideas and religion. Thus he had determined on his own volition to follow the ascetic path of a Christian and independence fighter.

Kangso, the home town of my family, produced a large number of progressive men of religion as well as patriotic champions of independence for Korea, my father among them. Ahn Chang Ho, who used the pen name of "Tosan," was one of the famous men born in Ryonggang, West Korea, which adjoins Kangso.

Recognizing that large numbers of renowned independence fighters were the product of the extraordinary spirit of the Kangso people, the Japanese police hammered an iron piling into the mountain behind the village, ostensibly to remove that spirit from resting there. I've been told that the Kangso people dug out the iron piling secretly and prayed to God to resurrect the spirit of the mountain that produced such famous men.

Apparently this was the reason the Japanese Governor General in Korea had assigned brutal policemen to serve at the station in Kangso. They became notorious as evil ones. When my brother, Won Yil, was arrested he was dragged to that police station and subjected to cruel torture. Kangso became even more famous because it had produced the Rev. Sohn Jong Do and Mr. Ahn Chang Ho, two of Korea's great freedom fighters.

After graduating from Sungsil School in Pyongyang in 1908, my father went to Seoul and attended the Hyopsong Seminary. In 1910, before graduating from the seminary and, by coincidence, on the eve of the annexation of Korea by Japan, he was assigned to take charge of a church in Jinnampho. In 1911, he was ordained as a minister and appointed roving missionary for Korean compatriots living in Manchuria, beginning that work while living in Harbin. In addition to that assignment, he put his heart and soul into the movement to free Korea from Japanese bondage and played an important part in establishing the Sinhung Military School.

In 1902, my father went to Vladivostok in the Maritime Territories of Russia. Approximately 300,000 Korean refugees were living in the territories at the time and he planned to do missionary work among them. Vladivostok, however, also was where zealous independence campaigners assembled. He met Sin Chae Ho there and they became friends. He also became involved in publishing *Haejo Sinmun*, the independence movement newspaper which was managed by Mr. Sin.

Katsura Taro, who later became prime minister of Japan, was visiting Russia at that time. My father and a man named Jo Son Hwan were sent to Harbin with instructions to assassinate Katsura when he passed through that city. However, Katsura had taken another route on his return from Russia and the plot was aborted. My father then went to Dalian, but he was arrested there by Japanese police who were on strict alert to apprehend and interrogate any newly-arrived Koreans because there had been a recent attempt to assassinate Terauchi, the Japanese Governor-General of Korea.

My father was charged with being implicated in the attempt to assassinate Katsura and he underwent extremely vicious torture. The large scar on his forehead was merely one vestige of the beatings they administered routinely. Unable to coerce him into admitting to something that had not occurred, the Japanese sent him into exile on Jin Island. Eventually he was released from banishment but was sent back to Seoul and kept under constant surveillance. There he worked as minister of the Jongdong Church for several years before I was born.

On the eve of the March First Popular Uprising in 1919, my father turned over the ministry leadership of the Jongdong Church to the Rev. Ri Phil Ju, one of the thirty-three persons who had signed the Declaration of Independence during the uprising. My father had been one of the original signatories, but he then had another greater responsibility: to help with arrangements to send the Prince of Uichin, Ri Kang, to the international peace conference at Versailles after the end of World War I.

Ms. Ha Ran Sa, the first "modern woman" in Korea, who had studied in the United States, once had accompanied Prince Ri Kang to a church service and, after hearing my father preach, became determined to follow his leadership in the independence movement. She was in the company of the Prince as he crossed the Amnok River on a third-class carriage. Although disguised, they were recognized and arrested by the Japanese police in Dangong, a Chinese town bordering Korea, and the plan to go to the peace conference thus miscarried.

Tragically, Ms. Ha Ran Sa, a short time later, was a guest at a function in Beijing where she died almost instantly after drinking a beverage which had been intentionally poisoned by a Japanese spy. Only my father had succeeded in gaining refuge in Shanghai unharmed. However, his days in Shanghai were a bitter experience which left his mind indelibly scarred.

He was one of the founders of the Korean Provisional Government in Shanghai. Along with Ri Kwang Su and others, he organized a provisional national assembly in the French settlement in Shanghai early in April of 1919, founding the Korean Government-in-Exile. Ri Tong Nyong was elected as its first speaker and my father took office as its first deputy speaker. A few days later, when the Provisional National Assembly of the Republic of Korea was officially inaugurated, my father was elected speaker and Sin Kyu Sik was chosen as deputy speaker.

I don't think it would be inaccurate to say that my father, who virtually directed actions of the national assembly, was the "parent" of the Korean Government-in-Exile. However, he served his relations with the new government without hesitation when a creative faction and a reformist faction became at odds and generated discord over government policies.

That action perhaps is the reason that some historians have omitted or downplayed my father's leadership role in the formation of the provisional government.

The parochial attitude of some members of the provisional government led to his decision to leave Shanghai and his position of leadership. The rift had deeply affected my father; the mental pain awas reflected in his eyes and applied a veneer of gloom to his face. That is why I didn't recognize him when we were reunited in Jilin. But I can recall the day when In Sil and I were sitting on his lap that he had asked us to solve a puzzle: "What is the most dreadful creature in this world?"

We ran through our best guesses: "Tiger ... snake ... ghosts, etc." "No," he counseled, very seriously. "It's man!"

He was heavily burdened mentally and thoroughly disgusted by the factional strife going on within the provisional government; people were grouping themselves as a "faction of Phyongan" or a "faction of Kyongsang," discriminating between people according to the provinces from which they hailed. Trembling as he spoke, he said, "When a small country is torn by feuds between dozens of factions, such feuding will make a ruin of the independence movement."

After liberation of the country, when founding the naval force in South Korea, Won Yil ensured that the provinces from which men and officers came would not be listed on the cards of their personal history. Etched in Won Yil's memory was our father's advice that one should not discriminate among people on the basis of which province they hail from.

Because he was a forthright and just man, my father had left Shanghai behind to go to Jilin to continue his struggle for independence for all of Korea. He had his own plan, shared by his close friend, Ahn Chang Ho, that the country's independence could not be won in a short time so the strength of the Korean people would have to be cultivated first. He believed, echoing the views of Mr. Ahn, that it was essential first to build large Korean settlements in Manchuria and in the vicinity of Shanghai to serve as a basis for life and the cultivation of the unified strength needed to achieve national independence.

In the spring of 1927, my father and Ahn Chang Ho, along with several other patriots, formed an anti–Japanese movement called the Peasant Cooperative, whose aim was to promote laying the foundation for national independence efforts among the Korean peasant masses living in Jilin province. Its initial goal was to improve the living conditions of the peasants to enable them to take part in the struggle against the Japanese.

The cooperative had three major objectives: (1) To improve employment opportunities to provide material life necessities; (2) To broaden education levels; and (3) To greatly enhance health and hygienic conditions. In order to attain those objectives, my father prepared large-scale plans to exploit the hydro-electric resources of the Songhua River and Lake Jingbo, and then began contacts with Chinese authorities to negotiate joint efforts by Korean and Chinese people to initiate a start-up of the project. He also spearheaded an attempt to bring foreign capital and technology into the project. However, all of those efforts were obstructed and eventually sabotaged by the Japanese imperialists.

Prior to the outbreak of the September 18, 1931, Manchurian Incident, my father had been pursuing the anti–Japanese struggle on his own. He had sold off all of his inheritance assets and land holdings in his native village in Korea and he had purchased fifty hectares of land in Emu county in the region of Dunhua and Jiaohe, China. He attempted to bring in Korean compatriots who were leading wretched lives elsewhere and enable them to settle into farming there. He planned, of course, to inculcate in them a fervent anti–Japanese spirit that would encourage them to support other anti–Japanese patriots.

The Rev. Sohn Jong Do in 1930 at age 49. Date of birth: July 26, 1882. He died in Jilin, China, on February 19, 1931.

The Japanese aggressors in Manchuria trampled upon that rustic aim! In February of 1931 my father died of illness under strange circumstances at the Oriental Hospital in Jilin. I learned of his death while at school in Beijing; Won Yil was aboard a German cargo and passenger ship at sea when he heard about it. Neither of us was able to attend the funeral ceremony. We never visited his tomb, nor were we able to investigate the circumstances surrounding how he had died so suddenly of an undetermined illness, nor could we learn what had caused him to age physically in such a short time. I was able to learn more of the details of his dying only when I met President Kim Il Sung on my first visit to Pyongyang. It was suspected that the Japanese had introduced slow-acting debilitating poison in his food during one of his arrests and imprisonment for interrogation.

Although many years had elapsed before we met again in Pyongyang,

The family of the Rev. Sohn Jong Do taken in 1917 in Seoul Jung Dong Methodist Church Compound shows the Rev. Sohn, my brother, Won Yil Sohn, who later became the Chief of Staff of the South Korean Navy, my mother, Park Shin Yil, and my sister, Jin Sil, who later graduated from the University of Chicago. In front of my mother is me holding a doll. This photograph was found in the library of Harvard University in Boston in 1955 by Dr. Youngho Choe.

the president remembered my family with warm and affectionate feelings. He was very grateful that my father had been able to get him released from the Jilin prison and recalled with apparent relish how my mother would cook a mouth-watering stew of bean curd and rabbit meat whenever he visited our house.

Calling my father the savior of his life, the president told me at Pyongyang that had it not been for him he would not have been released from the Jilin prison and, if the Japanese had been occupying Manchuria at the time, he would have been handed over to Japanese police, suffered great hardship and probably would have been killed. He had laughed heartily then, pointing out that if he had been turned over to the Japanese at that time there would not have been the anti–Japanese struggle, nor would there ever have been a Kim Il Sung existing in the world.

When Kim Sung Ju had been arrested and jailed in Jilin, the anti–Japanese spirit was running high and the crackdown on Korean revolutionaries and independence champions was becoming more intense, largely because reactionary warlords in northeast China had concluded a secret agreement to cooperate with the Japanese. My father tried every tactic to get Kim Sung Ju released, including visiting the Jilin military control station to placate Zhang Zuoxiang, the officer in charge, by slipping a huge sum of money into one of his pockets. Mr. Oh In Hwa, an official of the Jilin provincial administration, had accompanied my father as an interpreter and facilitated arranging contacts with important people. When my father, Choe Tong O and others guaranteed that Kim Sung Ju was not a communist, he was released.

The president never forgot that incident. He told me at our reunion that the first thing he did after his release from the Jilin prison was to visit my father's house in Niumaxiang to express his gratitude for getting him freed and to warn him not to stay in Jilin because the situation was becoming too threatening. Kim Sung Ju said he had learned of the assassination of a pastor in Jiandao while he was making preparations for full-scale armed struggle against the Japanese.

In our 1990s conversations, President Kim Il Sung asked me where my father's remains were buried. I told him that at first they were buried in a graveyard outside of the Beishan Gate in Jilin. Later, we had bought about 100 square meters of land at the eastern foot of Beishan in Jilin and reburied them there and we had also set up a tombstone in front of that grave. However, as the city expanded, the area of the graveyard was enveloped and we were unable to locate the grave again.

The president had frowned when I gave him that information and said that we should have kept father's remains. I learned later that, when the Patriotic Martyrs Cemetery was being built, the president had sent officials to Jilin to confirm whether my father's grave was still there. Kim Il Sung told me that he always had suspected that my father's death had been the result of murder committed by the Japanese police. Although the Rev. Sohn had suffered periodically from a gastric ulcer, the fact that he had died on the first day in the hospital created much doubt about the cause of his death, the president said.

He gave me a copy of the official document issued by the Japanese imperialists covering the death of my father. This was the letter which Ishii, then the Japanese Consul-General in Jilin, had sent to the Japanese foreign minister, Shidehara, on Feb. 24, 1931. The official document read:

> On the death of the Rebellious Sohn Jong Do:
> — Birthplace: Ohung-Ri, Jungsan Subcounty, Kangso County, South Phyongan Province, Korea
> — Address: Yaxiiya Dayaofang, No. 17, Jinyuhutong. Dongcheng, Beijing, China.
> — Date of birth: July 26 of the 15th Year of Meiji.
> In March of the 8th year of Taisho (1918), Sohn escaped to Shanghai in connection with the so-called independence movement inside Korea and involved himself in the independence movement, holding the

Left to right: Song Sil Sohn, Chi Chang Yun, his wife Jin Sil Sohn, and In Sil Sohn, in Seoul, Korea, in 1932.

Jin Sil Sohn (Mrs. Yun) with Chongsun and Wonhee (Michelle), photographed in Seoul, Korea, in 1935.

post of speaker of the National Assembly of the Provisional Government organized by Korean nationalists in Shanghai.

He then moved to Manchuria. He organized Christian Church in Jilin Province and established a church. While engaging in missionary work for several years, he joined the Hungsadan of Ahn Chang Ho and his faction in Shanghai and kept steady relations with the nationalists there. Last year he moved with his family to the aforementioned address.

Urged by Ko Hwal Sin, Oh In Hwa and others to come to Manchuria, he alone returned to Jilin on December 10 of last year. Staying in the Taifenghe Rice Mill situated outside the Dadong Gate, he repeated secret discussions with his comrades on the national movement. Then he had a relapse of chronic gastric ulcer and was admitted to the Oriental

Hospital on the 19th of this month. As he died on the very day, a funeral was held on the 22nd according to Christian custom with the attendance of 40 famous Koreans including his wife from Beijing (arrived on the 21st), his younger brother, Sohn Kyong Do, from his native place, and the Rev. Paek from Fengtian. His remains are now buried under the care of the Fengtian Public Hall (in Jilin) and are planned to be reburied in Korea.

After I had read this "official" Japanese report, I felt that some things about the circumstances of my father's death were becoming clearer. Frankly speaking, I was of the same opinion as the president now. Both of us were doubtful that the hospital to which my father had been admitted was in fact the Oriental Hospital which belonged to the Japanese. Father, who had the anti–Japanese struggle paramount in his mind while asleep or awake, would not willingly have gone to a Japanese-run hospital even in an emergency situation. And, if he had gone there, there would have been mysterious implications.

My doubts grew deeper with the passing of time until they have been churned into pent-up fury. Proportionate to this agonizing doubt has been the painful realization that this man, who had toiled fervently all of his life to free his country from deprivation, could have been the victim of an unnatural death. Moreover, time became a merciless factor in covering up the true legend of his patriotic struggle for Korean freedom. As his contemporaries and friends in the independence movement passed away, one by one, those who might remember the Rev. Sohn Jong Do could rarely be found to testify to this true phase of Korean history.

Should the Rev. Sohn Jong Do, a man who had lived and died for the sake of his nation, be forgotten by or be unknown to the rising generations in this way? This thought weighed heavily upon my heart ... the heart of his son!

However, some years ago Professor Kang Sun Ung, holding a doctorate in history, visited me at my home in Omaha, Nebraska, arriving without prior notice. I had been on intimate terms with him during our days at Northwestern University in Chicago. Our worlds of study were different; I was a student of medicine and he was a student of history. I was attracted by his honest and upright personality; he had been a zealous student devoted to his quest for knowledge and was so intensely occupied in his educational pursuit that he had remained a bachelor until his fifties.

We hadn't been in touch since I left Chicago ten years earlier. Dr. Kang brought out a videocassette and asked me to view it with him, explaining that it had been produced in North Korea and my father was portrayed in it. My wife and I were surprised when he explained that he

My Father, the Reverend Sohn Jong Do

This family photograph was taken in 1947. *Back row from left:* Won Tai Sohn, Mr. and Mrs. C.C. Yun, Kyung Doh Sohn, Mr. and Mrs. G.K. Shin, Won Yil Sohn, and Dr. R.K. Moon. *Middle row:* H.S. Kim, Y.S. Lee, my mother Shin Yil Park, E.H. Hong, In Sil Sohn holding Thom Moon and daughter, Sungja. *Front row:* Tom Yun, Haesun Yun, Myongwon Sohn, Michelle Yun, H.S. Sohn, Yong Sohn, Dongwon Sohn, and Yanghi Yun. Child in front center unidentified.

had visited his native area in North Korea on several occasions. On one of his trips, while watching television, he saw a film about the Rev. Sohn Jong Do and then had purchased the videocassette which he now was about to show to us.

As we watched, I could recognize familiar scenes of Jilin and my father's church which was still vivid in my memory. Then I saw "my father," wearing a mustache and dressed in a western suit; it was an actor, looking quite different from my father while playing him in the role. My father had never worn a mustache. However, I was moved to tears by the knowledge that there still were people who had not forgotten the Rev. Sohn Jong Do.

But questions did arise. The life story of the Rev. Sohn apparently has been forgotten in South Korea, but how can it be that communists of North Korea, where religion is said to have been eradicated by the "iron fist," still remember him? This was a puzzle I could not get answered until after I had visited Pyongyang, a decision I could reach only after long and mentally painful deliberation. Just as President Kim Il Sung was highly appreciative of my father's patriotic spirit and his contribution to Korean independence and remembered him fondly, North Korean people also have remained aware of my father's patriotic role in the fight to end Japanese occupation.

The president had told officials close to him, as well as historians and media writers, about the Rev. Sohn Jong Do. Moreover, he had written in detail about the patriotic spirit and exploits of my father as an anti-Japanese independence fighter in a separate section of his memoirs, entitled "The Rev. Sohn Jong Do," among his reminiscences of this century of Korean resistance to occupation and separation.

In the minds of the North Korean people who believe that patriotism is the most valuable thing, the Rev. Sohn John Do is indelibly remembered as a Christian of integrity, a savior of their president's life, and a leader of anti-Japanese patriotic fighters. I believe that is why North Koreans regarded me, an unfamiliar man, as their close friend as soon as they had met me, showing respect for me because I was the son of an esteemed patriot. Their sincere overtures moved me to tears on several occasions.

I have been very proud of my father and have tried to model myself after him but it wasn't until after his death that I clearly understood him fully. When I reached adulthood and felt the misery of our ruined nation as my own, I came to understand why he had chosen the ascetic road that he had followed. And I told myself, with understandable pride, that he had been an outstanding person.

On one occasion, when I was studying in the graduate class at Severance Medical College, I went to a fortune-teller with some of my friends. The Pacific War was at its most intense phase and everyone under those suspenseful circumstances would frequent fortune-tellers to obtain forecasts of their future. In an alley in Seoul, we found a tile-roofed house with a nameplate indicating that this was the home of a seer. A middle-aged man, clad in Korean clothing, met me at the door and ushered me inside. Looking intently at my face, he said that I would inherit a large fortune. I told him that my father was a minister and had devoted all of the family property to the independence movement and, therefore, not a penny was left to me. Glibly, he responded that a fortune consisted not solely of property but of my father's spirit and virtue as well. I was not unhappy with what he said because I did hope that I would inherit my father's indomitable spirit. The god in my mind was my father; my religious belief was founded on his patriotic spirit.

However, I have done nothing for him worth mentioning except that

I have sincerely respected and remembered him and in my everyday life have attempted to follow his example and do things for the sake of my nation. In the latter days of my life, I have had the good fortune to meet a man who has been even more devoted to my father than I have been.

That man was President Kim Il Sung. He not only respected and remembered my father as the savior of his life but he also inscribed him in the annals of Korean history as a patriot to be revered and remembered by posterity throughout the coming ages. It was President Kim Il Sung who had accomplished the national liberation from Japanese occupation which my father had aspired to achieve so earnestly all of his life and it was President Kim Il Sung who had built, in the northern half of the country, an ideal society in which all Korean people could live in harmony, helping and leading one another ... a society so similar to that which my father had attempted to build on the Songhua River in Manchuria.

All things considered, my father was a blessed man. I could not but admire him.

3
Jilin, China

Jilin is the seat of Jilin Province, one of the three provinces of Northwest China. Mount Xianging rises high north of the town ... a towering wall that holds off the cold winds to protect the village and the vast fields which spread southward from its foot. The Songhua River flows along the outskirts of Jilin which has thrived from its benefits and has been called "The City of Water" since ancient times. Jilin also is an old city that has many vestiges of historical and cultural value. Its famous scenic spots include Mt. Lungtan, Mt. Puda, Beishan Park and Jiangang Park.

The military control station which is situated in Jilin was established by Zhang Zuoxiang, the younger brother of Zhang Zuolin, who was the de facto ruler of Northeast China. Jilin was of strategic importance for the Fengtian warlords of China and its future was assured partly because the area's farming production was abundant year after year.

The town became known as the "Shanghai" of Northeast China because a great number of progressive social and ideological activists settled there. Many Korean independence champions and philosophers gathered there so Jilin became closely related to the Korean national movement. Eventually it became the stronghold of independence fighters affiliated with Jongui-bu and the leaders of Chamui-bu and Sinmin-bu.

It was understandable why Jilin attracted so many freedom fighters who were seeking a safe haven from the Japanese imperialists. At that time, Jilin had about 2,800 Koreans in permanent residence; this was the largest

Korean population in any city or town in northern Manchuria. After the occupation by Japan, Koreans who fled their native villages in search of a new way of life had moved deep into Manchuria, most of them by way of Jilin, where many decided to settle.

Jilin was also known as a small kingdom least affected by influence from the outside world because it was situated far from the south Manchurian railway. However, it did provide strategic access to the main travel routes, which perhaps was the reason it had become the den of bandits in olden times.

Perhaps the basic reason Jilin was favored as a haven by Korean refugees was that Zhang Zuoxiang, the military ruler in the area, hated Japan and for many years had welcomed Korean independence fighters who were opposing the Japanese. As the result of Zuoxiang's friendly overtures, Korean independence leaders made Jilin the base of their operations and the movement grew in strength while it operated from that city.

Among the well-known leaders living there were Hyon Ik Chol (also known as Hyon Muk Kwan), the chairman of the central executive committee of Jongui-bu; Kim Ri Dae, chairman of the Jilin local bureau; and Ri Ung, chairman of its military bureau. An Pung, commander of the First Unit of the military bureau, also resided in Sanfeng Inn just outside of the Kinkai Gate. Jang Chol Ho, commander of the Second Unit, was living on Tongtian Street, whereas Ri Tong Hun, commander of the special detachment of Jongui-bu, and Kim Ku, chief of the police affairs section of Jongui-bu, both were boarding at my family's house. Both Kim and Ri hailed from Kangso, the birthplace of my father. Ri Ok Chon, head of the police affairs for Jongui-bu, virtually lived at our house also. Kim Ku, Ko Won Am and Oh In Hwa were the independence fighters who were closest to my father during his days in Jilin.

Ko Won Am, whose original name was Ko Hwal Sin, hailed from Ryonggang in South Phyongan Province. He was seven years younger than my father and lived in Niumaxiang in Jilin. At one time he was a member of the central committee of Jongui-bu and an executive member of the organizational department of "The Only Party of the Nation." Later on, he served on the executive committee of the Korean Revolutionary Party, and in the 1930s joined hands with the Committee.

Ko Won Am, Ri Jong Rak, Hyon Jon Gyong, Cha Kwang Su and Choe Chang Gol formed a leftist force within the Jongui-bu and later on joined with Kim Sung Ju in the Communist movement to wage guerrilla warfare in eastern Manchuria.

Oh In Hwa hailed from Jinnampho, Pyongyang. He was nine years younger than my father but apparently they became friends while he was in Jinnampho doing missionary work. He took part in the anti–Japanese struggle and was active in raising funds for the Independence Army. He was sought by the Japanese police and took refuge in Manchuria but he was sentenced in absentia to five years of imprisonment. He was the only one among the Korean independence fighters to change citizenship, obviously to avoid being arrested by the Japanese police. After becoming naturalized, he was able to obtain an official position with the Chinese government and became an interpreter in the judgment section of the public security bureau's negotiation office of the Jilin provincial administration. He adopted Chinese dress and lived in a Chinese neighborhood.

Behind the scenes, Oh In Wha assisted the Korean independence movement. When Ahn Chang Ho was arrested on a visit to Jilin, and when Kim Sung Ju was taken to Jilin Prison, Oh In Hwa contacted influential people on their behalf. Ko Won Am, who had been arrested by the Jilin military control station in the fall of 1930, was also released thanks to the efforts of Oh In Hwa. Oh In Wha became naturalized and then obtained a Chinese government position so that he could be of assistance to Korean independence fighters who became involved with the law.

When the campaign to expel Koreans from China was launched in 1927-28 on orders of Chiang Kai-Shek, Oh In Wha was among those who frustrated the effort. The purpose of the order was to oust any Koreans who had not sought Chinese citizenship. Of the tens of thousands of Koreans living in Manchuria, only a tenth had applied. Chiang Kai-Shek's orders led to expulsion of refugee Koreans to areas on both sides of the Amnok River. Led by Choe Tong O, the "Association of People from the Same Province" was formed to oppose the expulsion procedures. Representing the association, Choe Tong O and Oh In Hwa, as well as others, contacted the Jilin military control station to defend the Korean compatriots living in China from such injustice. Their efforts persuaded the station authorities to declare that they would not enforce the order.

Whenever Koreans residing in Jilin were confronted with problems involving the law, Oh In Hwa would respond with enthusiasm to their pleas for help. I believe that was why my father held him in such great esteem.

After my father's death, Oh In Hwa was also assassinated. His killer was Kim Jong Yun, a lackey of the Japanese who concealed his actions by being a member of the Association of Korean Residents in Jilin. I still seem to expect to see Oh In Wha, dressed in Chinese clothing, opening the door to my house, asking, "Is the Rev. Sohn in?" On New Year's Day he would give In Sil and me gifts of money, which we usually spent on candies. He not only was intelligent and courageous but had a delightful sense of humor as well. He would prop me up on his lap and tease, "It's too bad your nose is too small, Won Tai. When you're sitting on the lavatory, pull your nose; then it will grow big."

How tragic that a man so full of humane feeling and so devoted to the welfare of his Korean compatriots should be murdered by a fellow Korean turned traitor.

Jilin was the haunt not only of nationalists but of self-styled communists. The leaders of the Tuesday Group and Shanghai Group of the Korean Communist Party came to Jilin often while attempting to broaden the influence of their respective factions.

Lee Jang Chong, a heroine of the Nationalist Independence Army, was residing in Ryu Kum Chong's place outside the Dadong Gate. Ryu was one of the leaders of the Tuesday Group. In a house adjoining Jang Chol Ho's dwelling on Tongtian Street, two boarders were Sin Il Yong and So Jung Sok, members of the Seoul-Shanghai Group. Sin Il Yong was an important leader of that organization. Jang Chol Ho, a widower, had married Mrs. Yun, a well-off widow who lived with her daughter in a large house next to his. While he was studying in Jilin, Kim Sung Ju also roomed in the small house. Thus Jilin became a melting pot where campaigns of all factions met while pursuing Korean independence, each in their own way.

It was understandable why my father had chosen Jilin as the base for realizing his ideal of a free Korea: it was because so many Koreans were living there and independence campaigners would gather there. Living conditions for Korean residents of Jilin were wretched and made even more difficult because they were not given elementary legal protection. As a result, they were subjected to violence committed by mounted bandits and even by Chinese authorities.

After becoming settled somewhat comfortably in Jilin, my father built a Methodist church on the bank of the Songhua River. With the joint efforts of independence campaigners, a church sanctuary and minister's office of about 170 square meters were constructed of wood and brick materials. He immediately established a kindergarten and primary school to educate his fellow Koreans.

A Roman Catholic church had been established by the French on a street by the Songhua River but its parishioners were Chinese for the most part. My father's church was the only one available for most Koreans and he continued to promote religion and education for the Koreans, using the church as his base for both. My elder brother, Won Yil, and Kim Sung Ju were teachers in the Sunday School. I attended classes taught by Won Yil; he lectured about General Ri Sun Sin and the history of Korea more than about Jesuitism so Sunday School really was an institute to promote the spirit of independence for Korea.

The Jilin church became a refuge for the thousands of wandering Koreans who fled to Manchuria. Helpless immigrants, independence fighters fleeing oppressors, and others without means of a livelihood ... anyone in need of material assistance as well as religious support called at the minister's office for help. There was a large Chinese cauldron in the kitchen of our house and my mother cooked rice and soup in it day and night to provide food for these wayfarers. Our house gave them a place to rest and to sleep. As they left for their next destination, my father would empty his pockets of whatever money he possessed to help them meet their traveling expenses.

Nearby my father's church was the Sanfeng Inn and adjoining the inn was the Taifenghe Rice Mill. The innkeeper had two sons, Ri Tong Hwa and Ri Tong Son, and a daughter, Ri Kyong Un. Ri Tong Son was my age and Ri Kyong Un was a close friend of In Sil. The four of us enjoyed frolicking in the piles of rice straw heaped in the frontage area of the rice mill. We would roll around in the straw and pellet sparrows and pigeons with our slingshots ... carefree moments in the lives of small children in an alien country during times of duress in their parent's homeland.

Father was also engrossed with his ideal of building Korean settlements, a project that involved spending his own money to facilitate negotiations with Zhang Zuoxiang. My father had inherited a considerable fortune but he would not spend it to sustain the needs of his own family. I have no pleasant recollections that my brother, my sisters and I ever ate our fill at mealtimes, but I do remember that we would dip our bread in water to make it more palatable. At such times, my father would say that when his negotiations with Zhang Zuoxiang were successfully concluded, we would be able to purchase land to provide a livelihood for Korean compatriots, to cultivate crops and to build a hydroelectric plant ... and then we would be well off!

My father lived very frugally while pursuing his far-reaching plans. Of necessity, to improve our family's condition mother obtained work sorting rice at the rice mill to supplement our food needs. I went to the mill on some occasions to help her; it was not a simple task to sort rice while squatting in the cold of winter. When I asked her one day why she kept on doing this hard work, she sighed heavily and said, "What can be done then? I have to earn every penny I can in this way because your daddy's money goes into one of his pockets and comes out through the other." His money was spent for the poor Korean compatriots and for the independence movement!

In those times, the Independence Army received its war funds from the Koreans. Bills to be paid were also sent to our house for handling. Those invoices, sheets of paper about 9×12 centimeters in size, were issued by the Jongui-bu. My mother would pay them without exception.

Most pastors were not very well off financially during the days of the independence movement but the clergymen were zealous patriots and devoted their property as well as their untiring efforts to the cause. As a result, many of them were arrested, subjected to cruel torture and died before reaching 50 years of age from the residual effects of their mistreatment. In contrast, the stooges of the Japanese imperialists lived comfortable and lush lives in clover.

An opinion survey conducted several decades ago among girl students in Seoul sought information about what kind of career job they would prefer a prospective husband to hold. A career as a government officer led the list and to be the wife of a clergyman was the least favored among choices submitted.

Among the many young people who studied in the United States some seventy years ago, one young man fell in love with a clergyman's daughter. In his final year of schooling, the boy received a letter, written by his parents from Korea, telling him to abandon his plans to marry her because she was the daughter of a poor clergyman who was dedicated to the independence movement. Instead, his parents advised him to complete study on his doctorate and then return to Seoul and marry a rich man's daughter. Accordingly, the youth broke off from his sweetheart, returned to Seoul and did wed the daughter of a rich man ... a pro–Japanese collaborator! A love story written by Yi Kwang Su recounted the situation but, contrary to the facts, portrayed the girl as the one who was the betrayer.

A recent survey showed a complete reversal of the marriage intentions of girl students. A clergyman is now the favored prospect for a husband. Oddly enough, the church has been transformed into an agency which collects money. I don't understand why God turns a blind eye to this practice. Nevertheless, I am proud of the fact that my father was not a minister who collected money, but a clean-handed patriotic minister who donated his last penny to the cause of independence for his native land.

My mother courageously smiled in the face of hardship; she was proud of her husband and was happy to share his burdens although he contributed all of the family property and assets to the independence movement while she toiled to earn the meager money needed to support him and to feed, clothe and educate her children. Mother was not a simple woman and, thanks to her, my father was able to devote his energies to seeking independence for Korea without a heavy burden of worry about his family's welfare. In her way, my mother fought shoulder to shoulder with him in the cause of independence.

It was early in January of 1927 that Kim Sung Ju came to Jilin when it had become a theater of political activities of Korean nationalist independence fighters, communists of the early days, and patriotic people of every description. He had left, in mid-course, from Hwasong Uisuk School in Huadian, China, where cadres of the Independence Army were being trained. Kim Sung Ju had come to Jilin in search of a new theater for his activities because it had become the Mecca for all people who aspired to help win independence for Korea.

Thus the relationship between the future President Kim Il Sung and the family of the Rev. Sohn Jong Do took root. One day my father told mother that the son of a friend of his had come to Jilin to study. Since his father had died, the boy's mother had supplied him with school expenses by doing sewing for others. "But how much can she earn? We will have to supplement his funds and take special care of him," my father explained. Unnoticed, my mother sighed as she willingly agreed, saying only, "I see." Both of my elder sisters were studying in other places and Won Yil was a boarding student at the Wengueng Middle School. In Sil and I also were attending school and it was not easy to support her sons and daughters, let alone take on another burden. Yet such was the personality of my mother that she did, willingly!

I was too young to have known about the friendship between my father and Mr. Kim Hyong Jik, the father of Kim Sung Ju. He was ten years younger than my father but they both had attended the Sungsil School. However, after graduating, Mr. Kim did not enter a religious order but devoted himself to the independence movement while serving as a teacher and later as a surgeon. He had organized the Korean National Association in Pyongyang and had rallied the early membership in West Korea before eventually expanding the organization to other areas in the homeland and abroad. For this activity, he had been arrested and subjected to cruel torture. As a result of injuries inflicted on him by the Japanese police during his arrests and the severe frostbite he suffered while attempting to escape from them, Mr. Kim died at the young age of 32 years.

While operating from Fusong, Mr. Kim had been active in the Maritime Provinces of Russia and in Shanghai where, probably, he first became acquainted with my father. However, I believe that it was in 1925, during a meeting held in Jilin to organize the Korean Revolutionary Party, that they had become close friends and formed an extraordinary relationship.

Beyond the fence bordering our church property was a restaurant called the Ryongnam Restaurant, as I recall. It employed a boy of about my age as an odd jobs helper. One of his chores was to wring the necks of chickens to be prepared for dinners. Whenever I heard the squawking of chickens being killed, I would climb up on the fence to watch the beheaded fowl flapping their wings and hopping in frenzy about the enclosure, bleeding profusely. I would shudder at the gory sight, yet would continue to watch with fascination. That sight has been engraved in my memory, as has been the imagery of the people whom I saw shedding their blood and suffering deprivation for the cause of national liberation.

The leaders of national independence efforts in various places eventually realized that unity among their ranks could be accomplished eventually only by bringing themselves together in common agreement on their purposes and their ideologies. The leftist force in Jongui-bu provided the initiative to convene a meeting in Jilin. The Tamodu Youth Party, led by Jong I Hyong, also expressed its support for a merger and sent its representatives to the session. (Tamodu, in the dialect of the Koguryo Period, means "restoration.") It was a strong, influential organization. The leftist force of the Chondoist religion from Seoul and leaders of the Hyongphyongsa, an organization of butchers (the lowest class of society with about 20,000 members), also came to Jilin for the meeting. Others attending were independence fighters from the Russian Maritime Provinces.

Kim Hyong Jik was among the planners who founded the Party and led to its implementation, and my father gave it his full support. I have been told that Mr. Kim had difficulty traveling to Jilin for the meeting because he was seriously ill and had to depend upon a cane to stand or to walk.

Selected as chairman of the new Party was Yang Ki Thaek, an important man in the Sinmin-bu. Lee Jang Chong had traveled back to Seoul to bring Mr. Yang, who had been hiding there in Mr. Chong's house, to participate in the meeting.

Kim Hyong Jik, exhausted by his efforts to help the Party get organized at Jilin, died the following year. Yang Ki Thaek and the independence campaigners in Jilin were deeply moved by the death of Mr. Kim and showed special concern for his son. Kim Sung Ju had been entered in the second year class of the Yuwen Middle School in Jilin through the auspices of Jang Chol Ho, Oh Tong Jin and my father, all of whom were good friends of his father. While Kim Sung Ju attended school in Jilin, he was boarding at Oh Tong Jin's and Jang Chol Ho's houses. My father provided a room for him in the church annex and also paid for his school expenses whenever needed.

With religious charitable funds and his own philanthropic funds, my father had built a kindergarten and a primary school building attached to his church to help children of poor Korean families, but his special care for Kim Sung Ju exceeded general charity. My father patronized him not only because Kim was the son of a dear friend but, most of all, because my father was impressed by Kim's apparent eminent qualities and he prayed that the lad might have an important role to play in Korea's future. Father's own life experience had given him a background which enabled him to understand and evaluate the character and capability of people and his assessment of young Kim led to his decision to help the youth attain greatness in his maturity. My mother also was favorably drawn to Kim. She apparently was attracted by his kind, humane and affable nature. Whenever he visited our house, mother would prepare a special meal which she knew he would like most. There were a number of young students in Jilin who were said to be unusually talented. My father treasured them all and gave them his support but the fact that he had designated Kim Sung Ju, a newcomer, for the chairmanship of the Association of Korean Children in Jilin, I think, indicated that my father expected something much greater from him.

There were times when my father suffered great mental stress. Although he had applied all of his inheritance to strengthening the national independence movement, the increasing aggression by the Japanese imperialists had taken its toll and the support in Korea was on the decline. Observing this development, many people, including my father, sought new strategies and hoped, with God's blessing, for some kind of cataclysmic event that might herald the dawn of freedom for the nation. Subsequently, their eyed turned to young people.

4

The Association of Korean Children in Jilin

Some people have asked me if it is true that President Kim Il Sung of North Korea actually had begun his struggle for national independence while he was still in his teens. Of course it is true, but it was in the more complicated sense of experience, not simply knowledgeability. The question cannot be answered in a few words of explanation for those who are unfamiliar with that period, those who have not experienced the tribulations endured by Korean patriots during the occupation years under Japanese imperialism. There is a great difference between knowledge and experience.

I was the son of a patriotic Korean pastor who was strongly anti–Japanese. If he had lived in comfort on the fortune he had inherited from his ancestors as a Confucian scholar or as a government officer I might have become a totally different Sohn Won Tai. But my father chose to leave the noble family lineage and become a Christian clergyman. Like many other Protestant clergymen in those days, he became active in the anti-Japanese struggle, his heart burning with patriotic fervor. What I saw, heard and experienced from the day of my birth was the aura of anti–Japanese feeling and the spirit of resistance to imperialistic occupation to avoid living in slavery, an aura of enthusiasm for an independence movement dedicated to win back Korea from Japanese domination.

I feel no need to write in greater detail about what influence this exerted on my outlook on life, my soul and my personality. As I grew older my experience broadened but my heart and mind were indelibly scarred forever by two horrible events, one on that day of the March First Popular Uprising in Pyongyang when for the first time, as a very young boy, I saw the blood of Korean compatriots spilled ruthlessly in the public square, and the other on that day when I witnessed the same bloody brutality on the public square in Jilin. Both experiences left lasting pain deeply embedded in my heart as I witnessed the continuing humiliation and misery of my ruined nation, decade after decade.

The misery of seeing one's homeland deteriorating into ruin became more intolerable while I was living in an alien country. There the people spoke a different language, observed different customs, and were foreign in appearance and demeanor. There was a deep feeling of humiliation provoked by the looks of contempt and the frequent use of unfamiliar words uttered thoughtlessly but with obvious derogatory implications.

Korean and Chinese boys in Jilin frequently engaged in group fights. These altercations usually were started when the Chinese called the Koreans "Gaolibangzi" (a derogatory slang word for Koreans) refugees from "Wangguonu" (Chinese for a ruined nation). Those were deliberate humiliating taunts. Sometimes the combatants bloodied each other but the Koreans would never show their pain although they might be bloodied, suffer broken bones or have their clothing torn. The wounds, by comparison, were not as painful as the humiliation they bore in their hearts.

On rainy days we children would stay indoors, usually in the back room of someone's house. Talk most often was about the native villages we had left behind and it wasn't uncommon that tears would be streaming down our faces. Misfortune brought maturity far too early to boys of twelve or thirteen years. We would sing a nostalgic and deeply pathetic song which had been composed by Won Yil (when he was fifteen years old) and Pak Il Pha, about Beishan:

> Don't cry, innocent children in a foreign land.
> When spring comes, dry grass will be green.
> Never feel disappointed, my parents, brothers and sisters.
> When we grow up and win back our country
> We will return to the motherland in happiness.

Kim Sung Ju was two years older than me but three years younger than Won Yil. Although about our age, he was different from us. He was not content merely to lament the loss of his country and let others try to win back its freedom ... he was the son of Kim Hyong Jik, the renowned independence campaigner and indomitable anti-Japanese fighter!

At fifteen years of age, Kim Sung Ju was already determined to restore Korea by his own efforts and, young though he was, he had already begun to put his mind to formulating plans to accomplish it. He was blessed with exceptional qualities including the talent to translate knowledge and experience into practical avenues of performance. That difference is what separated Kim Sung Ju from the rest of us boys about his age in the pursuit of our destinies.

Kim Sung Ju was already planning a practical struggle to win back Korea's independence. His strategy was clear: to accomplish this, the whole nation would have to be closely united in order to create the great strength of common purpose needed to defeat Japan. This he realized while still in his teens, and he was already putting some of his ideas into action. He was forming various organizations, both legal and illegal, rallying children to become active in children's associations, students to enroll in student societies, and all young people to support youth organizations. The Association of Korean Children in Jilin was one of those projects.

I was a member of the Association of Korean Children in Jilin. In the spring of 1927, several years after my family had settled in Jilin, I was attending a provincial primary school but was being a failure in my first year. I had been an honor student during my enrollment in the Kwangsong Primary School in Pyongyang but because I did not know the Chinese language I found studying very difficult in the Chinese school. Fortunately, as I gradually learned the Chinese language and became familiar with the local customs, my school records began to improve.

One spring day I was told that a meeting of Korean children was planned to be held at my father's church. Returning from school, I hurriedly ate my lunch and then hastened to the church where a large number of children had already gathered in the church yard. I recognized some of them but there were many of about my age who were unfamiliar to me; they were students from boys' and girls' middle and normal schools, and some older youths from colleges. There had already been a children's association in the area, operating under the patronage of nationalists affiliated with Jongui-bu, but it existed in name only because it had inept leadership.

Although the independence movement and missionary work occupied most of my father's energy, he still paid special attention to the educational needs of Korean children growing up in the province. Despite his pressing need for money at all times, father had been able to build a primary school in which to educate Korean boys and girls whose families were too poor to send them to provincial schools. He also had provided a room in connection with the church for use as a kindergarten. These projects resulted not only from his religious spirit of charity and philanthropy but also from his patriotic desire to assure that the future generations of Koreans would be well prepared to serve as educated citizens. Not all of his aspirations were achieved as fully as he had wished, partly because he was involved with so many other concerns.

The enormity of his activities required finding capable people to assist in leadership roles. He had been seeking, for instance, someone to take over responsibility to direct the children's association. When Kim Sung Ju arrived in Jilin my father almost immediately designated him for the job. Kim Sung Ju, for his part, had already been contemplating ways to breathe new life into the almost dormant association.

Many independence fighters and the parents of the children had come to the church to show support and congratulate them on their activities, and had taken up seats in the back rows of the church hall. On the platform were Jang Chol Ho, an independence fighter, my father, Pak Il Pha, Kim Sung Ju and one other student whose name I don't recall. After some opening remarks by those on the platform, the assembled group formally created the Association of Korean Children in Jilin, elected a slate of committee members and then unanimously chose Kim Sung Ju to serve as its chairman.

Kim Sung Ju took over the podium, acknowledged the action of the assembly with thanks, and then outlined his goals for the association: its aims, immediate tasks to be accomplished, and the rules under which the organization would be governed. Fluent in the Phyongan provincial dialect, he challenged the boys and girls to unite as one to devote themselves to winning back the independence and honor of Korea. His use of the Phyongan dialect, which I understood, gave me an intimate feeling about him. I felt as if I were meeting someone I knew and liked from my native village.

When the program and rules of the association had been promulgated, the delegates formed sections and classes. This action was well organized — sections were put in charge of association affairs, public relations (propaganda), culture and sports. Classes were formed by districts and schools, and messengers were assigned to interlink the classes. After attending that meeting, I met with Kim Sung Ju frequently; in fact, I followed closely on his heels whenever I could.

A radical change took place in the lives of the boys and girls of Jilin. After school hours, we would gather at my father's church to hold debating contests and take part in storytelling and in book report meetings. The debates were serious events on subjects ranging from whether a girl should have her hair bobbed to very serious deliberations on how best to wage the independence struggle for Korean freedom.

The association even operated a small library. A room for the library was provided by the rice mill keeper, the father of Hwang Kwi Hon, a good friend of In Sil. We plastered the walls with clean white papers and built bookshelves to transform the room into our library. Some of us brought books from our homes and some of the middle school students purchased books for the library with money they had earned working at railway construction sites.

I had an unexpected and profitable experience that spring while walking along the banks of the Songhua River. It was a spectacular sight as the thawing masses of ice broke into large and small floes which were tumbled along by the surging river currents. I had the preposterous thought that I could ride all the way to the West Sea on a large block of ice but as I trotted alongside, absent-mindedly contemplating such a dangerous prank, I saw a large carp floundering on sheets of ice which had been washed onto the river bank. I grasped the fish without encountering much resistance for it apparently had been stunned by the crushing churning of the ice blocks. It was unbelievably larger than the silver carp that I caught on the Pothong River!

With the aid of three companions, I tied the fish on a strong stick and the four of us carried it back into town. People passing by asked if we had caught it by ourselves and we were elated at the curiosity it aroused. Suddenly the rice mill keeper appeared and asked if he could buy the carp and, after slipping some money into my pocket, he carried it away. When Mr. Oh In Hwa visited our house on New Year's Day, he would give In Sil and me handsels but the fish money in my pocket felt much greater than the handsels had ever felt; more importantly, it was the first money I had ever earned through business in my entire life.

I intended to buy books with the money and donate them to the library but Kim Sung Ju advised me to give it to my mother because it was the first earning of my life. When I gave it to her, my mother became radiant with smiles and she said, "So this is your earning, eh? You're better than your father." I was never happier than on that day!

There were various books in the association's library: such Korean story books as *The Tale of Sim Chong* and *The Tale of Jang Hwa and Hong Ryon*; Chinese books including *Three Warring Kingdoms* and *Deep Sigh*; and revolutionary books such as *Mother*, *The Iron Flood*, *Blessing* and *An Authorized Life of Ah-O*. I was permitted to read those books in the library because I was a member of the children's association.

Childhood pleasures I remember well included picnicking in Jiangnan Park across the Songhua River, mountaineering on Mt. Lungtan, and playing games as soldiers in Beishan Park. The Songhua River and Beishan Park were favorite recreational gathering places for association members. The community of Jilin boasted about its availability of fresh water, its mountains and its many historical relics. Because the Songhua River flowed along the outskirts, the city had been called "A City of Water" even in ancient times. The river cascaded and swirled down from the rugged hills but calmed to a large but gentle flow as it passed the city. In the summertime we caught fish there but mainly it was a place to swim and enjoy water fights.

Jiangnan Park, situated on the opposite side of the river, was a famous recreation area. It was lush with greenery, maintained hundreds of beautiful flowers in its botanical garden, and provided a zoo and various amusement facilities. Many children were unable to enjoy the pleasures of the park, however, because they did not have money to pay the charge for admission.

Shortly after the association was formed, a picnic was planned to be held in Jiangnan Park. Everybody was caught up in the excitement of anticipation for several days approaching the picnic. Early on that day I went to the church meeting place carrying the food my mother had prepared for me. We formed ranks in the church yard and headed for the ferry landing where we would be taken by boat across the river. On the way, marching along the streets, we loudly sang the "Song of the Association of Korean Children in Jilin." I do not remember who wrote the words and composed the music but I do recall that the refrain was:

> Let the 20 million Korean compatriots unite
> To win back the country, and
> To build a new country on the land of 3000 ri.

We were mesmerized by the beauty of the park, its green leaves shimmering in the sunlight, the flowers which everyone wanted to gather up in their arms. Hand in hand, we walked around the park, breathing in its entrancing aromas and feasting our eyes on its splendor. After a while, we gathered around on a spacious lawn and played children's games such as hide and seek and pass the handkerchief.

Eventually, we organized a game of soldiers, dividing into a "Sea" team and a "Land" team. Kim Sung Ju was commander of the "Land" team and I got to be a member of his team; in those days I always wanted to be on his side! I liked his smiling, handsome face and the warmth of his voice.

When I was beside him I felt at ease and wanted to enjoy his affection although I didn't know the motivation at that time. Kim's team always bested the "Sea" team. It was a children's game but apparently did require intelligent organizational skill. He told me, "You, Won Tai, hide under that pine tree and come to the rock on the right!" or "If you are located by the enemy, take the initiative and act!" We followed his tactics and won the game each time.

Even the girls played the soldiers game. I still remember cheerful, courageous In Sil and her apple-faced friend, Hwang Kwi Hon, running through the trees as swiftly as squirrels.

Those who know about my relationship with President Kim Il Sung when I was young have asked, "What was your strongest impression of him in those days?"

I answer them in this way:

> In the days in Jilin we were boys and girls alike. President Kim Il Sung also was a boy; he was cheerful and passionate, and he enjoyed reading and playing.
>
> They say that all great men are not in born; They scale the height of greatness at long last by growing gradually from immaturity and climbing from a low position. That can be true.
>
> But what I can confirm is that, already in his boyhood, Kim Il Sung was possessed of leadership. He had the qualifications and traits of a leader and he had an exceptional skill of attracting people. That attractive power should not be called a skill but a natural endowment.
>
> He was two or three years older than most members of the children's association and about the same age as some of them, but he always cut a conspicuous figure among them. He looked like a crane in a flock of chickens.

5

My Thoughts on the Soul of the Nation

They say that a man in the closing years of his life lives on memory. I often trace in my mind the days in Jilin when I was as innocent and unstained as grass sprouting in the springtime, participating in sports, giving art performances, speaking out on my ideas on the floor during debating contests and arguing pro and con on various subjects. The recollection of those merry and happy days fills my heart with warmth.

At such moments I ask myself, "What have those days brought to my life?"

A Korean proverb states that a promising tree is recognized when its seed has produced the first leaf. This means that an excellent man is distinguished from his childhood, denoting the importance of the environment and education he experienced when he was young.

In those long-ago days we lived in an alien land far from the motherland but not for a moment did we forget the deprivation in the country and in the home communities we had left behind. Our lives were cast solidly in that mold. Although we were young, we talked about independence for Korea whenever we spoke of home; we played as soldiers of the Independence Army whenever we played; we sang those songs appealing for restoration of our deprived homeland whenever we sang. Although we lived in a foreign city and country, we learned about the history of Korea and did not abandon the Korean language despite the fact that Korean children who were attending Chinese schools had to speak and study in the Chinese language and learn all about China's history and geography.

Under these circumstances, independence fighters in Jilin expended great effort to assure that children would be raised to be Koreans and become a reserve source for the Independence Army. The Korean primary school, built under the auspices of my father and supported by independence fighters, taught the Korean language, Korea's history and geography. The instruction materials were prepared by Korean leaders. I recall that Kim Sung Ju and members of the Ryugil Association of Korean Students participated in preparing and editing the class manuals.

The children's association members who were attending Chinese schools also were able to learn about the history of their motherland during storytelling and readers' meetings organized by the association's leaders. I still remember one storytelling meeting in particular. It was held in the classroom of the Korean primary school and the subject was a discussion about famous men whom Koreans revered the most. We all had a chance to proclaim a leader of our choice, some of us making a long speech but others merely stating, "I worship Sun Yat-sen!" or "I worship Zhuge Liang!" Most of the boys favored Sun Yat-sen.

Then Kim Sung Ju took the floor.

"I worship such famous generals of our country as Ulji Mun Dok, Kang Kam Chan and Ri Sun Sin," he said. He was only a young boy but his audience was attracted to him. He appeared to be more mature than his age group and he also was further distinguished by his apparent intellectual stature. He described events of a battle on the Salsu River which was commanded by Ulji Mun Dok and the one at Ku Ju castle commanded by Ri Sun Sin. On another day, he had related in detail the exploits of Jong Pong Jun during the Kabo Peasant War. I can still repeat the many stories that I learned about in those meetings. At one time, Kim Sung Ju also organized a readers' meeting to discuss the contributions of General Ri Sun Sin whose career was one of the main chapters of the history textbook provided for study in the Korean primary school.

The association members read many Korean history books to prepare themselves for discussions to take place during upcoming meetings. The group was particularly interested to learn about the turtle-shaped ironclad warship, the first of that type ever built, which was used in naval battles during the Imjin Patriotic War against the Japanese. Some members fashioned models of the turtle ship out of clay; others sought to learn more about the general by talking to independence fighters about it. Everyone, it seemed, wanted to come to that meeting fully prepared for discussion.

There was great evidence of Korean pride shown at the meeting during discussion of how the Koreans had defeated the Japanese aggressors by designing and using the first iron-clad warship of record in world history. But Kim Sung Ju counseled pointedly that Korea was able to emerge victorious in that war not only because Ri Sun Sin was a courageous and very competent general but because all Korean people had united as one to put up stubborn resistance with no regard to the risk or their own lives. That united effort was the lesson to bear in mind because that is the only way Korea will be able to win back its freedom, he emphasized.

During that turbulent period of Korean history, Japan had captured and occupied 3000 ri of Korean land and was forcing Koreans to worship Japanese ancestors in an effort to obliterate Korean history and transform the country into becoming Japanese. The Japanese even attempted to ban use of the Korean language, both spoken and written. There in Jilin, as we discussed the history of our motherland, our young hearts became imbued with the soul of national pride and our sense of national dignity was enhanced.

Another program designed to inculcate the soul of the national pride and a fervent patriotic spirit in the hearts of the members of the children's association was a short course in the Korean tongue. Most of the boys and girls living in Jilin then had been born in China and had never been to their motherland. Because they attended Chinese schools, wore Chinese clothing and spoke Chinese, a considerable number of those children did not know the Korean language.

My father's church conducted a Sunday School for children. In addition to teaching the Christian doctrine, the school also provided instruction on the history and culture of Korea. Kim Sung Ju was a Sunday School teacher. So was my elder brother, Won Yil, and I was in his class when the special short course was included in the Sunday School curriculum.

Kim Sung Ju inaugurated the opening of the short course with an explanation of its purposes. He explained that the Japanese had forbidden Koreans to use their language, either written or spoken, while attempting to make Japanese the "mother tongue" as a replacement. Kim Sung Ju asserted that "We must never yield to the Japanese; learning our language is a good defense of the roots of Korea and we must always confront the Japanese with courage!"

The short course continued for more than three weeks and when it concluded many of the Korean children who were attending Chinese schools had become capable of writing, reading and speaking Korean although encountering some difficulty in the beginning. Their reading material was the Korean magazine *Orini*. Perhaps the most valuable achievement of the short course was that it taught the children that they must not forget their own nation, no matter where they might live.

During the summer holidays, the children's association members went to the rural villages to teach the Korean language. One village, called Liudawen (meaning "Six Big Gates" in Chinese), was a community of six large Chinese landowners whose residences featured six big gates. Korean farm families who worked in the fields lived in 20 of the houses. The community, located some six kilometers west of Jilin, had neither a Korean nor a Chinese primary school. Members of the children's association went to the village on holidays to teach the Korean language to Koreans living there. For those who did farm work during the day, classes were taught at night.

The children's association promoted a variety of art group performances, including singing and dancing performances of "Pride of Thirteen Provinces" and "Unity Pole." The theme of both of those plays stressed the need for all of Korea to unite in order to achieve its independence.

The association also staged dramas. I had a great interest in dramas and once had a role in a play that condemned a man who collaborated with the Japanese. In the script, a soldier of the Independence Army is arrested because an enemy agent has betrayed him to the Japanese. The soldier's compatriots are enraged and sneak into the collaborator's house, bind him securely and interrogate him. Won Yil played the soldier who interrogated the enemy agent; he was quite accomplished as an actor. My role called for my appearance at a corner of the stage as an extra to make a murmuring sound; that was my first and only stage appearance as an actor!

The drama group performed another play which I can recall. A girl named Pok Sun (also the title of the play) lives with her stepfather and mother in poverty, which the girl resents deeply. Her stepfather is a heavy drinker and beats both the child and her mother brutally. Abused and finally driven out of her house, Pok Sun wanders about the streets until she finds employment as the servant of a landlord. Unable to tolerate the demeaning insults and mistreatment from him, she flees once more and resumes a wretched life in the streets of the city. Eventually she is saved by a benevolent pastor and is able to attend school while living in the pastor's house.

Members of the Ryugil Association of Korean Students in Jilin, while they were middle school students, staged a play entitled *An Jung Gun Shoots Ito Hirobumi*. The play, performed in the hall of Middle School No. 5 in Jilin, enjoyed great popularity and the hall was filled to capacity at each performance. I worshiped An Jung Gun. I was born after my father had been freed from banishment and had returned to live again in Seoul. Not very tall or strong, I was a quiet and mild-mannered boy, a boy of few words. My mother fondly nicknamed me "Reticent," and she would smile and tell me that "several old men are in your heart" because my thoughts were so deep.

Revering An Jung Gun as the most courageous of men, I would picture in my daydreams performing such laudable deeds as those of the martyr An. I must have had such dreams because my father had been arrested and tortured so badly by the Japanese following the attempted assassination of Katsura Taro. All my sisters and my brother also worshiped An Jung Gun and my two older sisters established close relations with the widow of the martyr An while they were studying in Shanghai. At that time they were living with my father in rented quarters on the same street on which Mrs. Kim Maria, An's widow, also resided. An's son and daughter, Jun Saeng and Hyon Saeng, were about the same age as my sisters and the four of them were as close to each other as brothers and sisters. My sisters, in their letters to us, kept us fully informed about the An family and I always considered the martyr to be close to my family and his deeds to be a model of patriotism.

Several times when I attended a performance of the play, I would become so excited that, in the scene when An fired at Ito, I would rush unconsciously to the stage. On those nights I would become An Jung Gun in my dreams and would shout, "Long live Korea's independence!" so loudly that I would wake myself up, only to find my mother looking at me with concern as she wiped my perspiring face. This was typical of my boyhood when I dreamed of defeating Japan and liberating Korea almost by day and by night. It is clear to me now that all of the things I heard and saw, sensed and breathed, became the cornerstone of my outlook on life.

Because my father was an anti–Japanese independence fighter, I grew up in a strongly patriotic home environment. He brought up his children sternly. Although he continually stayed out of the house and seldom gave his children face-to-face instruction, his ascetic lifestyle, the livid scar on his face, his eyes full of mental agony, and his heavy, labored footsteps all served to instill a strong feeling of patriotism in us all. Because every freedom fighter dedicated to the independence movement came to Jilin, all of their talk concerned how to conduct efforts to regain Korea's sovereignty. Thus, as I grew up in an independence fighter's family and lived among independence champions, I hated Japanese imperialism and detested its lackey collaborators from my earliest days. I am sure that the crystal-clear, patriotic soul which remains in my heart was nurtured in the main by the education provided by the Association of Korean Children in Jilin.

I cannot remember Kim Sung Ju merely as my boyhood friend. He was my brother and senior, the teacher who shaped the course of my life.

When people are asked what is the most valuable thing in their life, the answers will vary. Some will say it is money and wealth because one has to eat and live; another will say that it is the obligation owed to parents, brothers and sisters, spouse and children; still others will say it is knowledge and the personality one has been gifted to possess. Jesus Christ taught that one should love God, one's neighbors and even one's enemies. Buddha Sakyamuni instructed his followers to overcome their selfish desires and cherish benevolence. Confucius taught the ideal of humanism, and Socrates is remembered for his aphorism that a person should know himself. There is nothing wrong with the teachings of the ancient saints but I count first among all the doctrines the one I learned in my days in Jilin: that a man should not forget, even for a moment, the affection for and the obligation to his motherland.

One's motherland is what his mother is to a man. Whether she is rich or poor she still is his mother! Just so, his motherland is forever his motherland. Just as he should not, and perhaps cannot, forsake his mother, he cannot forsake his motherland. Just as he cannot choose his mother, he cannot choose his motherland. Just as he has only one mother, he has only one motherland. During my days in Jilin, I often shed tears for my motherland which was, figuratively, bleeding and groaning under the oppression of the Japanese imperialist occupation. Today I feel pain in my heart for my motherland because it has been divided into two segments.

When Kye Sun Hui, a girl from North Korea, defeated a Japanese player (claimed to be the strongest Judo athlete in the world) during the 26th Olympic Games held in Atlanta, Georgia, and was awarded the gold medal, all Koreans in both North and South Korea and in the United States cheered in national unity because the rising generation of the North "had thrown the Japan Islands over her shoulder!" Those cheers and tears of joy were the indication that an undivided soul still exists in our nation!

A man without love for his nation is nothing but a poor man however wealthy he may be, and a man who has lost the soul of his nation is no better than a castrated animal, alive though he may be! I contend that a man who cherishes the love for his nation and lives up to his obligations to his motherland with unstrained conscience is a man who leads a true life.

While living in Beijing, China, and in America, I gave a great deal of thought to the matter and have tried my best to live a true life without losing the soul of my nation. But that was not the case at all times; practicing is surely more difficult than thinking. I had lived in Seoul for a number of years after my motherland was "liberated" at the close of World War II, and I have lived in the United States since 1949.

My two sons, Jong Ho, who was born in 1945, and Jong Guk, and my daughter, Young Hui, have lived in the United States since they were small and are not well-versed in the Korean language. I must accept responsibility for that. They became well-adjusted in American schools, they were well-mannered and studied their new language and subjects diligently. When Jong Guk was attending a middle school in Chicago, Illinois, I once was selected as "Father of the Year," perhaps because Jong Guk had won an award for a composition in which he had written: "My father and I do not talk much. We talk in our minds. I know full well what kind of a man he wants me to become."

I am proud of my children. I have never beaten them or scolded them harshly. I always assumed that they naturally would take after their father! I had rationalized that there was no way they could become well-learned in the Korean language as they grew up in the United States. This put me in an awkward position during one of my subsequent meetings with President Kim Il Sung.

During one of our meetings, President Kim Il Sung asked me how many children I had and what they were doing. I told him that my eldest son, Jong Ho (Carl), was a pathologist like myself, that Jong Guk (Rickey) had been working for an architectural firm after graduating from college, and that my only daughter, Young Hui (Younghi), had graduated as an art major from a university in Wisconsin.

He said that it was "ideal" that I had two sons and one daughter, and "wonderful" that my eldest son was following his father in the pathology profession. Then he asked me to bring all of them with me on my next visit. I replied that I would like to do that but none of them had much knowledge of the Korean language and, to make matters more difficult, both of my sons were sporting mustaches.

On my previous visits to my motherland, I had noticed that no Korean men, not even the old ones, wore mustaches. For that reason and their language deficiency, I had not given thought to taking them with me although they had implored me earnestly to do so after hearing about and seeing video accounts of the visits I and their mother had enjoyed in Pyongyang, especially about the grand reception, which even the president of a country would be envious to receive, given to us by President Kim Il Sung and the Korean people.

They were also very eager to tour the Kumgang mountains, Mount Paektu and other scenic areas of our motherland, but they were unaware of why I hadn't been willingly to take them with me.

"Please bring them so they can see what their motherland is like," the President had said. "You say that they yearn to visit the motherland, so you should bring them here even though they do not speak Korean now. If they visit Pyongyang frequently they will get to know more about their homeland and they will learn Korean on their own. Please bring them free from constraint."

My wife and I, so moved that we were close to tears, then had decided that we would bring our children along on our next visit but, sadly, President Kim Il Sung passed away so suddenly that we had no opportunity to introduce them to him. However, in July of the year he died, I returned to our motherland with my children as he had wished me to do. I took them to Mansu Hill and together we bowed solemnly before the bronze statue of the president, after which I conveyed to them what Kim Il Sung had urged: "You must learn our language without fail!"

I suddenly felt my heart breaking: they understood! They put their minds to learning Korean. Of course they couldn't master the language perfectly in the brief time available but they began to speak and understand simple sentences although they couldn't communicate fluently in Korean. On returning from a tour of the Myohyang Mountains, Young Hui told some acquaintances at the guest house, "Myohyangsan jal wattawatsoyo [We have gone to the Myohyang Mountains]" when it would have been correct to say: "Myohyangsan jal gattawatsoyo [We have been to the Myohyang Mountains]." This slight difference in meaning amused her listeners. I joined in the laughter but I could feel tears welling up in my eyes as I recalled that the president, who had been a teacher of the mother tongue during those days in Jilin, had urged me to bring my children to Pyongyang and encourage them to learn their motherland's language and cultural history. A person who has been close to the teacher who has taught and given him leadership, both in his innocent days and his gray-haired days, should be called a happy man. In this sense, I am an unusually happy man!

6

An Unfading Picture in My Mind

Whenever I think back to the days in Jilin, one scene comes to my mind's eye. It is one of those pictures which, no matter how often it is viewed, leaves one wanting to see it again and again. In Sil and I were squatting in an alley off a busy street in Jilin eating jiangzi guoji under a blazing August sun, and Kim Sung Ju was standing there looking down at us, smiling affectionately. In later years, when I longed to see him again, I would look through the picture albums of my days in Jilin. When I could not find him in any photograph, I would close my eyes and recreate that scene in my imagination.

On another sunny day in 1927 or 1928, In Sil and I went to Kim Sung Ju's boarding room in the annex attached to my father's church ... or it may have been when he was living in the house of an independence fighter, I cannot remember which. We didn't have an appointment but, looking through an open window, we found him lying flat on the mat-covered floor solving mathematical problems. Impulsive In Sil burst into laughter.

In Sil was quite lively as a youngster. Always as tall as me, In Sil appeared to be more grown up than others in her age group. She and her friend Hwang Kwi Hon were very active in the children's association. Being the youngest child in our family, In Sil was inclined to be a little pet at times but was always a willing helper for her mother. An outgoing person, she had a joyous personality, as opposed to my more docile behavior. She made family life more pleasurable with her delightfully infectious laughter.

I was frightened easily when I was young. At times during the night, when there were rapping or trickling sounds from the roof I would feel my hair standing on end and, terrified by stories about ghosts, I would be afraid to go to the toilet, located in the corner of our back yard, unless In Sil accompanied me. In other situations, whenever I wouldn't do something she wished me to do, she would threaten me, saying, "Or else I won't go to the toilet with you anymore." She could be quite independent and, at the same time, lovable.

At the sound of her laughter that day, Kim Sung Ju raised his head, saying, "Ah, it's you, Won Tai, and In Sil too." Then he gathered up his books, greeted us warmly and ushered us into his room. There wasn't a bookshelf or a table or any other furniture in his Spartan room; in one corner there was a heap of his many books. We wondered if we had interrupted his studying but he told us he didn't feel like studying mathematics anymore so we had come at the right time. We asked if he had times when he didn't feel like studying and he replied, "Is there anyone who enjoys studying all the time? I'm also a human being, and I especially don't like solving exacting mathematical problems."

When Kim Sung Ju smiled, a double tooth slightly showing between his lips and dimples appearing in his cheeks, he was a very handsome person. I envied him! He looked around to see if there was anything to serve as a treat for us. As he lifted a folded newspaper, an army of ants was swarming about in a scattering of bread crumbs. In Sil again was convulsed in laughter and Kim Sung Ju grinned broadly as he suggested that we go outside for a walk. Into the street we went, each of us holding one of his hands tightly.

I was ecstatic, pleased beyond description! Although I had met him frequently at children's association meetings and group playground activities, this was the first time that I had walked alone with him. I felt that my body was floating in air. In Sil was delightedly walking along with a bouncy gait.

She had had her hair bobbed and was wearing a one-piece flower-patterned dress. Until a short time prior to this, she had been wearing her hair in a braid. There had been a debate at one of the children's association meetings on whether or not a girl should have her hair cut in the bobbed style. Hwang Kwi Hon, a cadre leader, had her hair trimmed boldly and it gave her a refreshing appearance. And then In Sil got her hair bobbed.

On this memorable day, we chose to walk along a relatively quiet alley although it was somewhat crowded with kiosks manned by peddlers of sweet morsels and ice-candies. Kim Sung Ju found enough money in his pockets to buy three bowls of jiangzi guoji, a traditional Chinese food. This consists of pieces of partly-risen dough which are fried in oil, like a twist of bread, and then are served in sweetened bean soup. People could be seen eating this traditional food in every Chinese restaurant: a culinary Chinese tradition. We squatted on our haunches against a yard fence and ate our food. When I dipped the jiangzi guoji and put it in my mouth I relished the sweet taste. In Sil also found that treat deliciously palatable.

I have never forgotten that taste. Whenever I thought about President Kim Il Sung in later years, I would recall the memory of that day when the three of us squatted against the fence eating our treat in the alley. When I wrote a letter to President Kim Il Sung some 60 years after we had last seen each other, I mentioned that experience, saying, "I'm still grateful that you bought me and In Sil jiangzi guoji when I was a primary school pupil in Jilin. You were attending the Yuwen Middle School and I was a pupil in the Provincial Middle School No. 4. When In Sil and I went to visit you at your boarding room, even though we were interrupting your study of mathematics, you greeted us very cordially."

I reminded him of this when I met him on my first visit to Pyongyang and, after a moment of reflection, he said, "Yes, I remember that I did; you're right!"

Feeling as though I had returned to my youthful days when I had eaten food in an alley with Kim Sung Ju, I told him, "Many years have gone by since then but I still long to have a taste of jiangzi guoji once again." And, playing on his affection although it might have been inappropriate during a conversation between two gray-haired old men, I asked if he would provide that treat once again.

Smiling broadly, he said, "Yes, yes, I will buy…. No, I'll have some cooked for you on your next visit. I'll teach my men how to cook it for you." Then, as if he suddenly had been reminded of it, he added, "And I'll serve you some bingtanghulu, too!"

Bingtanghulu is a wild fruit dipped in sugar water and threaded on a skewer. That day when he bought jiangzi guoji for me and In Sil in Jilin he had also purchased two skewers of bingtanghulu with his remaining change. In Sil and I each ate one on our way home. Jiangzi guoji and bingtanghulu are two names that remind me of those unforgettable days in Jilin. With those two names, President Kim Il Sung, the father of his country, and I, an aging pathologist, were transported in mind back to the long-ago days when we were rosy-cheeked youngsters.

The president sat back in his chair for a moment, immersed in the world of memory, before continuing:

> You may recall that I visited your house several times. The Rev. and Mrs. Sohn always greeted me warmly and did their best to make me feel at home. I still remember with pleasure eating the rice cakes your mother prepared with an herb called jondugi. I had gone to your house with Sin Yong Gun one time and your mother asked me to have a taste of her rice cake, saying it was made with herbs In Sil had picked in Beishan Park. When I said it was delicious, your mother said that the herb also grew on Moran Hill in Pyongyang. It had soft down on its blades but had neither scent nor toxicity. After liberation, I told my men to make rice cake mixed with jondugi, but they didn't even know the name of the herb! Since eating your mother's rice cakes, I haven't enjoyed its taste for more than sixty years.

After inquiring about my mother, long deceased, he remarked that it brought to mind a song that we had sung in those days:

> Sprouting out in early spring
> With downy clothes,
> It is jondugi
> For cooking rice with.

Continuing his reminiscing, President Kim Il Sung said that on several occasions when he had visited us my mother had cooked bean curd and rabbit meat stew, a delicious food which tasted little different from chicken stew. He recalled that we had raised rabbits of various colors to be slaughtered for cooking. Another time, he said, he had eaten a meal of sand launce, a food not easy to find in northeast China. He also was served sand launce at the Jang Chol Ho home whenever he visited that family because they knew he liked it so well.

As he recounted those experiences I felt I was reliving those days once more, and I commented that the president had "quite a remarkable memory."

"How can I forget those days? I will not forget the people who helped me during those difficult times … not until the end of my life," he said, adding, "Time deprives us of many things. Nearly everything fades somewhat in memory with the passage of time … but not the beautiful, humane feelings with which we take care of one another. That feeling does not fade." I was moved to tears by his sincerity.

Later that evening, when I was busied with personal affairs, I was informed that I shouldn't make plans for breakfast in the morning but should wait until I was contacted again. Bright and early, an official messenger came to our guest house bringing jiangzi guoji sent by the president. So, sixty years after my days in Jilin, President Kim Il Sung once more had treated me to that delicious food.

A few days later we went on a sightseeing trip to the Kumgang mountains. While enjoying the scenic places in the mountains, we once more had the pleasure of savoring bingtanghulu; the president had sent some to us and it arrived while we were viewing the Kuryong (Nine Dragons) Ponds. As my wife and I enjoyed our skewers of bingtanghulu, I thought how happy we would be if In Sil were with us, reliving that day in Jilin when Kim Sung Ju had bought some as a treat for us.

The president asked about In Sil when we were talking about the family of the Rev. Sohn, so I told him that she was living in South Korea and was holding a responsible position with the Red Cross organization. He urged me to have her with us, if possible, when we returned for the 80th birthday party which he was planning for me.

News about my visit to Pyongyang soon reached Seoul and In Sil was able to view a video recording of my sojourn. Dr. Moon, In Sil's husband, celebrated his 80th birthday in the United States. I met with her then and gave her a full account of my visit to North Korea and conveyed President Kim Il Sung's personal greeting to her and her husband. Later on, the president sent her a gift of a sinsollo made of gem stone. In Sil had sent him a book, *Invitation to the Benefit of Life*, which introduces secrets of longevity. Kim Il Sung told me that he would follow the instructions given in the book.

7
A Campaign to Get Ahn Chang Ho Released from Detention

A major event that took place during my days in Jilin was the efforts to get Ahn Chang Ho released from detention. He had been arrested on a visit to Jilin. My father and Ahn Chang Ho were very close friends. He hailed from Ryonggang and my father was from Kangso, both of those places being near Pyongyang. Both Mr. Ahn and my father, the Reverend Sohn Jong Do, were famous in their lifetimes among leaders who grew up in West Korea.

I do not know how they became friends but they had maintained business relations for many years and it was probably after my father went into exile in Shanghai that they began to work closely together in the independence movement. The Rev. Sohn Jong Do was the speaker of the National Assembly of the Korean Provisional Government in Shanghai and Ahn Chang Ho was director-general for home affairs and chief administrator of the labor bureau of the provisional government, so they were in close contact and on very good terms with each other.

In August of 1919 my father inaugurated the Korean Red Cross Society. The list of 78 sponsors included Ahn Chang Ho. Subsequently my father became the second chairman of the society, succeeding Ri Hui Gyong in that position. The society strengthened its support in the Christian community throughout the country and lent positive assistance to the anti–Japanese struggle by maintaining close relations with the government-in-exile in Shanghai and various independence organizations. It also made overtures to join the International Committee of the Red Cross.

The Rev. Sohn maintained close relations with the Hungsadan organization formed by Ahn Chang Ho. The Hungsadan had succeeded the Sinmin Association which led the national movement and the new cultural movement in the last days of the Yi Dynasty. The Hungsadan's goal was to prepare for a national revolution. It had been organized in 1913 at Los Angeles, California, largely as the result of Mr. Ahn's leadership.

When he was working in Shanghai as director-general for home affairs of the provisional government, he also continued his leadership of the Hungsadan. He asked my father to join the movement and, to signify his full support, the Rev. Sohn presented the Shanghai office with a symbolic gift of four pots of rare flowers. After joining the organization in 1922, my father organized the Provisional Far Eastern Commission of Hungsadan and was elected to its five-member board of directors along with Ahn Chang Ho, Cha Ri Sok, Ju Yo Han and Lee Kyu So. The commission published literature monthly to disseminate information on policies and activities, planned or in progress, to keep its Korean compatriots well informed.

After my father left Shanghai and settled in Jilin, Ahn Chang Ho expanded the independence movement throughout northeastern China. Their close relationship continued, and I saw him several times when he visited our house in Jilin. He and my father would talk endlessly through the night and always seemed surprised by the breaking of dawn. Sometimes they practiced Thaeguk-kwon, a type of martial arts. In Sil and I would peek through an opening of a door to watch them, covering our mouths with our hands to stifle our laughter. When our mother would reproach us with stern looks we would steal back to our room.

Ahn Chang Ho lectured at a political meeting in February of 1927 at the Dadong factory, which made machinery for the manufacture of straw bags, straw rope and rice threshers. It was a small factory of brick wall construction. The factory also was engaged in grinding buckwheat into flour; still another activity was honing the edges on hoes and sickles. The owner of the factory was a Korean named Choe Il.

The lecture was given in a former warehouse building, about 400 square meters. A single door provided entry at the front and another was located at the rear of the building. In the front of the hall was a platform about one meter high, with stairs leading up to the right side of the stage. Long wooden benches, apparently recently made because they still smelled strongly of resin, provided seating for about 300 people.

I went to the meeting early and took a seat in the front row. Choe Man Young, the manager of the Taifenghe rice mill, was already there and I took a place beside him. I was very excited to be attending the meeting; Ahn Chang Ho was a very important leader in the independence movement and he was a close friend of my father. Whenever he came to our house he would pat me on the head and pull my nose playfully, so I considered him to be an acquaintance of mine.

Soon the hall was filled to capacity by a crowd of about 400 people; those who couldn't find a place on the benches stood along the walls or sat on the floor. The meeting began with a memorial service for the martyr, Ra Sok Ju, conducted by people representing the Jongui-bu, the Sinmin-bu and the Chamui-bu independence fighters, as well as public figures from northern and southern Manchuria, and Korean businessmen of Jilin. The crowd included many young people. My father, however, was attending to matters in Eng Mok county and missed the lecture.

Ahn Chang Ho spoke about the future of the Korean nation and his audience listened with breathless attention. He reviewed the history of the nationalist movement, its success and its bitter seatbacks. Then he challenged his audience to try to determine what could be learned from the past experiences and to consider what strategy should be adopted for the future.

Being a primary school student, I couldn't fully understand his message, but I was captivated by his facial expressions, his persuasive voice, and the aura that surrounded him and permeated the lecture hall. His oratory had something mysterious about it that gripped his audience's hearts. I believe it reflected the spirit of the man — a man of passion for justice who had struggled throughout his life cherishing the love for his pitifully deprived motherland.

My father preached excellent sermons. Many people, including Ms. Ha Ran Sa, had been deeply impressed by them. When I was a child I enjoyed hearing him preach; his voice resonated in the tone of a plaintive song, revealing the sorrow that evidently burdened his mind, plucking the heartstrings of his listeners. Ahn Chang Ho's oratory was as stimulating as my father's. I felt like weeping at times when his words seemed to be tugging my heart.

Mr. Ahn said he believed the strategy that would best serve the independence movement should be to avoid scattered and spontaneous activities and to devote that energy to developing unity for the long-term struggle. He emphasized that independence could not be won by bloody localized struggles under the present circumstances. Instead, he said, the whole nation should unite to cultivate joint strength. He said the economic foundation for Korea's independence should be laid by building a water power industry on Lake Jingbo, aided financially by loans from the United States, France and other powers, and by promoting the farming industry of Korean residents in Manchuria. I was totally mesmerized by his words about the national movement which he and my father were promoting.

At one point, some activity at the back of the hall brought a reaction of displeasure from the audience and heads were turned reproachfully toward the rear. I remember that a middle school student approached the podium, placed a slip of paper on the lecturer's table and returned to his seat. Ahn Chang Ho, after reading the message, paused in thought for what seemed to be a long time, while the audience wondered what was happening, before he resumed his lecture.

Fifteen years already had passed since Japan had annexed Korea. Patriots of Korea had resorted to all kinds of struggle against Japanese imperialism: petitioning the big powers, disemboweling themselves at an international peace conference, assassinating the chieftains of aggression, organizing a Righteous Volunteers movement and arming themselves with spears to form an Independence Army. Nevertheless, Japanese imperialists did not withdraw; contrariwise, they grew stronger day by day and sought to control the three provinces of Northeast China. Japanese police appeared everywhere that Koreans lived. They were in Hunchan, Dunhua and Longjing, prying into the lives of Korean independence champions, arresting and persecuting them. The oppression became more severe as time passed; more Korean blood was shed every succeeding day.

As the situation worsened, independence champions began to waver in their determination to work together in common efforts to resist the Japanese oppressors. They began to argue among themselves about what fighting strategy should be followed, and soon they were abusing anyone who disagreed with them. It was then that Ahn Chang Ho and others of the middle-of-the-road faction conceived the policy of cultivating the united strength needed to confront the Japanese imperialist occupation with renewed and effective vigor.

I learned later that Kim Sung Ju had submitted the questions to Mr. Ahn. The questions reflected the opinion of the group of students, seated in the back of the room, that they were not satisfied with what Ahn Chang Ho was proposing.

Later, when the Jilin children's association sponsored debates on the strategies of the independence movement, they took under consideration the methods used by Lee Jun and Ahn Jung Gun, as opposed to the "Theory of Cultivating Strength" being proposed by Ahn Chang Ho.

Kim Sung Ju explained to us a short time after the meeting that none of the methods under consideration were suitable at this time because the country was occupied by Japan. How, he asked, would it be possible to cultivate the strength of the Korean nation by promoting industry under the Japanese military occupation? How could education be promoted when even the teachers in the primary schools carried swords and were teaching only in the Japanese language? Where could we build hydroelectric power stations? Then he pointed out that history would show, from the failure of Lee Jun, that depending upon foreign forces would only be another road to national ruin, and that Korea could not win its independence by hoping for assistance from the big powers. It had been Kim Sung Ju who submitted those questions to Ahn Chang Ho at the lecture in Jilin. Mr. Ahn had not read the questions to the audience nor answered them during the meeting, possibly because he would have needed considerable time to prepare a response.

Unfortunately, he didn't have the opportunity to formulate a response if he had chosen to speak to the questions; police suddenly burst into the lecture hall through both the front and rear entrances. The Jilin military station had mobilized hundreds of gendarmerie (military policemen) and regular policemen; one of them appeared to be Japanese. That man leaped onto the platform and attempted to bind Ahn Chang Ho but a woman soldier of the Independence Army, Lee Jang Chong, climbed onto the platform behind the Japanese, knocked him down and urged Ahn Chang Ho to escape. Mr. Ahn, fully composed, remained on the stage, however, and permitted himself to be tied up. But when the policeman then tried to bind up Lee Jang Chong, she shouted "Hands off!" so sternly that he backed away from her.

Lee Jang Chong was a famous Korean heroine. She was the only woman soldier in the Independence Army and was praised as a beloved "red flower among the green." Her hair bobbed, she wore the blue uniform of the Independence Army, carried a pistol and rode a cavalry horse. Ms. Lee visited our house frequently and my mother liked her very much. With us, she would tuck up her sleeves and help mother with the kitchen work. I often wondered to myself if she hadn't taken a fancy to Won Yil. That could have been a groundless idea, of course!

While Lee Jang Chong was scuffling with the policeman, Choe Man Young, who was sitting beside me, told me to get up on the platform and untie Mr. Ahn. I scrambled clumsily onto the platform, with no thought of using the stairs, and found myself being bound up by the police; they were trussing up everyone on the platform or standing around on the floor. I was being herded outside with all of the others when Choe Man Young protested against arresting a young boy. Fortunately for me, I was then set free.

I went back into the hall where there was a scene of total confusion. White sheets of paper were scattered about on the floor and on the chairs. Thinking they might contain material the police would want to see, such as the Korea national anthem which was written on some of the papers, I went about picking them up. Standing alone in the empty hall for a long time, I felt highly indignant about the break-up of the meeting by the police. This incident, I realized, was a deliberate action of the Japanese imperialists aimed at cracking down on the Korean independence movement.

After learning that Ahn Chang Ho was going to conduct a large political meeting in Jilin among Korean compatriots and independence champions, the Japanese consulate had cabled that information to the police affairs bureau of the Governor-General of Korea in Seoul. That bureau then had asked Zhang Zuoxiang, the governor of Jilin province, to arrest Mr. Ahn as a political criminal and to turn him over to it. At the same time, the police affairs bureau had dispatched scores of policemen from its bureau at North Phyongan Province, Korea, to Jilin. So I was not mistaken in thinking that I had seen Japanese among the policemen entering the lecture hall.

The Chinese police were acting under the Mitsuya Agreement signed in June of 1925 between Zhang Zuolin, the dominant warlord in Manchuria, and Mitsuya, head of the police affairs bureau of the Governor-General of Korea. That agreement stipulated that the crackdown on communists and Korean independence forces in Manchuria should be conducted through joint efforts of the security authorities of Manchurian and Japanese police. Citing the agreement, the Korean Governor-General's police affairs bureau had requested Chinese authorities to arrest all of the communists and independence fighters attending the political lecture.

The arrests aroused great indignation among Koreans living in Jilin and the three eastern provinces of China. My father hurried back to Jilin as soon as he heard about it. He immediately went to the Jilin military control station and met with Zhang Zuoxiang, and then traveled to Fengtian to meet Zhang Xueliang to urge him to take effective action to have Ahn Chang Ho released. Oh In Hwa, in his role as an interpreter for the military control station, acted as an intermediary for my father.

Kim Sung Ju also took an important part in the efforts to have Ahn Chang Ho released. He contacted my father to advise that, in addition to bribing the Chinese officials with money in the negotiations, a more effective measure would be to bring pressure upon them. My father and other independence champions agreed with Kim Sung Ju on the need for such action and gave him their full support.

A Campaign to Get Ahn Chang Ho Released from Detention

A journalist, during an interview with me after my trip back to Pyongyang, had asked me if President Kim Il Sung had actually played a role in that effort when he was so young. He seemed to doubt that a middle school student could have had much influence. His doubt was understandable because he possessed little or no knowledge about the situation in Jilin in those days. He was completely unaware that the Korean nationalists were strongly influential, that the strength of the communists was not negligible, and that the influence of young people, especially among students, was the strongest factor.

There were several legal, and some illegal, youth organizations functioning actively. The mastermind of the youth and student movement was Kim Sung Ju. He enlisted the Association of Korean Children, the Ryugil Association of Korean Students, and other youth and student organizations in Jilin to help circulate letters of protest, to distribute leaflets and to organize and take part in demonstrations. Supporting the activities of student and other youth groups were the families of detainees, workers of the Dadong factory, workers of the rice mills, and most of the Koreans living in nearby villages. The support came from Koreans of all walks of life.

As the protests continued and grew in scope, the Chinese police released most of the people from detention three days after their arrest at the lecture hall. However, among 42 others still under arrest were Ahn Chang Ho, Oh Tong Jin, Hyon Ik Chol, Kim Ri Dae, and Kim Tong Sam. The Japanese ordered their Chinese counterparts to turn them over to their custody but the head of the Jilin police department denied that request because he feared a mass protest would occur. The provisional Korean government at Shanghai sent letters to both Beijing and Jilin urging the immediate release of Ahn Chang Ho. As a result of the joint efforts of every social group, Ahn Chang Ho was finally released after 20 days of detention.

From that day on, my father regarded Kim Sung Ju with special attention and later recommended him to be selected for the chairmanship of the children's association, recognizing that the youth was a dependable person who would serve in the national movement for independence.

When I eventually returned to Seoul, Mr. Ahn had already died after experiencing cruel hardship in Japanese-controlled prisons for a long time. I was told that the Japanese police had mixed pulverized glass with his food, fatally aggravating a gastric ulcer. To prevent an uprising if word of Mr. Ahn's death in prison reached the public, the Japanese buried his body surreptitiously before dawn in the public cemetery on Miari Hill. The freedom fighter Ahn Chang Ho died, vomiting blood, after eating poisoned food in Japanese-controlled prisons, and his theory of cultivating strength for national liberation remained only an echo pulsating in the universe.

About that time in Korea's troubled history, I began to hear news about General Kim Il Sung, now the last hope for the country's liberation, who was leading the armed fighting on Mt. Paetku. This brought to my mind the lecture in Jilin when his questions had not been correctly answered; now reality was providing the response in the gunfire of guerrilla warfare.

I learned that after liberation from the Japanese imperialism, pro-Japanese Korean collaborators had infiltrated the Hungsadan, which had been organized by Ahn Chang Ho, by pretending to be true patriots. Mr. Ahn's goal was to improve members by cultivating their minds but the insidious efforts of those traitors eventually brought about factional strife within the membership. Although differing from the philosophy of Ahn Chang Ho on some matters, my father did not form any organization of his own; in fact, he did not become a member of any group but strongly supported the goals that he could endorse.

After I left Korea to pursue my medical career in Chicago in 1949, I met an old man at a church service. His surname was Pak and he was a native of my province in West Korea. He informed me that a daughter of Ahn Chang Ho was working in a casino. I found her collecting admission fees, standing beside a shepherd dog, in front of the casino's iron entry gate. Finding the daughter of the great Korean patriot working in such a demeaning job to earn her living, I was unable to tell her a great deal about her father … I only wanted her to keep a beautiful picture of him in her memory. In our talk, I learned that her brother, Phillip Ahn, was an actor in Hollywood. I remember that when I was in grammar school in Jilin, Mr. Ahn Chang Ho discussed with my father matrimony between my older sister and his elder son, Philip Ahn.

When I visited President Kim Il Sung in Pyongyang, he spoke of Ahn Chang Ho with great affection. Ahn's birthplace was named Tosan-ri after his pen name. His sister, Ahn Sin Ho, a devout Christian, became an important official of the Nampo Committee of the Democratic Women's Union of Korea after the liberation from Japanese occupation.

While I was visiting the grave of Ahn Sin Ho in the Patriotic Martyrs Cemetery in suburban Pyongyang, I could not suppress the tears which were welling up in my eyes.

PART II

Hearing the Legendary Tales of General Kim Il Sung

8
The Crossroads of Our Lives

I spent my days in Jilin with Kim Sung Ju for a little more than two years, since my family had to move to Beijing because of Japanese oppression. It could be called only a dot in my lifetime but I am sure that my outlook was formed in those days and has remained unchanged throughout my life.

My friends of those days later followed their own roads through life. Won Yil, Hwang Kwi Hon, and Ri Tong Son all took their own course, just as I did. President Kim Il Sung followed his own road as well — the thorny road of armed struggle for the liberation of the motherland. The various directions of our lives and our aspirations were different from our youthful days in Jilin.

I cannot, in this book, give a full account of Kim Sung Ju's life, covering all of his activities and aspirations during his Jilin days. Although we met frequently during the meetings organized by the children's association, we lived our separate lives: he was a middle school student and I was a primary school pupil.

Kim Sung Ju not only was chairman of the children's association, he was in charge of the Ryugil Association of Korean Students and he organized the Anti-Imperialist Youth League and the Young Communist League, and guided the activities of both. The scope of his activity was very wide.

Hearing the Legendary Tales of General Kim Il Sung

In Seoul, after liberation, I happened to read *A History of the Korean Revolutionary Movement Overseas*, written by Choe Il Chon. The author was Oh Tong Jin's secretary. Mr. Choe had been active in Jilin with the independence fighters affiliated with Jongui-bu. He had visited my house often and I recall him as very intellectual and possessed of a most gentlemanly personality. My father had respected him as being a learned young man and a proficient writer.

Because the book had been written by Choe Il Chon, I read it completely without interruption. Choe Il Chon wrote, in part:

> Kim Il Sung (his original name is Kim Sung Ju) racked his brains for more than one year in Jilin as a leader of the youth movement. As he began to acquire social consciousness, his pure mentality began to experience agony. In those days the tendency to develop from the patriotic framework of yesterday to a revolutionary stage was pronounced in the circle of the nationalist movement and all organizations of the movement speeded up forming a single front. The theoretical confrontation between the group of the promotion association and the group of the conferential association in Jongui-bu meant development in the formation of the front. Meanwhile, Kim Chan of the Tuesday Group, Sin Il Young of the Seoul Group and Ku Ja Yong of the Shanghai Group emerged as leaders of the socialist movement.
>
> The boy Kim Il Sung's brain, nay, the consciousness of the student Kim Sung Ju, became critical of these two social tendencies and realized that he would be able to attain his end in the future through his own independent movement. Kim Il Sung, burning with revolutionary passion, thought everyone was his comrade and his leader. But it was sad that the society then did not acknowledge his aspiration. To be candid, the social phenomena just around him were far from understanding him, who was at a turning-point towards a new trend of thought.
>
> Braving through difficulties, Kim Il Sung sought after the theater and comrades where, and with whom, he would realize his ideal.
>
> Much was expected from him, and the activities of these organizations were positive. The support of the masses for Kim Il Sung, a man of passion and emotion, was great. It was not ordinary support; they loved the 19-year-old revolutionary as their own son and brother and he, in turn, promised that he would serve them with devotion.
>
> Looking forward to his future, his comrades made him a present of a pen name, "Il Sung," hoping that he would become a star of the Korean society. Hence, he went under the name of Il Sung.
>
> As the Manchurian incident broke out in 1931, he broke his long-drawn silence and, like the lodestar twinkling on the eastern sky, emerged cutting a conspicuous figure and holding the banner of the fundamental overthrow of Japanese imperialism and liberation of the small and weak nation in the East.

It was well written in that, in a few paragraphs, it portrayed the traits, activities, mental agony and searching of Kim Sung Ju, a promising leader of the youth movement enjoying the limelight in his days in Jilin. The more I read it, the more I felt that, although I had followed him as I would follow my brother, and tried to be near him, I had not understood his world in full. As I read Choe Il Chon's words the particulars of the events of those days flashed across my mind with fresh meaning.

This happened when I was returning home after enjoying for the third time the play of *Ahn Jung Gun Shoots Ito Hirobumi* being staged in the hall of the middle school No. 5 in Jilin. I was with members of the children's association, all of us walking along with chairman Kim Sung Ju at the center. Everyone was excitedly expressing their impressions gained from the play, and the gist of the comments was that more patriots like martyr Ahn Jung Gun were needed to bring independence to Korea sooner. I now recall that Kim Sung Ju had counseled us calmly: "Of course Ahn Jung Gun is a patriot and an heroic man, but I cannot agree with his method. Individual terror leads us to nowhere! Look, when Ito Hirobumi was killed another Ito Hirobumi appeared in his place!"

Kim Sung Ju already had found weak points in the activities of the preceding generation and was seeking an original method of struggle. Although he deeply respected Ahn Jung Gun, he did not agree with his method; nor was he pinning his hopes on the diplomatic activities being conducted by the Korean Provisional Government in Shanghai and some leading figures of the preceding generation; nor did he follow the theory of cultivating national strength proposed by Ahn Chang Ho and my father. Kim Sung Ju was of the opinion that the movement of the Independence Army was also outdated.

Kim Sung Ju believed that independence could not be achieved by such outdated strategies or by the passive attitudes of any movement involving a small number of dominant figures. He was formulating a clear strategy for the future struggle even in those early days. He was zealously reading books on Zhuge Liang tactics and Sun Tzu's *Art of War*. In retrospect, even then he apparently was making preparations for future guerrilla warfare.

The games of soldier which we had played frequently in Beishan Park were not merely childish play. We had sticks on our shoulders for rifles and wore grass-woven caps on our heads. The way we played was similar to military exercises. Hoisting a flag after the capture of a strategic height was particularly stimulating. We were divided into "Cuckoo" and "Oriole" teams; the leader of each team did not know which of us were his soldiers, nor did we know who our leader might be. The problem was for soldiers to discover who their leader was, and for the leader to identify his soldiers. Identification was achieved by recognizing a bird call correctly. Once a leader had assembled all of his men, the army would climb a specified slope and plant its flag at the peak. One had to use his brains and act swiftly in response to a bird call signal.

Time passed quickly in this pastime. Most children were dreaming of becoming soldiers of the Independence Army so the games were as serious as mock combat could be. Considering the frequency with which he organized such games, it is clear now that Kim Sung Ju was consolidating his plans even then to confront Japan with arms in hand. In my opinion, it was after that September 18, 1931, incident, when Japan occupied Manchuria, that he had made his final decision to resist Japan through a mass struggle with armed guerrillas.

At this point destiny divided both of us. With imperialist Japan's aggression in Manchuria impending, my father was making preparations to leave Manchuria for China proper. One day he called Won Yil, In Sil and me together and sat us in front of him. I still remember vividly what he said:

> Every Korean yearns for the independence of the country but it looks improbable that Japan will be overthrown and Korea will be liberated soon. We then will have to roam about for a long time as a ruined nation and be subjected to maltreatment. Even though we are compelled to roam about, we must not be subjected to humiliation. For this, everyone must cultivate himself.
>
> Qualifications are most important in the age of science and industry which will be used in the future. It is late for my generation. You must become competent men and women in different fields without fail. This would be the best method for bringing the independence of the country nearer.

I felt nervous at his words and looked up at him. His eyes, which always had been bright, were now dull. I abruptly realized that he was quite old. Because he had been away from home frequently for his independence movement and missionary work, he had not been paying particular attention to his children. Even when he was with us he rarely spoke to us in the way of giving us instruction. I think he went no further than giving us instructions out of his deep innermost thoughts.

Imperialist Japan was gaining strength with each passing day, stretching its tentacles even into China proper. The writing was on the wall: War with China was imminent! In contrast, the Korean independence movement was on the decline. For my father and other independence champions, Korea's independence, which they had long yearned for, now seemed to be even farther away.

Like many other independence fighters, my father did not put his children in the front line of the independence movement. He must have thought that the conditions were not favorable, that cultivating ability was a better way to achieve independence than the poor resistance being put up by the Independence Army. That is why he advised his children to become men and women of abilities.

On his advice, we went on to higher schooling. Jin Sil, the eldest sister, went to the United States to study, and Song Sil studied music in China. Won Yil specialized in navigation at Joongang University in Nanjing, and I studied biology at Dongwu University in Suzhou, pursued medicine at Severance Medical College in Seoul, and completed graduate studies in the United States at Northwestern University medical school in Chicago, Illinois.

Won Yil early on had shown characteristics of being a genius. However, he enjoyed sports and was more interested in playing games than in excelling at studies. Now, apparently shocked by my father's counsel, he went about his studying with a determination that made him the top student in his school. At first he thought he would like to become a medical doctor but, captivated by the seafaring activity he was witnessing in the port of Shanghai, he enrolled in the navigation department at the State Central University in Nanjing to pursue his ambition to become a naval officer.

This led to a life connected with the sea. Later he became one of the founders of the South Korean naval forces and became an admiral. His career brought him on voyages to Hamburg, Germany; the Mediterranean Sea; the Suez Canal zone; Singapore, Malaysia; Yokohama, Japan; and Vladivostok in the Russian territories. He had unusual linguistic talent and mastered Chinese, English, and German languages. His familiarity with the German language led to his appointment and service as an ambassador representing the Republic of Korea in West Germany after his term as Defense Minister.

Bearing my father's instruction in mind, I resolved to make my own fortune in order to contribute something to my miserable nation.

My family then had moved from Jilin to Fengtian because Song Sil had contracted an illness that required treatment which might be available at a hospital connected with Tong Bei University there. She had suspended her music lessons while attempting to recuperate at our house in Jilin, but our move to Fengtian was recommended by Sin Kuk Kwon, who would become my brother-in-law. Sin Kuk Kwon was a professor in the physical education department at the University.

Our family temporarily lived in the university's staff dormitory but later moved to Beijing. After finding housing for our family and getting In Sil and me enrolled in Beijing schools, father returned to Jilin to finish the undertakings he had launched there.

We received a letter from father, some time later, urging us, his sons and daughters, to study hard to be able to better serve the nation. At the end of his letters, he wrote: "There is hope for our nation; the Chinese authorities have allowed Koreans to buy land for cultivation, lay out Korean villages and engage in farming in Manchuria."

Apparently his year-long negotiations with Zhang Zuoxiang and Zhang Xueliang had been successfully concluded and he was filled with hope. Tragically, this was our last letter from him. Before finishing the undertakings in which he had invested his fortune and his energies, he died suddenly without having an opportunity to return to his family.

That letter was the "will" which he left to his sons and daughters. I was about to graduate from middle school and mother asked me which university I planned to apply to for acceptance. I told her I wanted to study engineering or architecture, but she asked if it weren't more advisable to become a parson, succeeding my father in that profession. She wanted one of her sons to succeed my father and believed that I, a boy of retiring disposition, was aptly suited for it. I did not want to become a pastor; I couldn't explain exactly why but I doubted that anything could be achieved through the preaching of sermons. Mother did not impose her wishes upon me.

"If that's your intention, what about becoming a medical doctor instead of an architect or an engineer? The medical field is a benevolent art," she counseled.

Thus I registered in the biology department of Catholic University in Beijing. A year later I transferred to Dongwu University in Suzhou and finished the preparatory course in medicine there.

Around that time, I received information about Kim Il Sung in the Shanghai *Dagongbao* newspaper. The paper devoted one page to the anti-Japanese armed struggle being conducted by guerrillas led by General Kim Il Sung in Manchuria.

"So he has embarked on that road at long last," I thought, and I tossed in my bed imagining how Kim Sung Ju would be sleeping and eating in the open in Manchuria. I was unable to sleep all that night. Even my soft bed felt uncomfortable as I imagined the hardships he was enduring.

Whatever the road they now followed, the friends of those Jilin days cherished one thing in common: the unstained soul of the nation they had learned to revere. Even though Won Yil had not met President Kim Il Sung, nor had he made friends with him officially or privately, both were alumni of Yuwen Middle School although they attended it in different years. Won Yil mentioned it in his *My Autobiography* which he contributed to the *Hankuk Iloo* publication.

Both President Kim Il Sung and Sohn Won Yil recounted in their memoirs the days they had spent in their youth in the same places during the same period, both undergoing similar experiences. Doesn't this mean that, despite a world of difference in their political ideals, views and careers, and despite the lapse of many years, there was something that joined them together in recalling the unforgettable days of their youth in Jilin when both were inflamed with patriotism?

When Won Yil came to meet his family in Seoul, 13 years after he had left Pyongyang and 16 years after he had left Seoul, he was detained in Jongno police station and suffered a hard time there. He was suspected of being a secret messenger of the provisional government in Shanghai. The police subjected him to brutal torture, beating and kicking him and forcing him to ingest huge quantities of water. They dragged him from Jongno to Pyongyang to Kangso while pursuing their interrogations, and he was almost dead when they set him free.

The torture the Japanese had inflicted upon him on a groundless charge, added to the suspicion surrounding the sudden death of our father from "illness," imbued him with bitter hatred of Japan. This deep-seated anti–Japanese sentiment found vivid expression in his refusal, after Korea's liberation, to accept Park Chung Hee's attempt to draw him into his camp after he had seized power in the May 16 coup d'état in 1961 following the fall of the Syngman Rhee regime.

The so-called "Revitalization" forces led by Park Chung Hee seized power and began the South Korea–Japan talks, kowtowing to Japan and extolling the forces that had insisted on revering the emperor during the Meiji Restoration in Japan. Won Yil watched these developments with increasing bitterness and eventually turned his back permanently on Park's maneuvers. Park Chung Hee graduated from the Kingjing Military School of Manchukuo and, as a soldier in the "Japanese puppet" Manchukuo army, had taken the lead in the punitive operations against Korean independence fighters and anti–Japanese guerrillas.

Jong Il Gwon, also a pro–Japanese collaborator, visited Won Yil's house three times, hinting that, initially, they would give him the post of foreign minister and then the higher position of Prime Minister. To each of these "overtures," Admiral Sohn Won Yil curtly refused. When Jong gave

Won Yil a long explanation about Park's request, he said earnestly, before departing, "You agreed, sir?" To which Admiral Sohn again answered curtly: "No, I did not!"

This strongly-spoken rebuff reflected his lifelong determination that he would not join hands with the pro–Japanese forces under any circumstances. It is well known that the leading newspaper in Seoul reported this affair under the headline: "Admiral Sohn Won Yil Refuses a Government Position."

I do not know how he felt about President Kim Il Sung and North Korea; however, immediately after liberation, when I was living in Seoul, I once visited his house. Guests there were his friends from the days in Jilin: Kim Kang, the son-in-law of Ahn Pung, was an independence fighter who taught English in the Yuwen and Wenguang middle schools; and Pak Il Pha had learned Russian from a White Russian officer. Pak Il Pha had been active in the Association of Korean Children in Jilin and later went over to North Korea and played an important role in translating Tolstoy's *War and Peace* and *Resurrection* into the Korean language.

Hwang Kwi Hon, a former member of the Jilin children's association, had returned to Pyongyang to rejoin President Kim Il Sung after living in Yanbian, China. Similarly, General Choe Tok Sin, a year younger than Won Yil as a student in the Wenguang Middle School in Jilin, also relocated to Pyongyang to spend his remaining days near the president. I, too, journeyed to Pyongyang to see him in the closing years of my life, after taking a long, long detour!

When I met the president after a separation of some six decades, I unleashed my long pent-up emotions. "I didn't fight in the front line of the anti–Japanese armed struggle," I said, "but I feel grateful that you have devoted your entire life for the sake of our nation."

President Kim Il Sung, laughing heartily, had responded:

> Everyone could not fight as a guerrilla; patriots are not only those who fought with arms in hand. It is laudable if a man resisted patriotically in those grave days without ever serving Japanese imperialism and, if he still cherishes the patriotic spirit of those days, such a man is a patriot!

The water that springs out in mountain valleys forms various streams which meander along their own courses until at long last they join in the sea. Likewise, the spirit of patriotism, whatever life it has experienced, forms a sea. The patriotic spirit reunited the president and me by some invisible ties even though we had followed different paths for a long time. That is why we could have an emotional reunion.

9
An Article Carried in the Shanghai *Dagongbao*

I shall write in greater detail about how I came to know about the anti–Japanese armed struggle of General Kim Il Sung through reports in the Shanghai *Dagongbao*. As I remember, it was when I was attending Dongwu University in Shanghai. How could I attend a university that was located in Suzhou, Jiangsu Province? Japan had already invaded China, occupying a large area in northern and southern China. When the Japanese army invaded Suzhou I was studying at Dongwu University, taking the preparatory course in medicine. To escape the invaders, the university moved its operation to Anhui Province but I did not go there; instead I returned to Shanghai and studied for one year at Zao Tung University where my brother-in-law, Sin Ku Kwon, was a professor. Subsequently Dongwu University returned to Shanghai and shared the facilities of the Da Lu Business Center. So I re-enrolled to continue my medical studies in Dongwu University.

Those were uneasy days worldwide. Following the invasion of Poland by Nazi Germany, Fascist Italy had annexed Albania. After occupying Nanchang, the Japanese army occupied Hainan Island. These kinds of events sent a chill into people's hearts and it appeared to be only a matter of time until Japan would occupy the entire territory of China. All Chinese and Koreans were apprehensive about these developments, fearing that Japan would swallow up the vast regions of China and expand its occupation to the entire southeastern Asian sphere. Independence for Korea appeared to be hopeless; even breathing seemed to be difficult.

In Shanghai, I was boarding at my brother-in-law's house. One day after returning from school I was scanning newspapers and magazines when I read this headline: "Kim Il Sung and His Anti-Japanese Struggle." It was on the third page of the *Dagongbao*, a newspaper which was printed in English in Shanghai. Controlling my excitement with effort, I read and re-read the article which covered an entire page. It reported in great detail the guerrilla warfare General Kim Il Sung was waging against the Japanese, leading thousands of Korean patriots under his command. I read this article many years ago so the name of its author escapes my memory. But it was the first time that a newspaper in China proper had made special mention of the career of Kim Il Sung as the leader of the armed resistance against Japan.

I was elated, and very emotional about it, to realize that Kim Il Sung, the hero of the anti–Japanese struggle whom even the Chinese people were praising publicly, was my friend of those days in Jilin, Kim Sung Ju. My delight rose even higher when I read another article, this one about Lee Jang Chong, the heroine of the Independence Army, printed on the same page.

I had an unforgettable image of her now: how she had tried to protect Ahn Chang Ho from the police when they had tried to arrest him after they had broken into the hall where he was delivering a political lecture in Jilin. The article reported that Lee Jang Chong, the only "Red Flower" of the Independence Army, would charge on horseback to the enemy's position, clad in a well-fitting riding habit, her bobbed hair flying, firing two pistols, one in either hand. That same courageous girl could be unassuming and considerate as she pitched in to help my mother with kitchen chores whenever she visited our home.

Reading about two of the most unforgettable persons of my entire youth in the same newspaper made me feel that my good fortune had been doubled. I rushed to my sister, Song Sil, to tell her about this exciting news.

"Kim Sung Ju, my friend back in Jilin, has been reported in the newspaper, Sister!" I almost shouted. "This is Kim Sung Ju, the former chairman of our children's association! You must remember him; he was the young man who accompanied us on the organ when we were preparing for art group activities in father's church. Kim Sung Ju is Kim Il Sung!"

I still remember the words of the recitative sung by a mother and son:

An Article Carried in the Shanghai Dagongbao

SON: "Where has Daddy gone, Mom, for so long?"
 The innocent youngster cried
 On his return home from school,
 Missing his father.

MOTHER: "Your daddy has gone to a far-away place,
 He teaches our people there.
 He'll soon come back flying a flag,
 Wait for him until then, studying hard."

SON: "How far is it…
 Russia, Manchuria, or wilderness?
 I'll go to him and
 Return with him, flying the flag."

Thinking back, I recall that this was a song of determination that Kim Sung Ju had composed for his mother. It reflected his determination to win back the country, carrying out the will of his father, Kim Hyong Jik, the independence fighter, and to return "flying a flag." Putting that determination into practice, he had organized a Korean army and was fighting the Japanese imperialists in the wilderness of Manchuria.

I had heard tales of the famous guerrilla commander, Kim Il Sung, long before I read the article in *Dagongbao*. By the latter half of the 1930s, the name of Kim Il Sung was mentioned frequently in newspapers and was being talked about among people. Yet, for some time I hadn't realized that the General Kim Il Sung of guerrilla warfare fame actually was the Kim Sung Ju of our friendship days in Jilin.

I had heard it first from Kim Ku, an independence fighter in the provisional government in Shanghai who became a close friend of my father. (Mr. Kim was not the Kim Ku of the same name who had held the title of chairman at Shanghai.) Mr. Kim had visited our house frequently after my father had died and he took special care of us. One day, when we were living in Beijing, he took me aside and whispered, "Kim Sung Ju, the chairman of your children's association has organized a Korean army. He is now General Kim Il Sung. Imagine! A general in his twenties! The Rev. Sohn did not mistake him; he said that Kim Sung Ju would be a great man."

My heart was surging when I learned that Kim Sung Ju at last was starting the armed struggle for freedom. How delighted my father would have been to hear this news; he had been so heartsick watching the independence movement falling into decline.

I didn't understand why Kim Sung Ju was being known now as Kim Il Sung. However, after talking with my brother-in-law, Sin Kuk Kwon, I became convinced that General Kim Il Sung indeed was the Kim Sung Ju of our Jilin days.

Older Korean people would be able to recall that Sin was a famous soccer star before Korea was reduced to colonial slavery. When I was kicking a grass ball barefooted and following Won Yil to his games, Sin Kuk Kwon was known in China as "The King of Soccer." I first saw him on the playground of the Sungsil School in Pyongyang. Sungsil was a famous soccer school and the Seoul-Pyongyang matches were annual grand events. One year Sin headed a team from Shanghai which came to play a friendship game. The event was so popular that even sniveling boys of my age went to see it.

Sin Kuk Kwon was tall, gentlemanly, and strongly patriotic. His original name was Ki Jun but he had changed it to Kuk Kwon, meaning he would restore the national sovereignty. (Kuk Kwon means "national sovereignty" in Korean.) He met my sister, Song Sil, when he was in Shanghai on a soccer-playing tour while heading a Korean team. Their romance blossomed while she was undergoing medical treatment at the hospital which was operated by Dongbei University where Sin was a physical training professor.

The University in Fengtian (the present Shenyang) had been established by Zhang Zuolin, a Manchurian warlord, for training talented people. After Zhang Zuolin was killed in a bombing assault, his son, Zhang Xueliang, took over the university which was being managed by his brother, Zhang Xueming. Zhang Xueming had attended the Communications Zao Tung University in Shanghai with Sin Kuk Kwon who, after specializing in physical culture in the United States and working at Yonhui College in Korea as a physical training teacher, joined the staff of the Shanghai university and became closely acquainted with Zhang Xueliang.

He was often invited to visit Zhang Xueliang at his house. Sin told me that on one visit he had seen many hams hanging in a storeroom and had learned that Zhang would eat only ham, that allegedly it was effective in treating hypertension. It was apparent that Kuk Kwon enjoyed a close relationship with Zhang Xueliang.

Although Zhang had withdrawn into the interior of China, deserting the three northeastern provinces after the Manchurian Incident (September 1931), he still entertained plans to return to the occupied territory. He missed his native place and was looking ahead for the opportunity to return to Manchuria. Both the Chinese and the Koreans shared a hatred of Japan and openly expressed their dissatisfaction with Chiang Kai-shek, who had failed to put up active anti–Japanese resistance and was believed by many to have virtually connived with Japan on its invasion of China. Thus everyone was intensely interested in the resistance efforts of the Chinese Eighth Route Army in Ya'an and the Korean guerrillas in Manchuria.

An Article Carried in the Shanghai Dagongbao

The reports of the struggle being conducted by Kim Il Sung, which were printed in the Shanghai *Dagongbao*, were in response to the interest of the general populace in efforts to stave off the Japanese invasion.

I believe that Sin Kuk Kwon maintained close relations with the Zhangs and must have acted as an intermediary between them and my father because the Zhangs had great influence in Manchuria. Sin married Song Sil after my father had died but the Rev. Sohn had known Kuk Kwon well and approved of him as a prospective son-in-law. As I mentioned previously, Sin Kuk Kwon told me that Kim Il Sung and Kim Sung Ju, my boyhood Jilin friend, were indeed the same person. Nevertheless I realized that this only confirmed the hearsay that I wanted to believe and I ought not to jump to a conclusion before I could see the truth with my own eyes. What made matters worse was that some people had said that General Kim Il Sung was old and gray-bearded!

Finally, I did get the factual substantiation I needed. I don't recall the date but the *Kyongsong Ilbo* newspaper published an article entitled: "Who's the Mastermind of the Attack at Pochonbo?" This appeared immediately after the battle had taken place and described the Kim Il Sung–led guerillas as "communist bandits." Under the subtitle of "Rebellious Father and Son," the writer explained that Kim Il Sung's original name was Kim Sung Ju, that he hailed from Pyongan Province and was 27 years old, and that he was the son of Kim Hyong Jik. I then felt certain the general was my friend, Kim Sung Ju, and I cannot adequately express my feelings when I read the detailed information of his activities in the *Dagongbao* soon afterward.

In those trying days when Japan was expanding its efforts to conquer all of the Asian continent and resorting to every evil scheme to forcibly obliterate the Korean nation, Kim Il Sung was the only ray of hope remaining for Koreans. The article in the English edition of the Shanghai *Dagongbao* assured me that, although the motherland was suffering humiliation under Japanese occupation, sooner or later Korea would become independent once more.

The people of my father's generation, who had failed to attain Korea's liberation despite all of their efforts, now were pinning all of their hopes on Kim Il Sung. I learned later that Kim Ku (alias Paek Pom), Kim Won Bong and others who were active in China proper were delighted when informed that the General's unit had crossed the Amnok River and attacked Pochonbo, killing Japanese occupation forces and police units, and thus rekindling the spirit of independence in Korea. They reported news of the victorious battle at Pochonbo in their newspaper *Jondo* ("The Future") under this headline: "Happy News of the Armed Independence Movement of Korea."

When I met Mrs. Ryo Yon Gu, daughter of Ryo Un Hyong, in Pyongyang, she told me that her father, after hearing the news of the victorious battle, had driven himself by automobile to Pochonbo and inspected the battlesite to ascertain the facts about the event. Ryo Un Hyong and Kim Ku had traveled to the north after liberation to discuss prospects for a reunified Korea. It is believable that their expectations were rooted in faith in the young hero of Mt. Paektu, General Kim Il Sung, expectations that had budded and grown as early as those days.

On my most recent visit to Pyongyang, I was struck with wonder again after reading an article about General Kim Il Sung in the *Sinhan Minbo*, dated September 3, 1937. The newspaper, published in the United States for Korean compatriots, had devoted two pages to the article, displaying Kim Il Sung's name prominently. What was surprising was that the paper, published by Koreans residing in the United States and distributed in American society, had printed the article.

The Rev. Hong Tong Gun, who was living in Los Angeles, California, reportedly had brought the newspaper with him on one of his visits to North Korea. On a previous visit, when he had mentioned reading the article, North Korean officials had asked him to find a copy and send it to them. The Rev. Hong went to extreme trouble to find a copy issued 60 years earlier, but he did and had carefully photocopied the moldy one he had found. As he shared the restored copy with others, it is reported that he had tears in his eyes, evidencing his regret that he hadn't shown the article to President Kim Il Sung before he died.

Following is an excerpt from the article:

> General Jon Il Sung, Commander of the 3rd Division of the Korean Unit of the Korean-Chinese Allied Volunteer Army; Fights Flying Like a Dragon and Dashing Like a Tiger.
>
> It has already been reported in our previous issue that the situation of the Japs in Manchuria is deteriorating in the Sino-Japanese war owing to the joint operations of the independence army of Korea and the volunteer army of China.
>
> Now a detailed Tianjin news dispatch says that the most courageous and efficient fighting forces among the Koreans and Chinese volunteers is the 3rd Division composed of Koreans and commanded by General Jon Il Sung, Korean. (According to newspapers in Japan and news from Korea, Mr. Kim Il Sung's armed force, operating from its base in Jiandao, crossed the border last June and attacked Pochonbo, Kapsan, to strike terror into the hearts of the Japanese army and police. The subsequent actions of his army were frequently reported by *Dong-a Ilbo* and other newspapers. Refer to the July 29th issue of this newspaper. The reports from China all call him Jon Il Sung and it is our conjecture that

the surname Kim was misreported as Jon, as Kim is a surname rare in China.)

The scope of operation of the army in northeast China is very wide and its power is quite strong as it is under a specially-organized force. Its soldiers' life and operation are characterized by the spirit of the Oriental man of military chivalry. To say between ourselves, not only do we feel the thunderous sound of their struggle but the Japanese enemies also praise them.

A Soviet military expert observed, "If China and Japan declare war formally against each other, the Japanese will need 200,000 troops to cope with the volunteer force in this one corner of Manchuria." If this observation is reliable, then they are truly a great force.

The Rev. Hong Tong Gun has done a laudable job for the nation.

After I read the article in *Dagongbao* I was anxious to hear everything I could about Lee Jang Chong, but not until I had visited North Korea was I able to learn about her later life. Her fate was no better than that of many other independence fighters. As the Japanese imperialists intensified their repression, rifts began to break out in the ranks of nationalist independence fighters. Veiled enmity was leading to the factional strife my father had been so apprehensive about; one compatriot would betray another to the enemy and sometimes even killed another. Incapable of adjusting to such changes, the movement began to lose vigor.

Lee Jang Chong's fate was caught up in this trend. Her outgoing spirit of patriotism and her unbendable will to follow the independence movement left no room for any compromise, so her support began to diminish. Aware of what was taking place in her relationship with the movement, Lee Jang Chong married the Chinese man in whose garret she had been hiding, and her glorified role as the "Red Flower" of the army in the independence movement came to an end.

It seemed likely that no one would remember her or the great contribution she had made for Korean freedom. She was living her married life in seclusion in a mountainside dwelling in an alien land — but President Kim Il Sung did not forget her!

Respecting her wish to live the closing years of her life and be laid to rest in the motherland for which she had devoted the prime of her life to the fight for freedom, President Kim Il Sung negotiated with Chinese authorities for her return to Pyongyang. In her eighties when she returned to her motherland, the former heroine of the Independence Army lived out her life in comfort under a government pension provided for her and other Korean independence fighters under the program inaugurated by President Kim Il Sung.

I visited her grave in the Patriotic Martyrs Cemetery in Sinmi-ri, Pyongyang. As I stood in front of the gravestone inscribed "Independence Fighter Lee Kwan Rin Lee Jang Chong," I was reminded of the article published in the Shanghai *Dagongbao* half a century earlier. Not having heard any news about her since that time, I mistakenly had assumed that the "Red Flower's" name had slipped from people's memory. However, thanks to a grateful President Kim Il Sung, she lay in dignified repose among other independence fighters and was acknowledged by her motherland as a heroine to be remembered by posterity.

When I went to Pyongyang to celebrate the 80th birthday of President Kim Il Sung, I met the son and daughter of Lee Jang Chong. They had journeyed from Xi'an, China, to pay their respects to the president on behalf of their mother. Meeting them caused me to reminisce on bygone days with special emotion. How could the patriotic sacrifices of Lee Jang Chong and many other independence fighters be extolled except in this way — a return to the motherland for comfortable pensioned retirement and an honorable burial in the Patriotic Martyrs Cemetery?

The armed struggle against Japan to free Korea from the yoke of slavery under the occupation, the rebuilding of his country under a caring and considerate government: such was the mission that the young man, Kim Sung Ju, had taken upon himself. It was the mission that the generation of my father, who had been making a great fuss in Jilin about the independence movement, had forsaken, whether unwillingly or intentionally. Kim Il Sung, the young man of my Jilin days, now had become the general in command of the 3rd Division of the Korean-Chinese Allied Volunteer Army, and would tread a bloody road for more than 15 years carrying out that mission.

10

In the Nagasaki Prison

When I was studying at the University in Shanghai in 1939, mother and In Sil lived in Seoul, Korea. Family life in Beijing had been very difficult. The family had not been well off originally and after my father's death the situation sometimes defied description. He had left mother no money for us because he had spent the entire inheritance he received from his parents on the independence movement. We managed to survive, thanks to help from my brothers-in-law. Before long, however, my mother went back to Seoul, accompanied by In Sil, to live with Jin Sil, her eldest daughter. Sohn Jin Sil was the only one of her children to be born in Kangso, my father's home community. After graduating from the Ewha Womans University, she continued her studies in Shanghai and then at a university in Chicago, Illinois. After marrying Yun Chi Ho's younger brother, Yun Chi Chang, she became a resident of Seoul.

I wanted to see my mother and In Sil and I was also eager to go to Korea because Won Yil was there and was planning to be married. I hadn't seen my brother for a long time.

In Shanghai, I happened to have become acquainted with a young Korean man named Kim Ho Mun. He visited me often and on one occasion I told him that I wanted to go to Seoul to see my mother but I didn't have the courage to go alone because I did not know how to speak the Japanese language. He immediately responded that his brother was about to end his visit in Shanghai and would be returning to Seoul soon so I could accompany him and have no language problems. I left Shanghai by ship on New Year's Day in 1940, accompanied by Kim Ho Mun's brother. After a long sea voyage our ship docked at Nagasaki, Japan, a port of call on our route to Seoul.

As soon as I had disembarked at Nagasaki, Japanese police appeared and without preliminary explanation walked me over to a maritime police station. I had no idea about what was going to happen to me but as I stood upright, a suitcase in each hand, I felt sickened and humiliated while a policeman scanned me from head to foot. I didn't have an overcoat so I had borrowed my brother-in-law's. The garment was too large for me and, although I had rolled up the sleeves to shorten them to my arm-length, the hemline of the coat almost swept along the ground. As a policeman was looking me over, I thought that he was treating me with contempt because of my unkempt appearance but I learned that he was being scornful of my upright posture. Koreans were supposed to be subservient.

He interrogated me in Japanese, which I could not understand, and when I did not answer his questions, he became angry, scowling fiercely at me and spitting out what apparently were words of venom and hatred. Koreans were supposed to be humble and obeisant in the presence of their Japanese masters.

Then he shoved me into a cell and locked me in. After liberation ended the occupation, I learned that Kim Ho Mun's brother was an agent of the Japanese police station in Seoul and Kim Ho Mun himself was an agent of the Japanese consulate in Shanghai. The cell was dark and so cold that I had to sit wrapped in a quilt.

At ten o'clock every morning I was called out and interrogated for about an hour while sitting in a chair placed in the center of a spacious room. The questions went on and on, repetitiously, like this: "When did you attend the Nanjing Military Academy?" ... "Which task have you been assigned by the provisional government in Shanghai?" ... "You're a communist, aren't you?"

Their questions seemed preposterous to me and I was too naïve to understand what they wanted from me. It was my good fortune that they didn't ask about my participation in the anti–Japanese demonstrations during my primary, middle-school and university days. Not long after my family had moved to Jilin a student demonstration campaign was launched under the slogans: "Down with Japanese imperialism!" and "Down with traitors to the nation!" The campaign was aimed at condemning Japan and the Chinese high officials who were being bribed by Japan.

When I was a student in a middle school in Beijing there was a fiercely conducted campaign against Japanese trade. I was given the assignment to persuade my classmates not to buy or use Japanese products. During the time I was enrolled in the biology department at Furen University, which was run by German priests, I had been elected chairman of the first-year students. The university's policy provided for the election of student chairman and vice-chairman in each department; at that time, most universities permitted students to form associations. The Beijing General Student Association organized anti–Japanese demonstrations which involved participation by students of all the universities, middle schools and primary schools in the area. Slogans were the usual ones: "Down with Japanese imperialism!" and "Down with traitors to the nation!"

Girl students were equally, if not more, courageous than boys. On one occasion, a girl student was making a speech on the roof of a streetcar when she was shot to death. My blood boiled at this atrocity and I became unafraid of the bullets. Many students were killed or wounded. A week later, I attended a memorial ceremony for the victims of the Japanese-controlled police assault. Hanging on the wall of the large classroom were the blood-stained uniforms of those who had been cut down during the demonstrations.

As I had from early childhood hated the empire of Japan, had supported the overthrow of its imperialism and had been a leader in the campaign to boycott Japanese goods, the Japanese police could have made a case for my arrest. Had they known those details about my past, they would have subjected me to cruel torture.

Apparently that information was not known by them. However, I was grilled every day at ten o'clock in the morning. When they became aware that I did not understand the Japanese language, an inspector who spoke Korean took over the daily interrogations; at other times policemen who knew Chinese or English did the questioning.

Then one day a Japanese of higher authority took over the inquisition. By that time I was disgusted with the stereotyped grilling and made no effort to respond with answers. Thereupon, he struck me hard on the crown of my head with a bamboo fencing stick. Losing consciousness, I fell off the chair. Recovering my senses quite a bit later, I felt that I was walking through a heavy fog. My memory of the past seemed to have disappeared but eventually an image seemed to emerge from a thick mist. It was Kim Sung Ju, his cheeks dimpling as he smiled affectionately.

I have wondered how this image alone could loom out of the depths of oblivion into which all memory of everything else in my past had disappeared. In retrospect, I believe that, apparently, the only person who could assuage my grief and pain by taking vengeance upon the enemy was Kim Il Sung, now engaged in fighting the Japanese imperialists in the forests of Mt. Paektu.

I thought: "He was right. Preaching a sermon or practicing medicine will lead us nowhere and cannot relieve our people of the suffering as a ruined nation or win back our deprived country. The only way is to fight with arms in hand!"

There were no windows in the cell so I could not see the outside world. I cannot adequately describe the stifling, uneasy feelings that immersed me in the silence and darkness of that grave-like enclosure. A round clock was hanging on the wall of the prison corridor. It was my only friend. I talked mentally with it, one-two-three, as its second hand ticked away the time. Sometimes the tempo seemed to be provokingly slow. Whatever my feelings, it relentlessly ticked away all day and all night.

I was reminded of a song I would sing in my childhood:

> Don't waste time,
> Tick, tock, tick, tock,
> Says the clock.

I composed words and set them to its tune:

> Don't forget,
> Tick, tock, tick, tock,
> Says the clock.

I can never forget the image of Kim Sung Ju as it emerged from the depths of my mental agony in that Nagasaki prison. During the long nights, I wanted to dream because only in a dream could I enjoy freedom and envision the dear people I was missing. Now I am rowing my boat to somewhere across the foggy sea. A light twinkles on the far-away mountain. Holding bags in both hands, I am falling down a waterfall! Now I wake ... this was just a dream!

A black chair has been placed in the middle of a clean room with white walls. Sitting on the chair, I am looking at the front wall. A door opens and a tall man comes in, silently takes me by the hand and leads me out of the room. We walk along a granite-paved lane and cross a green lawn. A clear stream flows across the lane from the right. The man picks me up and dips my feet in the stream and then puts me down on the lawn. He wears milk-white clothes and has long hair. He does not appear to be young. Then he disappears and never returns.

The day following that dream, a Japanese investigator informed me that I would be transferred to Seoul in about 1 week. Adding that it was confidential, he said that I had been confined in that Nagasaki prison for four months.

When I arrived by ship at Pusan a week later, another police detective took charge of me and put me on a train. About one o'clock a.m. we arrived in Tongdaemun police station in Seoul where the detective threw me into a detention room and locked the door. That was the way my motherland greeted her native son who was returning after nearly 20 years, as a detainee in a prison in Seoul the city in which I was born. The motherland, which I had yearned for while asleep or awake, had been turned into an immense Japanese prison!

I fell flat on the cement floor of the detention cell, my heart and chest consumed with pain. It was the start of angina pectoris, brought on by the cruel treatment, malnutrition and lack of exercise I had experienced in the Nagasaki prison. The Japanese also had made me the recipient of another "gift" disease, beriberi.

My entire family was set astir when it became known that I had been thrown into prison. Everyone did everything possible to get me released from detention. Jin Sil and her husband, Yun Chi Chang, apparently had the greater influence, assisted by Yun Chi Ho, and Yu Ok Kyom, who was the husband of the sister of Yi Wang's wife. All of them contributed a great deal because they had wide acquaintance among the Japanese police. Thanks to them all, I was released on parole after being held in detention for one year.

My parole required me to report to the police station at ten o'clock every morning to obtain permission to remain free under what is known as "house arrest." I had been transferred from a big prison to a small one but invisible chains shackled me tightly, giving me no freedom. It was the eventual fate of a ruined nation!

The angina pectoris which had been brought on by the conditions of my incarceration in the Nagasaki prison almost devitalized me later on. I always felt my heart was stifled and oppressed. In the mornings I felt as exhausted as if I had not slept and in university classes I would doze off from time to time. I consulted a physician at Severance Hospital and visited an internist when I was studying in the United States but neither could find anything wrong with my heart. However, their findings did not relieve the constricting sense of oppression. About thirty years later I consulted a specialist again and underwent a treadmill stress test. The diagnosis was normal so I accepted the possibility that my problem after all was not angina pectoris.

Then, in 1985, while playing tennis I felt a piercing pain in my heart and was carried to a hospital. A thorough coronary angiogram examination revealed that my right coronary artery was 95 percent blocked and the left tributary was 75 percent narrowed. To complicate the problem, the back muscle of the heart had been damaged and so hardened that it was not functioning. I immediately underwent coronary-artery surgery involving a double by-pass, and the symptoms subsided. The black hands of Nagasaki had pursued me even to the United States, tenaciously seeking to claim my life.

In my lifetime I was almost killed on three occasions. The first was in the summer of 1942 when I rescued a drowning man in the sea off Songjon in Kangwon Province. The second was in 1947 when I went to Sorok Island to treat lepers, accompanied by Hong Pil Hun, Sin Kwang Son, Jo Min Haeng and Choy Sun Hak, all fellow alumni of Severance Medical College, and a professor from the Ewha Womans University. After 5 p.m. one day, we all went swimming in the sea and I almost drowned while being carried out by the swift off-shore currents.

I "by-passed" my third close scrape almost without knowledge of it when I was a rotating intern at Severance Hospital following my graduation from the medical school in 1945. I was filling out case history sheets on patients of the surgical department when a first-year medical student phoned me to tell about a book he had seen, a confidential document of the Japanese secret service police. Listed in the document were thousands of people related to the independence movement. Among them were Sohn Jong Do, Ahn Chang Ho, Oh Tong Jin, Kim Ku, Kim Kyu Sik, Sin Chae Ho, etc. Also on the document's listing were the names of Kim Sung Ju (Kim Il Sung), Sohn Won Yil, and mine! Beside the name was written: "At large!"

The student's father was chief of the Seoul police station and, according to the student, the persons listed on the document were to be executed on one of three designated occasions. I was to be executed on the first occasion. That seemed quite probable because I was a son of Sohn Jong Do. The executed persons were to be buried in dug-outs in the streets. Those dug-outs were air raid shelters large enough to accommodate five people.

The student said that the first batch "consigned to hell" would be executed within three months. Had the liberation of Korea in August of 1945 by the defeat of Japan in World War II been delayed a few months, I would have been buried in one of those street dug-outs! During those several months prior to the Japanese surrender, a stranger, clad in a Japanese Kimono and carrying a menacing bamboo stick, would stroll in front of my house. Whenever I saw his threatening eyes I would shudder involuntarily although I thought he was merely keeping me under surveillance as part of my parole. Probably he was the detective assigned to execute me. Anyhow, I have had a long life!

11

Love Overcomes My Depression

Although I was released from the Tongdaemun police station, it was the same as being locked in a cage because I had to remain confined in my house day and night. I was living in Hyehwadong, Seoul, in the house my brother-in-law had built for my mother. Its surroundings had been thick with grass and wild berries, but other houses soon began to be constructed, one after another, until nature's ambience was changed to become typical of suburbia. Some of the dwellings were owned by high government officials who wore Japanese clothing, spoke the Japanese language and behaved like Japanese.

Those were trying times. Koreans were forced to change their names into Japanese ones; they were compelled to pay homage to Japanese shrines and bow in reverence in the direction of the Imperial Palace in Japan. I was also required to report to the police station every morning. Thus, I was looking for a chance to escape to a foreign country; at one point, I thought about trying to get to Won Yil, who was living in Shanghai.

Somehow, the police suspected my intentions and I was summoned to the station and handed a sheet of paper which contained all of the regulations which I would have to observe while living outside the prison on parole. I would not be permitted to outside of Seoul's city limits or attend any public or private gathering of people. I would also be required to report to the police station every morning at ten o'clock. I sealed my agreement to the restrictions with my thumb print.

I was completely distraught, almost to the point of losing my mind, as my plan to escape was thwarted in this way. I wanted to continue my study of medicine but that was impossible because I did not know the Japanese language which was mandatory in all schools. My sister, Jin Sil, suggested that I seek permission to go to Tokyo to learn Japanese; her proposal made good sense to me because I had become convinced that it was now impossible to escape to Shanghai. Anything to get free from my cage.

It wasn't easy to obtain permission to leave Seoul because I was branded "rebellious" by the police but, after people of influence stood up to guarantee my compliance, I was allowed to leave Seoul. I enrolled in a short course in the Japanese language at the International School attached to Waseda University. The school had been established to provide instructions in the language for second-generation Japanese born in America. I studied the language there for two years.

A girl student at the school apparently fell in love with me although I was unaware of it. She was a pretty and very kind-hearted Japanese girl who had been born in Hawaii. I didn't notice the attention she was paying to me, perhaps because I always walked with eyes downcast and was seriously devoting myself to studies and sports activities. My love at that time was exercise; I played tennis, soccer, and baseball and did a lot of ice-skating. I held speed skating championships in China in 1931 and 1932.

One day a Chinese student in the class approached me and winking in the direction of the girl sitting in front of us, said, "She seems to love you."

I looked at him in disbelief, wondering who could love this reticent fellow. Then he added that, because I was very good in sports, I was quite popular among the girl students.

"She has quite a passion for you, so I can't get anywhere with her," he continued.

I told him that he was wrong because she had nothing to do with me, whereupon he smiled meaningfully and responded, "What a fool you are!"

In retrospect, I think that he was probably right. She would always sit at a desk in front of mine; when we were on a class trip, she saved a seat for me beside hers; at times, she asked me to accompany her to a theater, having obtained two tickets; on other occasions, she would ask me to go to a restaurant for some Chinese food. Naively, I was suspecting that she might be a Japanese secret service agent; police detectives were keeping watch on me, even in Japan. While attempting to avoid close association with her, I studied her carefully. She didn't really fit the character of a Japanese agent and her eyes always seemed to be radiating affection, I concluded. Yet my heart could not respond.

One chilly winter day, as I was walking to the library, my hands stuffed in the pockets of my overcoat and my head down-turned as usual, I suddenly became aware of a tender hand joining mine in one pocket. Looking up, I saw her gazing at me, her eyes aglow. My mind struggled in confusion ... should I tell her to take her hand away, or should I take her hand in mine? The first option would be insulting, I knew, and, not wanting to hurt her feelings, I took her hand lightly in mine and withdrew them. Then I noticed tears welling up in her eyes and she seemed to be asking: "Is it because I am Japanese?" Was this true? In any event, I wouldn't be able to explain why I did not love her. I didn't know the reason, then.

A short time later, I boarded a train for a journey and again found her seated beside me. Another passenger, jostled off balance, stepped on her foot and she cried out: "Ayah!" That surprised me because "Ayah" is a Korean cry of pain; Japanese would say "Aita." Thinking it might be, I told her that I believed she must be a Korean.

When she departed for Wagayama Prefecture several days later to visit relatives, she left me a note stating that she would have something to talk about with me when she returned. I assumed that she was planning to ascertain whether her ancestors had come from the mainland. However, I returned to Seoul before she came back to Tokyo. I often wondered about what she had wanted to tell me. Was she going to say that she loved me? Or was it merely to let me know that her ancestors also were Korean? However, the one question that I never have been able to answer is: How could I have failed to fall in love with that affable and comely girl?

Thinking back on those days with some regret, I realize that I didn't feel real affection for any girl in my youth. The affectionate feelings that any girl might hold for me could not relieve me of the melancholy and mental agony caused by the Japanese occupation of my homeland. It was an unfortunate time for young people; there were many tragic experiences for youths; most young men were drafted and dragged to the Pacific War fronts. The cat's paws of Japan rummaged throughout the countryside to conscript Korean young men and send them to the front lines. Patriotic young Korean men were unwilling to sacrifice their lives for the Japanese tyrants who enslaved their country. Many went into hiding to avoid conscription.

One young man was spotted by Japanese detectives on Jongno Street in Seoul. To escape them, he dashed into the Hwasin Department Store, fled to the rooftop and took his own life by plunging headlong to the ground. It was a demonstration of patriotic spirit stating that he would not serve as cannon fodder for the Japanese empire; instead, he would courageously sacrifice his own life in protest. In that way, he was safeguarding the soul of the nation.

After reading an article about the event in *Dong-a Ilbo*, I went to the department store and bowed my head in tribute to that young man. Had there been many more like him in Korea, perhaps its independence would have been achieved much sooner. Nevertheless, as the nation was being reduced to slavery, its youth were being trampled down and falling in love was a luxury difficult to enjoy in those disagreeable times.

That tragic affair greatly shocked me. I was nearly 30 years old and I had given little or no thought to marriage. However, my mother was growing old and gray-haired. Whenever I saw her busying herself with kitchen work, I thought that I ought to marry for her sake but I could feel no compelling affection for any girl.

There were marriageable girls available, of course. One magazine printed a cartoon depicting several girls pursuing a male student at a medical school, shouting, "Please marry me!" All men who looked youthful had been conscripted for the Pacific War and only a small number of boys remained in the medical schools.

When I was attending Severance Medical College, a number of girls proposed to me. One was an Ewha Womans University teacher named Choe Ye Sun. She hailed from Kangso, my father's birthplace. Having studied in America, she was a modern girl. One day she confided to my sister that if she married Sohn Won Tai she would support him efficiently and make a famous man of him. I was unconcerned about her words.

However, a girl did enter my life when I was in the graduating class at medical college. One day in 1944, my mother returned from a dental appointment and announced that she had seen a girl there who was to her liking. She advised me, several times, to pay the young lady a visit. Finally, I resisted by asking, "But what if I don't like her after visiting with her?" To which mother responded, "Then it ends there!"

I was still reluctant, saying, "How can I say 'no' after I have met her, Mother? It would break her heart!"

Murmuring something like, "I seem to have been born stupid!" she appeared to be so disappointed that I did go to the dentist's office, if reluctantly, to assuage my feelings of guilt for causing my mother such unhappiness.

There, a girl with a face of peach color, wearing a white gown, greeted me with a smile. She was a student at Ewha Womans University and worked after school hours as a nurse in the dental office, which was owned by her brother. She was lovable, had a well-formed face, a smiling countenance and smooth complexion; well, she was as adorable as a chubby puppy. Somehow, there was an aura of freshness about her which was reminiscent of fruit blossoms in late spring. I wasn't inclined to make any quick judgment but I could think of no reason to reject her. Anyway, I reasoned to myself, mother is favorably impressed with her so I ought to follow her wishes. In other words, I would marry this girl who so charms my mother.

It was one of my finest decisions. The girl was Lee Yoo Shin, the wife who has shared my life some 55 years. She hailed from Sungsugu-ri, Pyongyang. Her father was a Christian presbyter in the church of Jangdae Hill in Pyongyang. The house in which she spent her childhood was situated not far from the Pothong River, and she had played in the same area of the city which I loved to recall in memory after leaving it when I was only seven years old.

After our engagement was arranged, I went with two classmates to the beach at Songjon, Thongchon County, Kangwon Province, for recreation and to recuperate. My brother-in-law, Yun Chi Chang, owned the villa in which we were staying. One evening, I heard someone knocking at the door, cautiously, it seemed; the silence that followed led me to wonder if I actually had heard the gentle rapping. But then a frenzy of cackling sounds broke out so I went to the door and opened it. Standing there was Lee Yoo Shin, holding a pair of live hens wrapped in a cloth. Reacting to my surprised looks, she said she had dropped by on the way back from her mother's maiden home in Cholwon, Kangwon Province. Her mother had sent the hens to her future son-in-law as a gift of health food because there was nothing else that seemed special enough to come from the countryside.

It was most gracious of Yoo Shin to have come such a long way, carrying those live hens without regard to tainting her honor as a lady, and I felt rays of warmth flowing into my heart. My deep love for her probably took root in my soul on that day.

I took her to the beach that evening. The moon flooded the whispering waves that were washing ashore to paint the sands a glistening silver. I couldn't think of anything to say to Yoo Shin. In novels and films, a man would caress and kiss a woman in such a romantic situation, but somehow I did not dare to make such overtures. I walked beside her, my head hanging down, hoping that there might be a stone in the sand over which she might stumble, so that I could put my arms around her to prevent a fall. But there were no stones on the beach.

When we had come upon a pine grove on our stroll, I gathered my courage and held her hands in mine and we sat down on the warm sands, side by side. The summer evening air was comfortable, but somewhat cool, and Yoo Shin pressed close to me apparently because she was a bit cold, I thought. But, as I hugged her closely to share the warmth from my own body, I became aware of a feeling of happiness that was a new experience for me. Yoo Shin later confessed that she too had felt as though her body was melting away.

That blissful moment didn't last very long. A policeman in a black uniform suddenly appeared out of nowhere and stood in front of us. He spat out: "Stand up! Follow me!" We did, having no alternative, and were taken to what obviously was a guard outpost. There we were subjected to a lengthy interrogation.

> Who are you; where are you from? Why are you on this beach in the dead of night? What the devil is love when the soldiers of the Empire are fighting desperate battles with the Americans? U.S. submarines intrude continually into the sea over there, and you sent a signal to them, didn't you?

The experience was abhorrent to us. Throughout the night, we were made fun of and harassed. However, when a messenger, sent to check on my statement that I was lodging at Yun Chi Chang's villa, returned and confirmed that it was true, their attitude changed. But my heart, which had begun to thaw, had become frozen again.

On our visit to Pyongyang in May of 1991, thanks to the consideration of President Kim Il Sung, we went on tour to the world-famous Kumgang Mountains, which we wanted very much to see. After bypassing Wonsan, our guide took our car onto a highway that followed along the seashore. Earlier on this drive, I had told our group about those romantic moments with Yoo Shin on the beach at Songjon.

After a while, our car came to a halt and Mr. Choe, our guide, suggested a short rest would be therapeutic before we continued on our way. A proverb counsels: "When in Rome, do as the Romans do." As we climbed out of our vehicle, the kindly, learned and humorous Mr. Choe suggested, smiling, that we look around at our surroundings. The beach, cloistered with thick groves of pine trees, somehow seemed familiar to me.

"Oh, this is Songjon beach!"

It was Yoo Shin who first recognized where we were. As we walked arm in arm, white ripples danced along the beach, wetting our feet. Forty-seven years had passed since we had strolled along Songjon beach a romantic first time, but the scene had not changed ... except that now there were happy people swimming offshore and young people dancing and frolicking in the pine forest.

I hugged my wife tightly, compensating in part for what I had failed to do on that long-ago walk! The head on my shoulder was gray now: Where had her vibrant black hair gone? Had youth left us so unaware of its departure?

Yoo Shin suddenly asked me: "Do you remember what happened on our wedding day?"

Do I remember?! We were married in 1944, but on that important day I almost spoiled my relationship with her. The ceremony was to be held at her house in Cholwon on the day before the popular Chusok Festival, when all trams and trains were crowded with passengers. I barely had managed to catch a tram to the railway station and it got there just as the train for Cholwon was scheduled to leave. In my haste to get aboard before my train pulled out, I got on the wrong one. I realized it was not the right train when it started to move out in the wrong direction. I jumped off, only to discover that the train to Cholwon was also beginning to get under way across the platform. I was frantic; if I couldn't catch my train, I would miss my bride-to-be as well. Running as fast as I could, I did manage to catch up with it and climb aboard.

Completing this narrative, I added, "If I had not been a skater and racer who had won a trophy in my middle school days, I might have missed marrying this lovely lady." This brought a burst of laughter from our tour group, so I was prompted to play the comic and commented, "Looking back, I think I regret having spent my youth much like a monk. I wish I had enjoyed as many love affairs as possible."

To which, Yoo Shin retorted, "The only man in my life has been you."

Happily, as we approached and passed our silver and golden jubilee celebrations, we have lived harmoniously like a pair of doves. My wife would understand any regretfulness associated with my youth that had passed so swiftly. How on earth could there be innocent youth and beautiful romance for prisoners behind bars? Deprived of their motherland, our generation had both its youth and its love downtrodden.

Silently praying that such misfortune might never befall the young people we saw enjoying, to their hearts' content, the pleasures on Songjon beach, I returned solemnly to our tour group.

12
To Testify to the Truth of History

A plane-tree was growing in the yard of our house in Hyehwa-dong, Seoul. My mother had brought it with her from Beijing when she returned to her motherland. There is a touching story about that tree. When my family moved from Jilin to Beijing by way of Fengtian, my father found a house suitable for the family and arranged for In Sil and me to be enrolled in school before he went back to Jilin to finish his work there. But, before he left, he planted a tree in the yard. It was a young sapling, its trunk thinner than my finger. He told us that both In Sil and I would be grown up by the time the tree would have grown enough to cast a shade. Then he asked mother to nurture that tree — and the children, as well.

Father never returned home to us. The following spring, when buds came out and its leaves, no larger than a baby's fist, glistened in the sun, mother would weep as she tenderly cared for the tree's growth. She was unable to bring father's remains with her when she returned to Seoul, but she did bring the tree. She had protected that tree with a mound of straw, held firmly in place with a necklace of white stones. As it matured, she would busy herself at chores under its shade and, as if in remembrance of father, seemed to fondle its bark, leaning against it when she took a moment or two to rest from her labors.

We called it Mother's Tree.

One spring, while planting the bole of the tree to protect it from insects, I wrote "1945" on it. Somehow, I had a hunch that Korea would become independent that year. Publications were headlining reports that Japan was winning one battle after another in the Pacific, but the signs of its eventual defeat were clear; no one would believe the propaganda. Fearing that the police, who continued to shadow me, might read my mind from the writing, I wrote "Mother's Tree" above the date I had inscribed. By chance, or inevitability, my hunch was proved to be right because on August 15, 1945, Korea was liberated.

Many of the people who worked in the Japanese Governor-General's department lived in Hyehwa-dong. Some of them were Koreans who were so pro–Japanese that they ate Japanese food, wore Japanese clothing and lived in Japanese-styled houses; they behaved like Japanese. The newspapers reported that their lifestyle followed Japanese fashion. Mother would stay away from gatherings of the so-called "patriotic circle"; she deeply disliked seeing the pro–Japanese Koreans wearing Japanese clothing, speaking in the Japanese tongue, and flaunting their pleasure to be doing so.

As soon as the surrender of Japan was announced, those pro–Japanese Koreans changed back to Korean clothing and cheered in the streets for the independence of the country. Many of them came to our house to bow in respect to my mother, the widow of the anti–Japanese independence fighter who had given his life to achieve it. Mother wept bitterly as she leaned against her tree, crushed by frustration and abhorrence as pro–Japanese elements came by, obsequiously offering patently insincere condolences.

With the landing of U.S. troops in South Korea, those who had been cooperating with the Japanese Governor-General moved swiftly into the military administration, cloaking themselves in the guise of friends of America. Their transition from pro–Japanese collaborators to pro–American colors was accomplished with all of the adroit skill of a chameleon, and for the same purpose: self-protection and aggrandizement.

Thanks to the blood and sweat, the sacrifice and dedication of real patriotism, the 36-year-long Japanese rule was brought to an end and liberation appeared, at last, to have come to Korea. However, the excitement did not last long. A new national tragedy, designed by foreign forces, had divided the nation into north and south segments!

In South Korea, where the U.S. Army had landed, a strange state of affairs was created: Pro-Japanese collaborators obtained the upper hand and slandered the patriots who had fought against the Japanese for Korean independence. Those pro–Japanese elements and stooges of Japanese imperialism had been driven out of North Korea but had now reassembled in the south.

It became difficult to distinguish between who was a patriot and who was a traitor to the nation.

The news that General Kim Il Sung, the legendary hero of Korean resistance to Japan, had made a triumphal return to Pyongyang became known in Seoul. At first, the newspapers carried the information under bold-lettered headlines, but then ensued a different period of rumors and gossip. One theme was that the General Kim Il Sung, who had made a triumphal return to Pyongyang, was a young man. Simple-minded people reasoned that this could not be so; he would have to be an old and veteran general because everyone had heard about the legendary tales of his guerrilla tactics from their childhood days and, in their opinion, a man would have to be very old to have achieved such fame!

I thought that if General Kim Il Sung was a young man in his thirties, he was, without doubt, the Kim Sung Ju of our days on Jilin. Yet, I hesitated to jump to that conclusion because I had not seen him with my own eyes. I also felt uneasy about it because there had been rumors that the Kim Il Sung who commanded the historic battle at Pochonbo had been killed in a subsequent battle and another man now was going under his name.

In those days, after my graduation, I had been lecturing on anatomy at Severance Medical College. Dr. Kim Myong Son, who had earned a Ph.D. degree at Northwestern University in the United States, was teaching physiology at Severance Medical College following his release from Japanese imprisonment. He had been arrested shortly before the Korean liberation and was imprisoned by Japanese police who considered him to be a patriot opposing Japanese occupation.

Dr. Kim advised me one day: "If you study in America for about two years and then return, there would be a road paved for you because your father was a renowned independence fighter and you're a friend of Kim Il Sung."

The doctor said he was certain that North and South Korea would be reunited sooner or later. When I asked him how he had come to know about all of this, he only smiled meaningfully, saying that there was nothing he did not know. He did not offer further comment and I didn't want to prod him for additional knowledge he might have about the political scene; I was happy enough to have learned through him that Kim Il Sung actually was Kim Sung Ju, my friend in those boyhood days in Jilin.

The false rumors about Kim Il Sung did not cease and it became obvious that they were being spread by pro–Japanese sources. At one point, the newspapers even carried a statement by Syngman Rhee, the man then in power in South Korea, that he would attack North Korea, but not Japan.

I once talked with Colonel Price, an American adviser to the South Korean army who had served under General MacArthur when he was in the Philippines. During our conversation, Colonel Price said it was "embarrassing" to him that Syngman Rhee continually insisted on fighting war with North Korea.

The "independence movement" that Syngman Rhee had conducted, while living an affluent life in America during the days of Japanese occupation of Korea, consisted of submitting petitions as a mendicant in lieu of diplomacy. After the liberation, Syngman Rhee strengthened his own political foundation by bringing together pro–Japanese elements and compradors of foreign capitalists. North Korea, where patriots had fought a long drawn-out struggle against Japan, apparently was a thorn in the flesh of his political administration. From that questionable background, many of the false rumors undoubtedly were disseminated intentionally to impair the prestige of General Kim Il Sung.

Engrossed in becoming a capable medical doctor, I was largely unaware of the inner workings of politics and its power manipulations, but I could not bear to see former pro–Japanese elements holding their heads high while plotting to harm the patriots who had fought against Japan to gain Korea's independence. Not disposed to buying favor of others with flattery, I was increasingly distressed by those developments. Fortunately, I passed scholarship examinations to pursue medical study in the United States, as did two other Severance graduates, and thus was extricated from my unhappy association with such a social and political atmosphere.

I left Seoul in the summer of 1949, destined for San Francisco. After studying English for a month at Mills College in Berkeley, California, I enrolled at Northwestern University Medical School which is located in Chicago. I took courses in anatomy, pathology, bacteriology and pharmacology at Northwestern and then had four years of pathology training in residency at Cook County Hospital in Chicago.

I once attended a party for Severance Medical College alumni in Florida. Meeting with school fellows after many years was an emotional experience; nothing could be more enjoyable than recalling those good old college days back home. Two young doctors brought me a cup of wine; they had been students at Severance when I taught anatomy there. They said they could never forget what I had told them during the first session of the anatomy class: "When you become medical doctors after graduating from college, you will be assigned to treat patients. The medical arts are human arts so you must learn sincerity and never resort to cunning! If you are cunning when studying medical arts, you will be cunning when you practice medicine; if you are not sincere when studying medical arts, you will become dishonest doctors. To entrust a man's life to the hands of such a doctor is dreadful even to think about."

One of the young doctors added: "As you said, we should not be cunning. I had a difficult time of it and I could pray to God zealously to enable me to pass my examinations, although even God can't do anything about that."

I was humbly pleased that they had kept in mind what I had said about the ethics of their calling and it was even more pleasing to learn, in later years, that my former students indeed had become honest doctors.

When I was attending Dongwu University in Shanghai, I had not taken the examination in physics because I had been ill. The professor of physics told me: "Although you did not take the examination, I have decided to give you a mark of 85 because you have done your homework of your own volition. Others copied the work of others, so most of them were wrong when one was wrong, but you were not one of them." He gave me good marks for my honesty; however, I have learned that not everyone in the world seems to be as just and fair as that professor!

Once, returning from a sightseeing tour in Beijing, the customs officials gave a sheet of paper to each person in our party with instructions to declare everything we had purchased. Others listed what they thought would get by without exceeding the limit; the customs would assess duties for anything over $400. I listed everything that I had bought and was the only one in our group who had to pay a customs duty. Sometimes it is disadvantageous to be honest; our worlds are really strange!

On my visit to South Korea in 1975, I was dumfounded to observe that falsity, masquerading as truth, was cutting a broad swath in the fabric of public awareness. I hadn't been to the motherland since going to the United States, not even when my mother died, and I wanted very much to see In Sil and my nieces and nephews.

Seoul had changed a great deal in the meantime. Although I could not often enjoy the scenery of the city in those days following liberation, I cherished in memory the atmosphere unique to Korea, despite its reek of poverty and backwardness. What had not changed in the least, I discovered, was that the pro–Japanese elements were still dominating affairs under the power structure headed by Park Chung Hee, the former officer of the Japanese army.

While leafing idly through *Chung-Ang-Ilbo*, I was startled to come across an article written by Lee Myong Yong, entitled: "Biography of True and False Kim Il Sung." My heart was beating so violently that I had difficulty reading it. The article was designed to "prove," by various methods, the "theory of a false Kim Il Sung." When I departed for the United States immediately after liberation, I hoped that those false rumors would disappear with the passage of time, the way fog clears off under a bright sun. I felt certain that true history would be authenticated and dispel the contrived false tales. Yet I was to discover, some 30 years after the country's liberation, that truth had disappeared, perhaps permanently, in the South where propagandists on the government payroll were employing deception and falsity to obscure and alter true history.

The fabricators of Korea's false history did not hesitate to exercise every disgusting means to spin an appearance of historical truthfulness and material credence in the fabric of their propaganda. Among their claims: That at least four or five men had carried the name of Kim Il Sung in the history of the national liberation movement in Korea; that the legendary anti–Japanese hero of Mt. Paektu, Kim Il Sung who struck terror into Japanese imperialists by attacking Pochonbo in 1937, was killed later in a battle with Japanese soldiers; that, subsequently, another man went under the name of the national hero; and that the present "President Kim Il Sung" of North Korea had been a subordinate of the first "successor," and was put into power under that name by the Soviet Union.

To prove their falsehoods were true, the propagandists cited various articles they had planted in newspapers and magazines, and repeated various conjectures beginning with "the theory of the murder of Kim Il Sung," naming various unlikely persons as eyewitnesses with inside knowledge as proof.

Despite being shocked by such chicanery, one thing delighted me: the propagandists thus were acknowledging that the name of General Kim Il Sung had been the source of courage, hope and faith for Korean people who longed for national liberation from the oppression of Japan; that Kim Il Sung continued to be the symbol of their hopes; and apparently, the anti-Kim Il Sung propagandists could not tarnish the bright image cherished deep in the hearts of most Koreans!

It has been shown clearly that, although masterful in fabricating misinformation in their efforts to "re-write" Korean history, they could not erase from the minds and hearts of the Korean people the truth that Kim Il Sung is cherished by the people of the country. The fact that the renowned general of the anti–Japanese struggle and hero of the Korean nation was President Kim Il Sung of North Korea undoubtedly had become an intolerable thorn in the side of those pro–Japanese Korean authorities who had usurped control following liberation. Obviously, in order to remain in power, they must have brought the false historians onto the public payroll in an attempt to tarnish the image of Kim Il Sung, whose image was outshining them despite such subterfuge.

Not having cheated or insulted anyone intentionally during my life, this underhanded political activity made me tremble with rage. I had not been fully aware that this had been taking place and was a common topic of discussion in so-called political and academic circles in South Korea, because I was outside politics, being totally engrossed in my duties as a medical doctor. I was lagging behind the times, so to speak, and the thought never occurred to me that this kind of deliberate fabrication of history would even be attempted. My relationship with Kim Sung Ju during our days in Jilin had been extraordinary and my reverence of him was near sacred. I had gone to the United States before the outbreak of the Korean War, far away from home and South Korea both in space and time. I had heard rumors that there were those attempting to defame Kim Il Sung, but I couldn't imagine such wicked fabrications were actually being created deliberately.

Some of the fabrications demonstrated that the authors had little common sense or knowledge. As an example: One wrote that a man named Kim Il Sung had participated in the independence movement as early as 1910 and identified him as a graduate of a Japanese military academy. I had lived in Jilin, where the leaders of the independence movement would assemble, and I had never heard mention of such a man. Had there been, he would have been very well known to Ahn Chang Ho, my father and the other leaders of patriotic groups who were active at that time. His name was never mentioned!

The name of General Kim Il Sung became the talk of the people only from the early 1930s when Kim Sung Ju organized and led the famous anti–Japanese guerrillas into armed resistance. There is no room for further argument about it. I can attest to that as an eyewitness of that part of history.

Another example: Various pictures of General Kim Il Sung, taken at different ages and under different circumstances, were used to "prove" these were different men. One, for instance, was when he was in his upper teens in Jilin; another when he was fighting guerrilla warfare in Manchuria; still another after liberation. His image in the days of the armed struggle revealed, above all, the effects of the rigors of those rugged days.

However, the men in the photos who were claimed to be different men, in fact were one man: President Kim Il Sung!

My reaction to this propaganda was simply this: How dare they run down and vilify the man who had undergone indescribable hardships to win back the deprived country and lift the nation out of ruin when they, themselves, had acted to ensure their own comfort and pleasure in disregard of the needs of their countrymen and nation?

I have tried to live honestly and, in good faith, have never attempted to interfere in others' affairs or politics. I have done my best to be faithful to my calling as a medical doctor. However, I could not remain indifferent to these issues concerning President Kim Il Sung. I realize that this, rather than being scientific or political, is a matter of morality and conscience for me. I had been his friend! For a long time, I did not know what to do. As a doctor practicing in the United States, I had no apparent means to confront the strong power of South Korea which had made this kind of deception and fabrication of history its state policy.

However, let me quote from a book written by Kim Hyong Uk, a former director of the Korean CIA during the regime of Park Chung Hee.

> Many people will be surprised at what I, a former director of the CIA of the Republic of Korea, have to say. Nevertheless, truth should be taken as truth. It might bring about a shock right now, but it is rather desirable in view of the long history of the nation.
>
> I knew that Kim Il Sung, in his twenties before liberation, had commanded anti-Japanese guerrillas and once devoted himself to anti-Japanese movement in the areas along the Amrok and Tumen rivers, belonging to the Northeast Anti-Japanese Allied Army of the Communist Party of China in the Manchurian region. I also knew that he had quite a number of organizations, though small in their size, in the three southern counties in North Hamgyong Province, including Myongchon and Kilju, and commanded the battle at Pochonbo.
>
> However, for some reason, the relation of his life has become the main theme of anti-Communist propaganda and education in South Korea since the government of Syngman Rhee. This has been intensified further as Park Chung Hee of the Republican Party seized power. Apparently the majority of the officials under Syngman Rhee who had been pro-Japanese and Park Chung Hee who had surpassed Rhee and hunted the independence fighters, serving as an officer of the Japanese army, wanted to ignore the records of Kim Il Sung. I feel ashamed to have failed to establish during my tenure of office a realistic and reasonable system of anti-Communist education in the way of recognizing his records and criticizing what should be criticized.
>
> The anti-Communist culture was so dreadful that even I, director of KCIA, was frightened and had to take care of myself in revising that Kim Il Sung was not a complete sham but real Kim Il Sung. The brand "pro-Communist" was a stigma as cruel as the punishment of Heaven in South Korea.

The foregoing quotation is from *Kim Hyong Uk Memoirs*, Korean edition, volume 2, page 272. If the powerful director of the Korean CIA dared not do anything with the issue, what could a commonplace man like me do?

Nevertheless, I did make up my mind to speak out about the truth, though in a low voice! I reasoned that if I told the truth to one person and to another, then perhaps one man would awaken ten, the ten another one hundred, and the one hundred another one thousand!

About that time, I received a letter from Dr. Youngho Choe, a professor at the University of Hawaii. Prof. Choe hailed from Yongchon and had a bowing acquaintance with me. After completing studies in Seoul, he received a doctorate in postgraduate work from Harvard University and then joined the faculty at the University of Hawaii where he specialized in the modern history of Korea. Dr. Choe's brother was a writer in Japan. His mother was living with a sister in his home town.

In his letter, he mentioned that when he was at Harvard I had told him about President Kim Il Sung's anti–Japanese struggle in the north. He was now requesting me to send him in greater detail whatever I knew about those times.

Professor Choe later published an essay entitled: "The Christian Background of Kim Il Sung's Growth." In his treatise, he stressed that a man had confirmed that President Kim Il Sung of the North was Kim Sung Ju in his days in Jilin, and that man was Dr. Sohn Won Tai, living in Omaha, Nebraska. He wrote:

> According to Dr. Sohn, the young man named Kim Sung Ju, who went to church regularly for a certain period as a teacher of the Sunday School, while attending the Yuwen Middle School in Jilin, is Kim Il Sung, the highest authority in North Korea. Dr. Sohn recalls that young Kim Sung Ju was active in the Korean community, especially among young people, and demonstrated remarkable leadership.

The preceding quotation is an excerpt from Professor Choe's *History of the Independence War of Korea*, Korean edition, page 30.

After the book was published, it became known far and wide that Sohn Won Tai, a pathologist in Omaha, Nebraska, had been a boyhood friend of President Kim Il Sung of the Democratic People's Republic of Korea. Many people visited my house or phoned me to ask whether President Kim Il Sung actually was the one who had lived in Jilin in those days.

This is what I have told them:

> President Kim Il Sung of the North is the Kim Sung Ju of his days in Jilin and the Kim Il Sung, hero and patriot, of many legendary tales about the dark days of Korean history. Those who fabricate stories to imply that these historical facts are false without exception are pro–Japanese elements and traitors to the nation who lived on Japanese

largesse while he was fighting against Japanese imperialism ... or their descendents!

As the saying goes: Seeing is believing! If I could meet with Kim Il Sung only once in Pyongyang and ascertain that he was the Kim Sung Ju of our boyhood friendship, that would mean more than could be implied in thousands of words. Because I seemed to be the only one able to do the job, I felt responsible to use all means available to me to testify to the truth of history for the sake of the nation and its posterity.

Having assumed the responsibility to be a judge of history, I realized that I must go to Pyongyang and meet with President Kim Il Sung. Only in that way could I fulfill my human and moral duties on his behalf. This would be the greatest action I could undertake on behalf of my country and nation. Thus I had made my final decision to go to Pyongyang.

13

The Road to Pyongyang

Pyongyang was the Garden of Eden in my heart. A dear place associated with my childhood, it felt like my hometown. From the old days, people of Kangso and Ryonggang assumed that they hailed from Pyongyang. In my case, my father started his career as a clergyman in Sungsil School in Pyongyang, and it was the last part of my motherland where I lived before taking up my life as a refugee in an alien land. Whenever I thought about Pyongyang I succumbed to nostalgia.

I always missed Pyongyang and was eager to go back there, if only once in my remaining lifetime. That desire grew more intense when I realized that President Kim Il Sung would be there. Apparently that had become the foremost reason that I was missing Pyongyang; candidly, I wanted to see him once again before my lifespan closed; it was an order from my heart that I could not disobey.

As events developed in Korea, another reason began to make a decision to return even more imperative: the duty I had assumed to testify as to the real truth of the history of the nation for the benefit of Korean posterity. This had become a moral obligation from which my conscience and all of my humanitarian impulses would not release me.

Nevertheless, a number of realities held me back from immediately implementing my decision. My greatest concern was whether communist North Korea would accept such a request from an ordinary American citizen. I was an old friend of President Kim Il Sung but, regardless of my personal ideals, I was not a communist. My father had been an independence fighter and there were no pro–Japanese or traitors to the nation in my family but how their status might be interpreted or defined by North Koreans could not be predictable.

For instance, my elder brother, Sohn Won Yil, had served as Minister of Defense in the waning days of the Syngman Rhee government in South Korea and I was not sure if the North would be favorably disposed toward me considering the situation that North and South remained in direct confrontation both politically and militarily. No matter how much thought I gave to that problem, I couldn't resolve my doubts. Worse still, I was a naturalized citizen of the United States, a country with whom North Korea has suffered antagonistic relations for half a century and against whom North Koreans, from toddling children to the aged, bear bitter resentment.

In the light of such political, ideological and conventional differences, I feared that the fact that I was a boyhood friend of President Kim Il Sung might not weigh strongly enough in favor of extending a welcome to me. I cannot explain the degrees of mental agony I experienced as I reviewed my entire past life as a Korean at home and in alien countries but, eventually, I overcame those barriers and determined to go back to Pyongyang to meet President Kim Il Sung. That decision was made in the mid–1980s when, well past 70 years of age, I knew that I had no time to waste; I didn't want to die without responding to the yearning I cherished in my heart to return to my homeland.

My anxiety was intensified by the knowledge that many Koreans residing in the United States had visited Pyongyang in recent years. Those persons were from families which North Korea would not consider as patriotic and their political views definitely were not pro–North. Nevertheless, on their travel to Pyongyang, they had experienced no feelings of being restricted; most of them returned to America with favorable impressions of North Korea.

One day, Professor Kang Sun Ung of the University of Wisconsin visited my home in Omaha. He had been to North Korea three times. On his most recent visit, he had been accompanied by his wife, whom he had married when he was in his fifties. He was exhilarated by his experiences in North Korea.

"It was a honeymoon to my native town, so to speak," he said. "The warm-heartedness of the people in my native village hasn't changed in the least. They even slaughtered a pig for a feast to welcome me! Upon returning back here, it seems that I have come back with my body alone, leaving my soul there."

He recalled that my father's native home was in North Korea and then strongly urged me to visit there.

My purpose of visiting the North had a special meaning to me. Professor Kang had gone back to visit his relatives and friends but my reasons were quite different. My desire to go to Pyongyang did not derive from nostalgia for my hometown and relatives. I did have some distant kinfolk in Kangso and the Pyongyang vicinity but we had had very little contact during the past 70 years and no family ties would draw me that far. Mainly, I wanted to go there to meet President Kim Il Sung, as I had confided to the professor during our discussion.

Professor Kang advised me to write to President Kim Il Sung and address my letter to him personally. Since the president was well-known throughout the world, the letter should get to him even if the envelope bore only his name, he said. I was interested in his suggestion and did write a letter in which I emphasized that I would appreciate the opportunity to visit him. I addressed the envelope to "President Kim Il Sung of North Korea" and I eagerly looked forward to a reply from him but none was forthcoming. That approach had failed!

Seeking a way to get to Pyongyang directly, I joined a tour group to Beijing, China. My real purpose was to find a way to get to Pyongyang. When the tour group departed to view the Great Wall of China, I feigned minor illness and remained behind. Then, guided by Wang Fu Shih, the son of Zhang Xueliang's advisor, I went to the North Korean embassy in Beijing by taxicab. An attaché greeted me cordially and I told him that I had been a boyhood friend of President Kim Il Sung as a member of the Association of Korean Children in Jilin, and that I would appreciate help so that I could meet the President in Pyongyang.

The attaché looked at me wide-eyed, apparently surprised that an old man from the United States had been a friend of President Kim Il Sung and wanted to meet him. He was not aware of me or my father, the Rev. Sohn Jong Do, and our old friendship ties with President Kim Il Sung. He listened carefully to my story and said that he would do his best to help me. I gave him a letter I had written to President Kim Il Sung and asked him to have it delivered. However, I received no news from the president; I learned later that the letter had never been delivered to him.

When I told the president about it on my visit with him in Pyongyang in May of 1991, Kim Il Sung said that he had not received it and he appeared to be quite angry about the embassy staff's ineptness in handling the matter.

Despite that failure on my journey to Beijing, I didn't abandon my hope of going to Pyongyang but my anxiety grew with the fear that something might happen to me before I could fulfill the mission I had charted for myself. Then one day, unexpectedly, General Choe Tok Sin came to my home in Omaha to visit me. He and Won Yil were very good friends. They had attended the same Wenguang Middle School in Jilin and both held important positions in South Korea's armed forces following the liberation. I had enjoyed no particular contact with him so I wondered how he knew that I was living in Omaha and why he had come to see me.

General Choe explained that he had seen a film featuring the Rev. Sohn Jong Do while he was visiting North Korea and, while there, also had talked with President Kim Il Sung. During their conversation, General Choe said, the president had mentioned the Rev. Sohn and Won Yil, adding that when he heard that another son was living in the United States he had asked the Rev. Kim Song Rak to inquire about him. The president said he had not received further news about me from the Rev. Kim.

General Choe said that when he returned to the United States, he inquired about my whereabouts and learned my location from Lee Byong Hyon. Dr. Lee hailed from South Pyongan Province and had participated in the independence movement in China with Kim Ku. Learning that Kim Il Sung was searching for me, I told General Choe that I had sent letters to the president on several occasions but that there were no replies for reasons I did not know about. He said my letters would not have been delivered to Pyongyang because there were no postal or telecommunication agreements concluded between North Korea and the United States. He surmised that the U.S. postal service might have sent my letters to South Korea, noting only the word "Korea." His reasoning quite likely was correct.

I decided to write another letter but to send it with some person. I had learned that the Rev. Hong Tong Gun had been to Pyongyang on several occasions and I made an effort to contact him. I got in touch with his wife, Mrs. Hong Jon Ja, and I explained to her that I would appreciate having the Reverend be a messenger to carry a letter from me to the president on his next visit. It was not long before the Rev. Hong contacted me to accept my request.

It was quite a long letter. I wrote:

> Dear President Kim Il Sung:
> Sixty years have passed since I took leave of you in your days in middle school and the members of the Association of Korean Children in Jilin. Despite the passage of time I still remember you and the association members. I remember Ri Tong Hwa, Hwang Kwi Hon, Choe Jin Mu, and Mr. Pak Yong Won who taught Korean in the Methodist school in Jilin. In 1944 I married Lee Yoo Shin, hailing from Pyongyang, and I have two sons and a daughter.
> I am still grateful that you bought me jiangzi guoji when I was a

primary school pupil. It is still vivid in my memory the days when the association members, divided into the "Sea" team and the "Land" team, played on the beach along the Songhua River.

When you were attending the Yuwen Middle School and I the Provincial Middle School No. 4, I visited your boarding room. You were solving mathematical problems and you greeted me gladly.

It seemed as if it was only yesterday when you told the association members gathered in Beishan Park about the independence movement, but 60 years have already passed.

The days when we were enthusiastic about the independence movement, though going hungry, were the most worthwhile and happiest days for me.

I shed tears at the thought of those who were devoting themselves to the independence movement and anti–Japanese struggle and even now writing a letter to you I cannot keep back tears welling up.

They devoted their life to independence for posterity with an ennobling spirit, but it is disgusting and disappointing to see the pro–Japanese and opportunists behaving in this complicated society.

I believe that you would know that my father, the Rev. Sohn Jong Do, continued his independence struggle in Jilin before dying in Jilin Province, without his family members present.

I attended the preparatory course of medicine at Dongwu University in Suzhou, China, and suffered in prison in Nagasaki, Japan, in January 1940. I was then transferred to a Japanese prison in Seoul and later released on parole. I was ordered to report to a Japanese police station at ten o'clock every morning; the practice created the agony and a sense of oppression deteriorating my heart. I underwent heart surgery five years ago and my health has improved considerably since then.

When I was attending a university in Beijing, the anti–Japanese movement of Chinese students was fierce. As the chairman of the student association of the biology department of the university and head of the inspection section of the Beijing Student Association, I participated in the campaign to boycott Japanese goods. The student association organized anti–Japanese demonstrations on many occasions and scores of students were shot to death by Chinese soldiers while staging street demonstrations, shouting "Down with traitors to the nation!" and "Down with Japanese imperialism."

In 1938 or 1939 the English-language newspaper *Dagongbao* of Shanghai carried a one page article titled "Kim Il Sung and His Anti-Japanese Struggle," praising you for conducting a daring anti–Japanese struggle in command of thousands of soldiers. It also carried an article about the independence fighter, Lee Jang Chong. Reading the inspiring article about you, I was very delighted and grateful to you.

Let me extend my heartfelt thanks to those who are working for the country and for the future of the rising generation.

With best wishes,
Sohn Won Tai

I gave the letter and an application for a visit to the motherland to the Rev. Hong Tong Gun in Los Angeles. He, in turn, entrusted it to a group visiting Pyongyang, headed by Dr. Sunoo Hak Won. In the application, I wrote that I would be going to Pyongyang to meet President Kim Il Sung, and I would be accompanied by my wife and three other people. I was told later that the president was very happy to receive my letter and instructed officials who would be involved to take immediate steps to invite me to come.

I was trimming the hedge in my garden one day in late April of 1991 when I received the news that President Kim Il Sung had invited me to come to North Korea to visit him. My strained mind at long last seemed to relax. I had been nervously wondering whether my request would be accepted and, now that the road to Pyongyang was opened so easily, all the stress disappeared instantly. My heart began to leap; I felt the greatest happiness, the ecstasy of joy, with my long-held wish about to be realized.

Before long, other thoughts crept into my mind to upset that tranquility. Would the president recognize me? Would he be able to interrupt his heavy schedule of state affairs to meet me? With what feeling and attitude would his compatriots receive me? Would I be able to meet my wife's brother and other relatives living there? Such thoughts stole disruptively into my sleep.

What worried me most was the uncertainty whether I could correctly understand the realities of North Korea and form an unbiased opinion of them. I wanted to meet President Kim Il Sung in person in Pyongyang, witness his government in operation, and make my own judgment based on my observations. However, I also realized that, because I had lived so many years in the western world, my outlook on spiritual, social and institutional ways of life might be challenged as biased or influenced, leading me to subjective impartiality in arriving at any judgments I might make.

I concluded, therefore, that in order to make an objective judgment on North Korea's social structure, I would have to maintain composure of attitude, speak frankly, and hold fast to my own conscience, my reasoning and my commitment to morality. This open-minded approach to making judgment, I was firmly determined to follow. Such was the thorough process of ideological and moral self-cultivation that I underwent while awaiting my forthcoming meeting with the president.

At long last, the day of going to Pyongyang arrived. I went on the trip with my wife; her nephew, Lee Hak Mo, a pastor in New York; her niece, Lee Hak Sun, a pianist; and Hak Sun's husband, Polish-American Chester Skiakowski, also a pianist. We changed planes at Los Angeles and flew across the Pacific Ocean, landing at the Narita Airport in Tokyo, Japan.

There we boarded a JAL plane for a flight to Beijing, China, where our entry visas to the Democratic People's Republic of Korea were awaiting us.

On the unforgettable 11th of May 1991, we boarded another plane. Our hearts swelled with a feeling that we were going to paradise as we flew over the Amnok River that marks the border between Korea and China. I was returning home after 70 years! We could see the motherland far below, once groaning under the colonial rule of Japanese imperialism but now adorned beautifully with green sprouts. A river could be seen streaming down to the West Sea through well-aligned dry fields. As the plane descended on its approach to the airport at Pyongyang, we could see vehicles moving along the streets and people working in the fields who were waving their hands at our plane — and us! As we touched down on the runway, I told myself: "Now I've come home!"

Truly, I had come back to Pyongyang after so many years, not along a straight road but by taking a long detour.

It was warm in Pyongyang. The airport, enveloped by the shades of sunset, was busy with passengers. We were greeted by Choe Jin Hyok of the History Institute of the Central Worker's Party of Korea. It was our first meeting but we hugged each other and didn't let go of one another for a long time. The Pyongyangites had accorded us a most hearty welcome!

We had our photographs taken to commemorate our arrival in Pyongyang. Mr. Choe told us that President Kim Il Sung was very happy about the news from me and was looking forward to our arrival. He also informed us that the president was in good health.

On our way to town from the airport, we relished breathing the invigorating fresh air. Ah … this is the motherland, my native place which I have yearned for so much, I thought happily. We were taken to the Sojaedong Guest House which had been built only recently. My wife and I unpacked our travel luggage in Building No. 18, one of dozens of detached guest lodges. The others in our party were put up in nearby Building No. 19.

I did a good deal of thinking on the first night of our stay in Pyongyang. Having left in my childhood, I had returned as a gray-haired man. I was reminded of the night when I had left the dear city. Although I had been happy to go to my father, I had felt sorry in spite of that. Was it because I had known what leave-taking from one's motherland meant? No, it could be likened to a baby not willing to leave its mother's bosom. Though rich or poor, one's motherland is something like a mother one cannot part with. A man cannot leave his motherland for good even after he dies. People scattered all over the world return at last to their motherland; I too, have returned, in my seventies, to the motherland I left at the age of seven.

That night, all of the apprehension and disturbing thoughts that had been tormenting me vanished. I forgot all of my cares and immersed myself in a kind of sheer trance. I felt as if I had returned to the days of innocent boyhood. Because I felt as if I was becoming young again, I slept soundly that night. I had thought that it would be hard to fall asleep because of the time difference of 13 hours between Pyongyang and the United States but I was wrapped in a heavy sleep before I knew it. It was not the sleep of a man fatigued from long journey; I had returned to my own house, my native town and to my compatriots … to Pyongyang which I had missed for so many years.

I now had come to anchor at my destined port at long last after experiencing the ups and downs of a long and rough sea voyage. What more could I care about? Forgetting all of the worldly cares, fully relaxed, I had a good night's sleep.

PART III

My Reunion with President Kim Il Sung

14

"Where Have You Been Only to Come Now?"

On the fourth day of our stay in Pyongyang, May 15, 1991, I awoke to a feeling of great happiness, possibly engendered by the pleasant fragrance of lilac flowers in the room. After breakfast, I was informed that President Kim Il Sung would meet with me later that day. I tried to remain calm although my spirits soared at the news that we would be seeing each other again for the first time since those days of our youth so many years ago.

A chauffeured automobile took me and my wife, Yoo Shin, swiftly through the central city and its suburbs, over low and high hills, and then into a peaceful, secluded valley. We motored on for some time before stopping in front of a beautiful residence, which was set in a wooded area overlooking and mirrored by a picturesque mountain lake.

Our guide led us through the main entrance where we stopped ... because President Kim Il Sung was standing in the foyer awaiting us. We were some distance apart but I recognized him immediately. Although he was nearly 80 at the time, he appeared hearty and his demeanor was refined. He approached, looking at me closely, as I stood silently trying to recall the image of his youth in Jilin when he was a handsome man of slender build. The rigors of bitter frost and chilling winds endured during his years on Mount Paektu had etched his brow and cheeks. His hair was now gray but I could see without difficulty the distinctive features of the young man I had admired so much.

President Kim Il Sung was also peering at me as if he were trying to find in the features of this white-haired elderly man those of the youngster who had followed on his heels during his days in Jilin. After a moment, in his deep and resonant voice, he said, "Ah, Won Tai, I remember you!"

He spread his arms and hugged me close, saying, "Where have you been only to come now after so many years?"

I was choked with emotion and unable to say a word as he clasped my face in his large, soft hands and continued to look at me with obvious pleasure. Then I remembered that even as a youth he had those kindly eyes, a snub nose and thick lips. My mother used to tweak his nose affectionately and I had nicknamed him "Reticent," reflecting the impression of his smile. His eyes expressed the exceptional warmth that I have cherished in my memory and now, sensing it again, I became aware of tears welling in my eyes.

While holding my head to his chest, Kim Il Sung asked what had caused my hair to become so white. His tone was so sincere that I instinctively responded playfully, just as his young friend of those Jilin days might have done: "My yearning for you, President."

He detected this subtle charade, his eyes twinkling, and murmured, "I understand, Won Tai, I am honored." At that moment I knew that our mutual regard had remained unchanged after more than 60 years of separation. Only then did I realize that other people had gathered in the room.

Kim Il Sung led us across the foyer to a large anteroom to meet Kang Sok Sung, head of the History Institute of the Central Workers' Party of Korea, and Hwang Kwi Hon, a member of the Jilin Children's Association. Hwang, beginning to stoop with aging, gripped my hand, saying, "It has been a long, long time, Comrade Won Tai."

I remembered Hwang as a lovable and lively girl with a roundish, oval face. She was now nearing eighty and was a grandparent like myself. I was suddenly aware of how time had flown by since our youthful years in Jilin. As we reminisced about our mutual friends, she asked about my sister, who had been a close friend at Jilin. She was pleased to learn that Sohn In Sil was now living in South Korea and was serving as a vice president of the South Korean Red Cross.

Turning to Kim Il Sung, I recalled the time when he had taken my sister and me to a restaurant and bought us jiangzi guoji, a delicacy resembling a doughnut served in sweetened bean soup. He said that he remembered Sohn In Sil well because she frequently had run errands between my father and himself.

From left: Dr. Won Tai Sohn, Kang Sok Sung (Chairman of the History Institute), President Kim Il Sung, and Mrs. Won Tai Sohn in Pyongyang, North Korea, May 31, 1991.

Sadly, I could not remember much about many of my friends in Jilin and had forgotten some names and details of my life there. So when I mentioned having had an altercation in the heat of a soccer game with Ri Tong Son, the eldest son of the Sanfeng Hotel keeper, Kim Il Sung corrected me, saying, "The hotel keeper's eldest son is Ri Tong Hwa; Tong Son was his second son."

Then I showed him a photograph of some people who had been active in the children's association at Jilin. I had kept it safely over the years and brought it to Pyongyang with me. Scrutinizing the photograph, he identified face after face, demonstrating his exceptional memory.

"This is Pak Il Pha, and standing here is Kim Kang," he said, pointing them out in the photograph. "And here is your older brother Won Yil."

I asked if he remembered having had a group picture taken after playing in a soccer game at Jiangnan Park, across the Songhua River in Jilin, and he responded, "Yes, I do."

This brought to my mind a question I had sought to have answered many times as I had looked at the photograph back in America: "Why had you not appeared in any of those group photos?"

Kim Il Sung smiled and explained that he carefully had avoided being included in group pictures.

> For example, when we went to Mt. Lungtan in Jiangdong, you all appeared in a group picture but I was not in it. At that time, while I was doing legal service through the student and children associations, I was also engaged in secret work for the Young Communist League. In those days, I delivered many lectures on the independence movement to boys and girls in rural communities. These were revolutionary activities so I avoided having my picture taken.

"I remember you well in Jilin, Mr. President. You were a graceful crane standing amid a flock of chickens," I said. "Tall and handsome, with dimples in your smiling face...."

Laughing heartily, he led us to the luncheon table. He selected several delicacies and placed them on our plates, urging us to help ourselves to appease our appetites. As the meal progressed, Kim Il Sung, wine glass in hand, looked back on days long passed into history. He began with a tribute to my father, the Reverend Sohn Jong Do.

"The Rev. Sohn Jong Do is the savior of my life," he stated solemnly.

My wife and I listened in awe as Kim Il Sung spoke of the great debt he owed to my father for helping him survive and press on in his life-long fight for freedom and unification of all Korea. This recognition and gratitude for my father, who perhaps was only one among many people who joined the president in his crusade over the years, showed great integrity and humility.

Our table conversation brought back many other people and events of the Jilin era: Shang Yue, a teacher at Yuwen Middle School; Li Guanghan, headmaster of the school; Choe Tong O; and several others. The president recalled that my brother, Won Yil, was attending Wenguang Middle School during the time that he had been enrolled at Yuwen Middle School. He said that he also had been aware that Won Yil had gone to Shanghai to continue his studies.

He smiled as he recalled having eaten rice cakes mixed with herb jondugi at my house. In Sil would pick the herb in Beishan Park.

"Your mother's affection for me was deep indeed," he commented. "When I visited your house, she would slaughter a rabbit and cook bean curd and rabbit stew for me; she knew how much I relished it."

He then turned to the events leading up to my coming to Pyongyang. When I explained that I had visited the North Korean embassy in Beijing and had provided officials with information about my plans, he was critical of the embassy staff's handling of communications. "They were irresponsible," he said grimly. "They may not have been aware of the situation but they should have reported it to me because it was a matter concerning The People."

He said he had been attempting to locate me before receiving my letter so, when the Rev. Kim Sok Rak of Los Angeles had visited Pyongyang, he was asked about In Sil and me. The Rev. Kim then had said that he had no knowledge about either of us but he had promised to inquire further about us. However, nothing more had been reported back to him, Kim Il Sung said.

I said that I would like to return next year to celebrate his 80th birthday. He thanked me and urged me to come, adding that many of his old friends had been visiting him in recent years. My wife, sitting beside me, commented: "That is because you are managing so many important affairs."

"No," he responded. "The People are managing big affairs and, as I am one of them, I am just doing my part."

The aphorism, "The People," was a basic tenet of his political philosophy. He often said that he believed the innate strength of The People would always prevail over individuals and ideologies. Even as a young man, when his elders had advised him to pursue studies in Russia, he instead went among the Korean people, intent upon educating and rallying them to the pursuit of a free and unified Korea.

We sat for hours discussing the history of The People's movement, while Kim Il Sung told us about many of their most cherished achievements:

> Although many people wonder why North Korea continues to favor socialism despite the fact that many eastern European countries have collapsed, after visiting our country and observing our progress they are better able to understand why we have pursued this course.
>
> For instance, North Korea has built the great flood control complex, known as the West Sea Barrage. It ranks among the greatest ocean, river, and land reclamation projects of this century. When an American financier inspected the barrage project, he was astounded to learn that all of the planning, financing and construction had been the work of the North Korean people. He said that he might have been interested in providing a loan of several hundred million dollars but one of several trillion, such as this project entailed, would be a different matter. He then acknowledged that the people indeed had built a truly world-class project on their own.
>
> In leading the revolution to rebuild our country, we did not want to be subservient to any of the great powers. The height of a mountain can be judged properly only when compared with those lower than it.

Kim Il Sung then spoke of his son, Kim Jong Il, who was serving as secretary in charge of organizational affairs for the Central Committee of North Korea. He said Kim Jong Il had recently proposed creating the Thongill Street project to provide housing for families living with other households, and was enlisting the entire country to work on the development which would make 30,000 family apartment units available within the forthcoming year.

I remarked that he must have undergone a great deal of adversity and difficulties over the years on behalf of the Korean people and Kim Il Sung responded: "Yes, if I said there have not been great troubles and difficulties to endure, then I would not be telling the truth — but there must always be someone to take on trouble in order to help the people."

Kim Il Sung's dedication of his life to improving the welfare of the Korean people helped me understand why he was held in such great esteem as the father of his country. And I felt that I was indeed fortunate to have had the privilege of visiting with him and thus gain a greater understanding of his philosophies. How fortunate that I now would be able to better understand Korea's needs and know in what ways I might contribute to the development and security of my native land.

"I hope you can come to visit me in Pyongyang every year," Kim Il Sung told me. "I will make board and lodging available while you are here and I would appreciate visits each year on your holidays. The people around me are younger and not very good companions for reminiscing. Sixty-one years have passed by since we saw one another; perhaps we can live another ten years or so, wouldn't you think?

I laughed puckishly and asked him to let me read his palm to find the answer to his question about our possible longevity. He smiled and asked if I really did know the art of palmistry. I had to confess I had learned a little from a fortune teller during the time I was studying medicine in Seoul.

My wife, sitting beside me, interjected with a little laugh: "Pardon me, Sir, but whenever Won Tai is charmed by pretty girls he tells them he would like to read their palms just so that he can hold their hands, I think."

Kim Il Sung laughed as he held out his hand, saying that this was the first time anyone had wanted to read his palm. Adopting the serious mien of a fortune teller, I told him that a significant line resembled a deep valley in a great mountain range and could be interpreted to reveal uncommon qualities possessed only by a peerless man of the world. Then I pointed out another line identifying qualities of leadership for which he would be held in high esteem in the future. And, peering more closely, I traced the life line in his palm and said that he would have a long life, perhaps well over 100 years. (In retrospect, my reading of his life line revealed my ineptness as a palm reader because, sadly, Kim Il Sung passed away three years later.)

Kim Il Sung smiled warmly, aware of the admiration and affection I held for him, and suggested that we plan to see each other every year. Then he said that he would like to visit with us again before we returned to the United States. When I asked him if it might not be difficult to take time for us, he laughed and said, "It would be a lie if I said that I'm too busy to visit later on. When a man does not feel like meeting someone, he might say he is busy."

My wife glanced at me through moist eyes, deeply impressed by Kim Il Sung's plain-spoken sincerity. That evening we walked leisurely through the lawn and gardens, relishing the fragrance of the lilac blooms, while silently contemplating the purport of the day's events. How many people, during their lifetimes, would enjoy the spiritual sublimity such as we were experiencing?

As if she feared to disturb my happiness, my wife softly caressed my hands, saying almost in a whisper, "Now I can understand your yearning to be with Kim Il Sung all of your life."

15

With the Mind of My Own Brother

After I had visited Pyongyang at the invitation of President Kim Il Sung in 1991, I discovered that I had become a topic of interest both in the United Stares and South Korea. Newspaper articles noted that Sohn Won Tai of Omaha, Nebraska, a boyhood friend of North Korean President Kim Il Sung, had been given a cordial reception by invitation from the president, bringing about a reunion after an absence of sixty-one years. Articles appeared in many newspapers along with a photograph of Kim Il Sung and me.

People generally reacted in astonishment and admiration, treating this reunion of boyhood friends as a rare event in world affairs. I was swept into a whirlpool of world concern as newspaper after newspaper assigned reporters to interview me. The mere fact that a physically fit President Kim Il Sung had invited his boyhood friend to visit him in North Korea dispelled many false rumors and premises about the president and North Korea.

The September 5, 1991, issue of *Dong-A Daily News* (the American edition of *Dong-A Ilbo*) carried an article about my meeting with Kim Il Sung under the headline: "Kim Il Sung Was a Real Independence Fighter." The story covered an entire page with subheads reading: "Old Man Sohn and President Kim" ... "President Kim Still Grateful to the Rev. Sohn" ...

"President Kim Healthy Beyond Expectation; Advises Sohn to Have Medical Check-up" ... "I Was Not Used as a Tool, I Only Told the Truth." The article was illustrated by two photographs, one showing the president with me at our first meeting at Pyongyang and the other of my wife and me posing with Kim Il Sung during a sightseeing tour in the Myohyang mountains.

As a result of these newspaper articles, persons in South Korea, who had been fabricating derogatory propaganda, found themselves in an awkward situation. Their misinformation, now having been refuted, had called attention to and recognition of what a great man President Kim Il Sung was.

The most prestigious business newspaper in the United States, *The Wall Street Journal*, reported my visit to Pyongyang in an article captioned: "Of the Two Friends, One Has Become a Doctor and the Other a Dictator." As I read this article months later, I wondered how the editors could have presumed that they could write about either North Korea or President Kim Il Sung's government without firsthand knowledge of the country or the president himself.

When I made arrangements for my first trip to Pyongyang in 1991, I had some misgivings about how my motives might be interpreted by the people of North Korea. My touring party was to include not only my wife but also Hak Mo, the son born to the first wife of the brother of my wife, Hak Soon, the daughter born to his second wife, and her husband, Chester Skiakowski. My wife's brother, Lee Yoo Sung, was critically ill at the time so it seemed to be possible that my plans might be misconstrued as a visit with him rather than the president. However, when we arrived in Pyongyang, we were cordially received by everyone because President Kim Il Sung had written about my father, the Rev. Sohn Jong Do, in his published memoirs and I was widely known among the people.

During our stay in Pyongyang, the newspapers and television stations followed my activities day by day. Everywhere that I went in North Korea, people apparently recognized me and greeted me warmly on busy streets, in the Kumgang and Myohyang mountains, and on the sandy beach in Songdowon. It was plainly evident that Kim Il Sung's guest was their guest and the guest of their sons and daughters as well. All seemingly were pleased to meet me and I realized that one could experience such a feeling of oneness only in North Korea where all of the people were one large family and the president was its respected head.

My wife, Yoo Shin, overwhelmed by this experience, asked me, "How can people here be so kind-hearted and good-natured? Every person seems to be one of character; how simple and honest the women are!"

"You once said that a child takes after his father," I responded. "The people seem to closely resemble President Kim I Sung."

While rearing two sons and one daughter, I had not spanked or scolded them once, and I don't recall ever seeing them quarrel seriously with one another. Their behavior was so exemplary that, at one time, I had been chosen "Father of the Year" in our community in Chicago. I was selected for this honor as the result of an essay written by my second son, Rickey, in a high school composition contest. As his parents, we of course were very proud of his accomplishment. That was the first time Yoo Shin had said that children naturally take after their fathers.

I would like to believe that North Korea is a good example of this principle. Since President Kim Il Sung was so tender-hearted and respectable, his people also have developed those qualities. The open-hearted, humane aura which so enthralled us in Pyongyang certainly imparts credence to such a belief.

On our second visit to Pyongyang in 1992, we felt so at home that we already were Pyongyangites in spirit. It was the eve of a great national holiday celebration of the 80th birthday of President Kim Il Sung. The whole country was festooned in colorful festival decorations.

We stayed at a spa in Onchon County some distance from Pyongyang. At one time, Onchon had been a part of Ryongang County which was famous for its hot springs. Our suite included a personal spa which President Kim Il Sung had reserved for us.

On April 22, Yoo Shin and I were invited to a luncheon which he had prepared himself. As he explained why we were given lodgings with the hot springs spa that usually was reserved for his own use, I realized that he was treating me just as he would treat his own brother, not as a formal guest of state.

"We have a shortage of guest houses on this occasion because many government and party leaders have come," he told us. "There are 4,800 guests and 2,000 members of art groups to be accommodated. In making recommendations for lodging, I emphasized that you were my personal guest and they should be certain that you have the spa that I always use."

He told us it was a rare salt spa bath and that its hot spring sea water contained radium which is efficacious in treating arthritis and neuralgia. Then he said we could have its use for a month or two if we wished.

This was our first meeting since he had been honored with the additional title of Commander in Chief. I congratulated him on this new responsibility and said that I was especially pleased to see him in such excellent health. He agreed that he was fit as a fiddle and said he was taking moderate exercise to remain that way. Then he advised me to play tennis, do regular walking and ride a bicycle "to prevent becoming senile," and abruptly asked me: "Won Tai, how old are you?"

"I'm 78 years old."

"That's right, you are two years junior to me and you'll be celebrating your 80th birthday the year after next. Please come to see me then. I'll prepare your 80th birthday table, so promise me you will spend the day in Pyongyang. Bring everyone with you: your family and all of your friends."

When I had visited with him in Pyongyang in 1991 he had extended the same invitation and now he was re-emphasizing his wish once again. Both my wife and I were deeply moved. We thanked him again and promised that we would make plans to do so.

As we were departing following the luncheon, Kim Il Sung asked when we planned to return home and I told him it would be before the end of May because I did have tax returns to file and we didn't like to leave our home vacant much longer. He appeared to be saddened as he asked: "Do you really have to go back to the United States?" His demeanor brightened as he quickly added: "But it is nice that you can come every year so we have a chance to talk like this, isn't it?

The president said that since his son, Kim Jong Il, had taken charge of major affairs, he now would be concerned mainly with external matters and he might be able to enjoy some leisure hours. Yoo Shin said she hoped that he would live a long time and be able to counsel Kim Jong Il as he assumed more of the president's responsibilities, and I assured him he would have many years of activity to come according to my reading of his palm.

Kim Il Sung laughed and asked again where I had learned to read palms. I told him I had picked up some of it from fortune tellers on the streets of Japan when I was learning the Japanese language in preparation for the Severance Medical College entrance examinations in the early 1940s. Yoo Shin then repeated her tongue-in-cheek accusation that I only practiced palm reading so I could hold the hands of pretty girls. Kim Il Sung was laughing merrily as we parted.

Recalling our conversation later on, I wondered what he had been implying when he asked if I had to go back to the United States. I told my wife that I thought Kim Il Sung was hinting that he wanted me always to be near him but Yoo Shin said she thought he wanted me to come back to North Korea to live and be buried. I wasn't sure how I would respond if he might ask that question again. I hadn't given any thought to settling permanently in Pyongyang and was unprepared to be confronted with the matter on this second visit. I reasoned that Kim Il Sung may have put his question in that way because he was emotionally reticent to part from the

President Kim Il Sung (right) bidding Dr. Sohn farewell, June 2, 1991.

old friend with whom he shared such intimate feelings. So I discussed my dilemma with Yoo Shin.

"If we make permanent residence in Pyongyang, the president will be very delighted," Yoo Shin counseled. "If he wishes us to come live and be buried here, then we must settle in Pyongyang. But I would wish that we could travel freely to the United States to see our children. There is no other worry for me."

I knew she was right. Different and conflicting social systems still prevailed in North and South Korea and a critical state of confrontation had existed for half a century. From a political viewpoint, I had not supported or opposed either side as I grieved over the tragedy of a divided motherland; I wished only for its early reunification.

My life in the United States was stable in every respect; I had not been persecuted for political reasons and I had been able to become an American citizen. Economically I fared well as a certified pathologist. There was a little prospect of amassing a great fortune in the manner of the "American Dream," but we are comfortably well off as an upper middle class American family. We own a comfortable multi-level dwelling, a hilly 70-acre forested tract, and an automobile. Our three children attended and were graduated from American universities, and the eldest is a certified pathologist in Los Angeles, pursuing a medical career in that city's expansive hospital system.

I even bought a few goats "to keep our lawn well manicured," as I would tell my friends.

Our property lies a few miles north of the Omaha city limits and we value the privacy afforded by being away from the clamor of big city life. However, the entertainment and shopping advantages of the metropolitan area are but a few minutes away and easily available to us if desired.

I was aware that we would benefit from a financial windfall if Omaha's suburban residential area might expand northward or new highway projects would encroach upon our estate. I really did not want that to happen; I was very contented with my life as an esteemed professional medical practitioner and a comfortably well-off American citizen.

Nevertheless, as I grew older, I became nostalgic about my homeland and, from time to time, I thought about returning some day to live in Korea and, at the end, to be buried there. However, I never had entertained plans to leave the United States and settle in Seoul where I once had lived and where my sister, In Sil, my nephews and other relatives now are living, or any other place in South Korea, where the pro–Japanese traitors are settled into power and continue to demean and castigate those who had fought for liberation of the country in the past.

After meeting with Kim Il Sung in Pyongyang and returning to Omaha, we spent a good deal of time recalling events of our trip and began making plans for another visit there. I felt that Kim Il Sung was a caring and loving person filling a place in my heart emptied with the passing of my father and mother and elder brother. But one thought deterred me: if I settled in Pyongyang I would not be able to visit my sister In Sil in Seoul.

The Japanese had occupied Korea and vast coastal areas of China following the military invasion in the early 1900s. My father, the Reverend Sohn Jong Do, was pastor of the Methodist church in Seoul. After becoming a victim, along with other Christian ministers and their church members, of Japanese persecution, he became involved in the independence movement. This had developed as the result of the brutal atrocities being committed by the Japanese who believed that all Christians were pro–American and therefore were anti–Japanese.

My father had been arrested, held in jail and tortured by Japanese military "occupation" authorities. He was so brutally tortured that he almost died while imprisoned. I was born in Seoul on August 11, 1914, and was only four years old when my father fled to China to escape from Japanese persecution and to continue his church mission as well as to work in the independence movement. By the end of World War I, many thousands of Koreans had fled to China, most of them joining the independence movement as freedom fighters and taking up arms to assist Chinese citizens in restricting the Japanese infiltration of Manchuria.

My father helped to organize the Provisional Korean Government in Exile at Shanghai. One of the patriotic Koreans in that group was Mr. Ahn Chang Ho, the father of Philip Ahn, the noted American movie star. Syngman Rhee, who was in the United States to petition for Korean independence at the League of Nations' post-war meetings, was elected president of the Provisional Korean Government.

When the Japanese expanded their occupation of eastern China, Mr. Ahn was arrested in Shanghai and taken back to Korea where he mysteriously died while imprisoned by the Japanese authorities. It was widely believed among Korean patriots that Mr. Ahn had been fed rice mixed with ground glass while in prison in South Korea and that this was the cause of his death.

While the Chinese Nationalists, led by Chiang Kai-shek, fought the rising forces of Mao Zedong, the Japanese strengthened their occupation of Manchuria. For several years, my father continued his work as a Methodist missionary in Shanghai and as a member of the Provisional Korean Government. Then he went to Jilin where he established a Korean Methodist church and at the same time secretly engaged in the Korean independence movement. However, the harsh treatment and terrible tortures he had received while imprisoned in Jilin, until eventually being released, had left continuing physical problems which eventually led to his death in December of 1931. His patriotic Korean friends believed that he had been poisoned by the Japanese. He was only 50 years old when he died after a lifetime devoted to helping Korea to achieve independence from Japanese occupation and to become unified as a democracy.

I attended grammar school in Jilin, Manchuria, where I learned both English and Chinese languages. There was a good relationship between China and America then. The missionary schools provided textbooks and teachers for language classes. There was no Cold War prejudice during that period, and the level of public education in China at that time was believed to be superior to that in either Japan or the United States.

I entered Catholic University in Beijing in the mid–1930s. This was a private school run by German Catholic priests. However, the following year I transferred to Suzhou University in Suzhou. Then I matriculated in pre-medical study in the department of biology and moved to Shanghai after the Japanese troops had invaded Suzhou.

A man named Kim came to visit with me quite often. I was not aware at the time that some Koreans were collaborating with the Japanese and spying on their fellow Koreans. I thought this man was just being friendly and I mentioned to him one day soon I would like to visit my mother in Seoul. She had returned to Seoul after my father's death. My friend became very enthusiastic about this and told me that there wouldn't be any problem to make arrangements because his brother was also planning to go to Seoul and I could accompany him.

We embarked by boat for Seoul. I became aware that my "friend" was a traitor spying for the Japanese against Koreans when Japanese police arrested me when our boat docked at Nagasaki, Japan. My "friend's" brother who, I later learned, was a Korean traitor operating as a Japanese police informer in Seoul, had disappeared, his mission accomplished!

I was held in the Nagasaki prison for about four months. Every day at ten o'clock in the morning, inquisitors came to plague me with questions, beating me senseless on the head with bamboo flails when my response didn't please them. They would torture me again and again by beating me with bamboo sticks until I fainted. While I strongly wished for independence and a unified Korean nation, I was at no time involved in the secret movement and had nothing I could reveal to their satisfaction.

Eventually, I was transferred to a prison in Seoul and, about a month later, released on parole with the restriction that I could not leave Seoul.

All Koreans were required to speak Japanese under the occupation; it was the compulsory language in schools. Having been educated in Jilin, I had learned English and Chinese but not Japanese. To pursue my medical education at Severance Medical College in Seoul, I would have to know the Japanese language. Fortunately, I was given special permission to enroll in the Waseda International Institute at Tokyo to learn Japanese. There were perhaps 300 second- and third-generation Japanese students, from families residing in the United States, also enrolled at the institute.

I completed two years of the language study and then, in 1942, I returned to Seoul and matriculated in Severance Medical College, which was run by Presbyterian, Methodist and Canadian missionaries.

After graduating with a medical degree from Severance Medical College in 1945, I was retained as an anatomy teacher and served on the staff of the department of anatomy of Severance Medical College in 1946, 1947 and 1948. During those years I also taught English classes for medical students and the School of Nursing.

There were no doctors tending the people on Leper's Island, which lies off Korea's southern tip. Five of us responded to a call for volunteers. Mainly, our duties entailed teaching the afflicted lepers about how they could help themselves and each other.

After I had been on Leper's Island about a month, I heard from my sister, Jin Sil, informing me that the United States State Department was offering scholarships for university study in the U.S. She told me there had been about 400 applicants already signed up for written and oral examinations, so I had to return immediately if I wanted to apply. I arrived back in Seoul just in time for the first day of written exams. Another day of oral interviews followed. Among the 400 who were competing, I was one of the fortunate twenty selected to receive scholarships.

In August of 1949, I began my life in America by matriculating at Northwestern University's graduate medical school in Chicago, then the second most populated city in the United States. Northwestern University conferred a Master of Science degree upon me in the spring of 1951, and I became a resident in the department of pathology of Cook County Hospital in Chicago in 1952.

I practiced in the Cook County Hospital and West Side Veterans Administration Hospital and also taught at the University of Illinois until 1972 when I left Chicago and moved to Omaha, Nebraska, to accept a staff position with the pathology department of Bishop Clarkson Memorial Hospital. In addition to my responsibilities at Bishop Clarkson Memorial Hospital I also taught pathology classes for the Omaha medical branch of the University of Nebraska, Lincoln.

In 1986, I retired from my affiliation with the Bishop Clarkson Memorial Hospital after sixteen years of service. This brought to a close my lifetime of medical study and practice which spanned almost half a century, including thirty-seven years of study and practice in the United States, most of that time as an American Citizen.

After our luncheon with Kim Il Sung in Onchon, we visited with him on May 7, a fortnight later. The president had invited us to join him for a meal in the Okryu restaurant to savor the famous Pyongyang cold noodle

President Kim Il Sung (right) greets Dr. and Mrs. Won Tai Sohn on May 7, 1992.

dish which was created there. I told him then that we had decided to come live in Pyongyang where I could be near him. He expressed delight that our decision was based on our affection for him.

"Thank you. It is very kind of you to think so fondly of me," he said. "When you come I will have a companion to chat with about bygone days. There are some older people around but they all have worked under me and are uneasy about chatting freely and I find it difficult to communicate with our young people. We could go hunting and fishing together; if you don't know much about hunting, I could teach you."

Kim Il Sung told Yoo Shin not to worry about being unable to visit with her children in the United States.

"You have relatives here and in South Korea as well as your sons and daughter in the United States, and you can take a trip to America and South Korea when necessary," he said.

Our worries thus dispelled, I commented jocularly that all that remained to be done then would be for him to provide us with a straw-thatched house in Pyongyang which we could inhabit.

"There are no straw-thatched houses in North Korea. Even in rural communities there are only modern dwelling houses. So I cannot fulfill your request," he responded.

Tongue-in-cheek, I teased him, "That is not true. There is a straw-thatched cottage in Mangyongdae."

"But you know that you can't have that dwelling: The People wouldn't permit it," he replied, laughing as he directed attention to Kang Sok Sung (Soong) and Choe Jin Hyok (head and deputy head, respectively, of the Party History Institute), who were dining at a nearby table.

I knew that the president's birthplace was a national shrine to which great numbers of North Koreans, as well as people from all parts of the world, made pilgrimage the year round. To North Koreans, the birthplace of Kim Il Sung was what Jerusalem was to Christians and Jews, Mecca and Medina to Muslims, and Sakyas to the Buddhists.

Kim Il Sung patted me on the shoulder and said I would get a nice house and receive fine treatment when I came to the motherland, adding, "I will drop in to visit you now and then," and, as an afterthought, asked, "What will you serve me then?"

"I'm not sure how to make noodles with frozen potatoes, but I can prepare Pyongyang cold noodles which you like so much," my wife interjected.

The president said that both cold noodles and warm noodles would be delicious if Yoo Shin prepared it herself. Then, as he was helping us to replenish our plates, he commented that our table was arranged "luxuriously, in the style of a banquet being hosted by a president," but when we were settled in Pyongyang he would be treating us to foods, not as a president but as plain Kim Sung Ju. I agreed that would be a good idea and appropriate for our close friendship; then the president, obviously quite pleased, summoned the waiter and asked for one more glass of blueberry wine.

The waiter admonished this idea: "No, you mustn't." But Kim Il Sung insisted. "Two or three glasses are all right for me. I'm feeling pleasant."

The two of them seemed as close and respectfully informal as a grandfather and grandson might be. I envied their comfortable relationship.

"Mr. President, I feel a bit awkward when you address me as Mr. Sohn Won Tai, and I call you Mr. President. I would like simply to call you "Brother" and would you please call me by my first name?"

"I understand and I agree with you," Kim Il Sung said. "From now on, I'll call you Won Tai and you call me Kim Sung Ju."

Whenever we met after that, the president greeted me with, "Hi, Won Tai, how are you doing?" Are you all right?" Although I thought of him as a brother, I found it difficult to call him "Brother" when we were not

Myohyang Mountain in May of 1992: President Kim Il Sung (center) explaining a large rock on the top of the mountain to Dr. and Mrs. Won Tai Sohn.

alone. Government officials and journalists were at hand whenever we met so I was not comfortable calling him "Brother Kim Sung Ju" or "Brother Song Ju." This familiarity brought back the close feelings of our relationship in the long-ago days of our youth in Jilin.

He asked about my situation in retirement. I told him my monthly income was about $6,000 and he commented that it was not a small sum. Then he turned again to my plans.

"You should not come back to Korea merely because it is my wish," he said. "But please come if you feel like living here. Your pension is not a small one, so don't be in a hurry to come here. Live there, enjoying your pension, and when you feel too infirm to travel back and forth to visit here, then make arrangements to come back to your motherland and be buried here."

In retrospect, I have wondered how anyone could disparagingly call him a dictator, this man who holds all of his countrymen in highest respect. I had looked to him as an older brother; never in our relationship had he stooped to coercion or made unreasonable demands upon me or anyone else that I was aware of.

The corruption in South Korea's highest government levels, involving theft of perhaps a billion dollars of public funds by two previous presidents, became known in the early 1990s. Unquestionably, this was only the tip of the iceberg of corruption at all levels of South Korea's puppet political structure which had taken possession of power in the transition from Japanese occupation to post–World War II occupation as a pseudo protectorate of the U.S. and its Western world allies. The Cold War against communism that consumed the political attention of the United States also brought it into a conspiratorial relationship with South Korea to oppose North Korea's efforts toward a peaceful reunification. That resulted in a tragic "permanent" division between North and South at an arbitrary line of demarcation at the 38th parallel, militarily guarded on the South by so-called neutral armies of the U.S. and other nations, along with South Korean military units, and on the north by North Korean soldiers.

The propaganda from South Korea attempted to portray Kim Il Sung as a dictator who was holding his countrymen in bondage by the harshest of measures. But in the 1990s the true character of the South Korean political regime was revealed as it waged bloody reprisals against citizens, many of them students and factory laborers who were demonstrating in support of their democratic right to freedom of speech. Heavily-armed police and military troops were being sent against student demonstrators supporting the reunification of Korea and working people asking for better conditions in which to work and for a more just return for their labors.

Another example of barbarity, which shocked most of the world but not the United States, occurred in September of 1996. That was the slaughter of 25 or more North Korean seaman who made their way to shore after their submarine had foundered in the treacherous rocky off-shore waters of the West Sea only to be hunted down and massacred by South Korean military and civilian police. South Korea justified the action by claiming that the men were spies. No such brutal action was taken by North Korea following its capture of the U.S. spy ship *Pueblo* (January 23, 1968), it might be pointed out.

Who, I have asked myself, is acting the role of a ruthless dictator: the powerful South Korean political regime? Certainly not the revered leader of his people, Kim Il Sung, who led North and South Korean patriots in their fight for Korean freedom against the Japanese and their collaborators for so many decades!

Yoo Shin and I pondered these many considerations while trying to decide what to do about our lives. In the end, we made up our minds to continue to live in our Nebraska home for the indefinite future. But we also pledged ourselves to do everything in our power to denounce those who were making a profession out of fabricating lies and distorting the truth about Kim Il Sung and North Korea and to present a true and honest picture of the man and his people to the world.

16

A "White House" on the Mountain

It was June of 1993, only a year after Kim Il Sung had promised to provide a magnificent dwelling for us in North Korea, that we returned to Pyongyang once more. After supper one day soon after we had arrived and were getting settled in the temporary quarters, Mr. Choe of the Party History Institute told us we should move immediately to our new house. Work on that dwelling place had only just begun before we left for home a year ago but we had been taken to the site by the builders the president had assigned to the project. Although it seemed improbable that construction could have been completed so soon, Mr. Choe insisted that we pack up and move there from Building 18 of Sojaedong where we were staying.

We assembled our luggage and helped to transfer it to a waiting automobile which took us through the center of Pyongyang to an expressway in the suburbs. Our car soon left the freeway and turned onto a narrow road. It was late in the evening and darkness limited our view but we sensed that we were headed into a valley shadowed by a huge mountain. Suddenly a brightly lit house appeared in the black void surrounding us. Two stories high and brilliantly aglow, to us it was a fairy tale palace in a magical forest setting.

An elderly man and a comely young woman, whom we assumed were caretakers of the place, came to greet us and told us that we would be living here. They guided us to a suite which had been a large drawing room and bedroom. We learned later that this suite had been used by presidents of other countries during their visits to Korea. It was a large house and, understandably, the furnishings were luxurious.

The caretakers led us on an inspection tour through other rooms on the first and second floors. There were ten guest rooms, including one reserved for vice presidents and others specifically assigned for use by Jong Ho, the eldest son; Jong Guk, the second son; and Yong Hui, the daughter. The other guest rooms were reserved for people who might come with me to North Korea, or visit me during my stay there.

The mansion also had a billiard room, a table tennis room, and a spacious lounge to accommodate casual socializing as well as privacy for intimate discussions. At one corner of the foyer was a doorway providing access to a dining room which easily could accommodate medium-size banquet groups.

"This is your house," Mr. Choe announced.

I was overwhelmed by the grandeur of the place and awed to be told that this was my house, the one that Kim Il Sung had promised to provide. "I have become a millionaire in a single day; this house would cost millions to build in America," I was thinking. And I hadn't even viewed the landscape surrounding it yet! Exhausted by the day's amazing events, I fell peacefully asleep that night without being aware when reality diffused into my dreams.

Early the next morning I hurried out of the house to view the landscaping. There was a large artificial pond which we hadn't noticed as we arrived last night. Mr. Choe was already there, standing at the water's edge. The view of the house from where we were standing was breathtaking. The grounds were landscaped with pine-nut and a variety of other fir trees, and lilac bushes and multi-hued flower gardens. Everything vied to share the glory of perfuming the air and adorning the pristine white beauty of the house, itself a vase of alabaster delicately painted and lacquered to lend beauty to the earth as if on a mantelpiece.

"This is a wonderful house; it's a White House, so to speak!" I exclaimed, expressing my thought aloud as I tried to visually absorb this beautiful scene.

Mr. Choe explained that it was one of the houses provided for visiting heads of state and was used by President Kim Il Sung on important state occasions.

"Then I've become a president!" I said in jest. "This is too much for me; I've never been a government official, let alone a president. I'm only a medical doctor."

From left: Mrs. Won Tai Sohn and Dr. Won Tai Sohn in front of their house in North Korea with Y. K. Lee and Ki Yong Lee, in June of 1993.

Mr. Choe smiled as he replied: "Nevertheless, each time you have come to Korea you have been accorded the respect due a president although you haven't had a title. Why don't we name you president of a country? President of Omaha, or President of Nebraska?"

We both laughed as I explained that Omaha was a city and Nebraska was a state and neither had an official of that capacity. Therefore I would be able to accept the honorary title of President of Omaha. I said that this might make the elected mayor of Omaha a bit nervous but there would also be no reason to fear I would attempt to usurp his power inasmuch as I could be "President of Omaha, U.S.A." only in Pyongyang, North Korea.

For the historical record, that is how I became President of Omaha with residency in my White House in Pyongyang.

A year earlier, after Kim Il Sung had said he would provide an excellent house for me in Pyongyang, Mr. Choe had accompanied me to a hillsite on the River Taedong some distance from Mangyondae. This overlooked the river lowlands of the valley and was cloistered on three sides by mountains. The location had been left undeveloped although it appeared to be ideal for important government uses.

Mr. Choe had told me this site had been chosen by Kim Il Sung and he had been instructed to take me there to obtain my approval or disapproval. If I liked it, Mr. Choe said, construction would be started immediately. As I looked the terrain over, downhill from above and upward from the riverside, I was troubled by the thought that I was imposing a burden on the president by having him build a new home for me and Yoo Shin.

A few days later, Mr. Choe took me to the Paektusan Architectural Institute which is the leading school of architectural design in North Korea. Its research teams had designed such monumental structures in Pyongyang as the Tower of Juche Idea, the Arch of Triumph, the Mansudae Assembly Hall and the Grand People's Study House. The chief of research, who guided us on a tour of the institute, brought out a blueprint for my inspection.

He said the plans provided a main house for my wife and me, a detached dwelling for my sons and daughters, and a third house for my guests. Auxiliary facilities would include a tennis court, a swimming pool and a hothouse. A fishing camp on the river also was a part of the plan. Then the three of us motored to the proposed site where the design chief pointed out the locations selected for the various buildings, each to conform to the topography. This plan was in sharp contrast to the layout of the Sojaedong Guest House where we were then staying.

When I met the president afterward, he asked my opinion of the location and the various aspects of the plans. I told him everything was so outstanding that, in addition to providing housing for me and family guests, he would be able to use the facilities for more important matters also.

"It is a most desirable place and I have been withholding it from development until now," he agreed. "I stopped a project from being carried out for that property at one time. You might say that I spared the site for your house."

I thanked him and asked to be allowed to take a copy of the blueprints back to the United States with me, and I did. On my next trip to Pyongyang I went back to the site on the Taedong River. Building locations were already bulldozed, some pillars were in place and construction work was in full swing. One worker said everyone was helping speed up the project because "an old friend of President Kim Il Sung, Sohn Won Tai, would be living in this house."

I praised the men for their work and they said they would speed up even more so that I could be able to move in about the same time next year. There seemed to be an endless stream of vehicles on the expressway in front of the construction site. The project supervisor, noticing my apparent concern about possible traffic noise, said plans included a sound-baffle wall which would block the view of the house as well as mute the sounds from the freeway. I said that I was grateful for that but I was troubled by one other thing. What could be lacking in the plans for this wonderful house? The workmen seemed to be implying that question by their demeanor and subtle glances.

"How can I idle my days in this wonderful place?" I asked them. "I need something to work with. Can you lay out a small garden off the kitchen and erect a hen house alongside?"

They laughed and agreed that it was a good idea so together we marked a site for a hen house and a kitchen garden where I could grow garlic and lettuce.

How then did we come to live in a palatial residence quite the opposite of the one where construction was in full swing? A moving story is associated with my "White House" on the mountain.

One day President Kim Il Sung was talking with leader Kim Jong Il about the house on the River Taedong in which the Won Tai Sohns would be living. Kim Jong Il agreed that it was a good idea to build a new house for me at the Taedong site but, even if the work were expedited, construction could not be completed and the house furnished adequately as early as expected. Therefore, for the time being, Won Tai would have to be accommodated in a guest house in the city center as had been done on previous visits. Kim Jong Il then suggested that a fine guest home already built should be reserved as a residence for the Sohns.

The president was satisfied that such a change would eliminate any chance of problems arising to upset his plans to host my 80th birthday party so if a guest house with a spacious banquet hall were given to me he had no objection to following that course.

Actually, the site on the Taedong River was quite a distance from Pyongyang residential areas. Even if the house could be erected ahead of schedule, a great deal of additional work would remain to be done such as installing electricity and laying water supply and sewage facilities. All of these related construction projects were further complicated by the building site being located such a long distance from access to existing service installations. In consideration of my age, they decided that all of these auxiliary projects should be completed before the house was occupied.

Thus, toward the end of June in 1993, I moved into a house which was equal to an official residence of a president and, thanks to the thoughtfulness of President Kim Il Sung and Kim Jong Il, I was being accorded all of the amenities due a president.

In Pyongyang, I learned that Kim Il Sung had initiated a program which provided status of vice premier for veterans of the anti–Japanese armed struggle. That knowledge was conveyed to me during a visit with

Hwang Kwi Hon, a former member of the Korean Children's Association at Jilin. Now she was living in comfort in a luxurious house on the River Pothong, receiving all of the benefits due a vice premier. I also visited Mrs. Ryu Mi Yong, widow of the late General Choe Tok Sin, and discovered that she too was being accorded the same benefits.

I was being accorded even higher status, I realized, because when I went to the Kumgang and Myohyang Mountains on a sightseeing trip, I was given a guest house in which Samdech Norodom Sihanouk of Cambodia had stayed at one time.

In July, President Kim Il Sung came to visit me. He had visited us several times in Pyongyang but this was his first in our new home. Yoo Shin and I rushed to greet him where he was standing in the hot sunshine. His first words were, "What do you think of your house; do you like it?"

My wife and I assured him that it was so magnificent that we were at loss for words to thank him properly.

"If you like it, then everything is all right," he said. "The fresh air here is good for one's health so I made certain this house was provided for you."

He questioned us further to assure himself that we didn't think it was inferior to the newly-built place on the River Taedong. I expressed my deep-seated feeling that I didn't deserve such a wonderful house and, being an ordinary person who had done nothing for the nation, I was feeling ill at ease at being treated so lavishly.

The president looked at me for a moment and, as we walked slowly toward the house, almost to himself, quietly said, "I owed the Rev. Sohn a great deal but I have not done anything for him."

I was deeply moved by his earnestness and now realized that his affection for me was not merely as an old friend. In talking with Kim Il Sung about the death of my father, he once told me that many people who had fought for independence of the country had died before their time. He said that the Japanese killed Mr. Ahn Chang Ho by feeding rice mixed with glass dust while holding him in prison. Now, whenever he was able to locate family survivors of such patriotic independence fighters, he was attentive to their needs. Thus Ahn Chang Ho's sister, Mr. Ryang So Bong's son and Mr. Lee Jun's son all were living in North Korea and being benefited under the president's special treatment for veterans.

The depth and breadth of Kim Il Sung's concern for his people could be likened only to an ocean which takes all rivers of the earth into its bosom and then replenishes the clouds with vapor so that the life-sustaining waters can be returned to earth as rain.

We chatted informally in our lounge, the time passing quickly. When the president stood up, preparing to leave, Yoo Shin was mortified and apologized for not having served him anything to eat.

"Don't worry," he said. "I'll come again soon and then you can treat me to some of your excellent food." He was smiling as he took his leave.

He dropped by our house in June the following year but we only had time to talk for a few minutes in the yard before he and I left together in his car. I had been hoping for an opportunity when we could entertain him properly with delicious foods elegantly prepared and served. Regretfully, that never happened. This was the last time that President Kim Il Sung would drop by my house to visit.

The news that President Kim Il Sung had provided a wonderful house for me became widely known among Koreans in the United States, and it was accepted as additional proof that the president was taking utmost care of me even though none had any idea how grand the house really was. The father of my eldest daughter-in-law, Dr. Kim, a resident of New York, was of the opinion that my house was one befitting an elder statesman. My father had contributed all of his property and wealth to the independence movement and President Kim Il Sung in this way had bequeathed a valuable heritage to me, the son of the Rev. Sohn Jong Do to whom he owed so much.

Dr. and Mrs. Kim and Ryu Jae Myong, who lived in New Mexico, were my guests on their visit to North Korea and I recall Dr. Kim's comment at that time:

> When I was told that President Kim Il Sung had given you a house, I took that information at face value. But this house surely represents the great consideration and solicitude with which President Kim Il Sung and Leader Kim Jong Il hold you.

During my first visit, the president had given me many gifts, among which were a gold wrist watch with his name inscribed and a jeweled picture. When I went to Pyongyang to pay my respects following the death of Kim Il Sung, I was informed that Leader Kim Jong Il had stated that my house was a legacy left to me by the president and would be well cared for during my lifetime and succeeding generations of my family.

The house in the mountains is a great material legacy. But a far greater and invaluable spiritual legacy which I have received from the inimitable President Kim Il Sung is an appreciation of those noble traits that guided his life and his unwavering belief that man should cherish and practice ennobling morality and fidelity at all times.

17

For the Benefit of the People

When I first embarked for Pyongyang in 1991, a number of persons opined that the president would not recognize me, nor would he meet with me, and I would come back empty-handed and disillusioned. Some people also warned me that the DPRK was a hermetic communist state where I would experience considerable restrictions on what I would be able to see, say, hear or do. After meeting President Kim Il Sung, however, I knew that I had been right to visit Pyongyang and witness everything myself before passing judgment on the country and its government. The ancient peoples were perhaps correct when they coined the old adage that "seeing is believing."

I found everything quite the opposite from what I had been told in the United States. From the moment of my arrival until my departure to return home, I did not experience any restrictions. President Kim Il Sung gave me a warm-hearted reception and everyone, including those people who were assigned to guide and attend to my needs, was most indulgent and trying their best to make me feel comfortable and at ease. Once I had set foot in Pyongyang, I became completely relaxed. There were no ceremonial formalities required of me and I felt at home in my house where the freshness of the air alone was exhilarating. I no longer felt like a guest. How good it was to be home after so many years of living under or escaping from Japanese occupation and the subsequent military-political settlement that had divided Korean people against one another.

On my way to Pyongyang, I thought a great deal, with some trepidation, about the derogatory (as well as deliberately misleading) propaganda about North Korea and President Kim Il Sung which was being circulated in South Korea and in the United States. On the other hand, not all of the media were being derogatory. The *New York Times* had published an article under the headline: "Korea Produced a Hero of the 20th Century." Many other newspapers and broadcasting stations had also given him favorable recognition as "an outstanding politician of the 20th century."

Nevertheless, Kim Il Sung had also been the object of many insults by political enemies in South Korea and the United States. Those parties did not speak well of him and this inflicted pain upon me because, although I did not believe the diatribes, I had no evidence to refute or disprove their charges. More and more, I had felt a need to go to Pyongyang.

What became apparent to me at once was that North Korea truly was exercising its inherent right to independence while holding firm in its desire to maintain an exalted level of national dignity. I believe that all of this was being achieved as the result of President Kim Il Sung's unswerving integrity and leadership. Subsequently, after visiting Pyongyang several times, I learned more about the Juche philosophy of President Kim Il Sung and its application in the development of independence for Korea.

During our first discussion, the president explained his opposition to permitting or seeking alliance with the great powers in Korea's struggle to attain independence, its reconstruction and the establishment of Juche as the basis for government by the people. He explained that when he was engaged in the revolution in Jilin some people had advised him to go to the Soviet Union to learn the communist theory of government.

"But, young as I was then, I was convinced that Korea should be liberated by Koreans themselves, so I refused to follow their advice," he told me.

"I said the Russians might be well-versed about their revolution but that wouldn't necessarily apply to the Korean struggle for liberty," he continued. "And I told my compatriots that if I studied Russian there was a danger that I might become pro-Russian. You know that Koreans over the ages have strongly resisted any Russian influence over their affairs."

I enjoyed listening to Kim Il Sung discoursing on the way he believed Korea should proceed under independence. It was well known in the days of Japanese occupation that most of the leaders of the Communist Party of China had studied in France or Russia. But Kim Il Sung sincerely believed that he could better serve his compatriots by remaining in Korea while learning how to successfully wage the struggle for its independence. His political idealism was deeply rooted in the love and pride he held for his country.

On various occasions, Kim Il Sung told leaders of eastern European communist countries, following the collapse of the Russian oligarchy, that he was continuing to lead Koreans in their own way by establishing Juche as the basis for government conduct and by owing nothing to the large communist powers in achieving that goal.

His comments reminded me of a phrase I had read in a first-year textbook in primary school and I quoted the maxim in Chinese. The President smiled as he interrupted the saying:

"When a large dog leaps, a small dog also leaps," he said, but added, "A country that copies what a big country does, like a small dog that leaps when a large dog leaps, cannot have its own independent ideas and, if it only does what others do as it reconstructs its country, it can only end up in ruin."

Kim Il Sung said that China, involved in the revolution throughout its vast lands, had followed a dogmatic relationship with Russia and thus represented an example of one big country worshipping another large country without giving proper thought to the role of its own intellectuals. As a result, those intellectuals experienced a great deal of hardship during China's cultural revolution.

"We did things in a different way; we regarded our intellectuals as a motivating force of the revolution," he said. "That is why the mark of our party bears a writing brush along with a hammer and sickle."

Factionalists criticized Kim Il Sung, claiming that he was too stubborn and was doing everything in his own way. They wanted to follow what the Soviet Union or the Chinese did.

"But I did not heed nor yield to their demands," Kim Il Sung said grimly. He said that he had asked himself and his opponents how Korea could wage its fight for freedom without intellectuals to provide leadership. The veterans of the anti–Japanese struggle were capable, brave "sharpshooters" but they did rely on intellectuals nevertheless, he pointed out.

The president recalled a visit by Wang Dingnan, China's secretary under Mao Zedong. Some years after China's cultural revolution, the secretary had come to North Korea and, at one conference, had commented that the banner of the Democratic People's Republic of Korea, with the hammer, sickle and writing brush emblem, "was not only creative but wise as well," noting that it recognized the importance of intellectual guidance of a country's leadership.

Kim Il Sung remarked that North Korea has well-educated intellectuals and he didn't think it would be advantageous to remold them into a rigid political philosophy. Surrounded by such major powers as the United States, the Soviet Union, China and Japan, the DPRK has been living in its own way without deferring to any of them, he pointed out. The propriety of its ideology and its achievements are apparent because there are no foreign soldiers in North Korea and no country has any influence on North Korea's politics, he explained.

Kim Il Sung emphasized, as an example, that when Soviet leaders ruled the roost and east European socialist countries were her satellites, Russia had no posture in North Korea, nor did North Korea join the COMECON (Council for Mutual Economic Cooperation) economic alliance, choosing instead to build an independent economy through efforts of its own people. The West Sea barrage represents a prime example of the success of that policy. Another monument to its citizens' accomplishments is the Tower of Juche Idea on the bank of the River Taedong at the center of Pyongyang. This is the highest stone tower in the world, and its torch flares day and night as a symbol of Kim Il Sung's contribution to North Korea's achievements.

The Juche philosophy asserts that a man is the master of his own destiny and has the power to determine and achieve the goals he sets for himself. President Kim Il Sung has expounded this idea throughout his political and personal life. This is also the basic political philosophy of North Korean society.

Kim Il Sung authored the Juche philosophy and built an independent new country on those principles. I would profess that the true greatness of the man is determined by the greatness of his own philosophy and ideology. The Juche philosophy, I believe, is the innate bonding faith of the entire Korean people. It values, above all else, the independence of the country and a society in which all citizens join in efforts to ensure that everyone shares in national prosperity. Basically, this identifies the spirit of patriotism in North Korea.

Kim Il Sung emphasized that Koreans, as a principle of national pride, should believe that Korea stands first among the countries of the world. Every nation holds a belief that it is a superior country. I have heard much about the pragmatism of the Anglo-Saxons and I acknowledge it to be true to a certain degree. The Japanese people talk much about the superiority of the Yamato nation; the Chinese have claimed superiority of the Chinese nation; the Russians have asserted that theirs is a great and powerful nation and a leader in the arts and sciences. Such feelings of national superiority have been used to justify national chauvinism and aggression against and oppression of other nations. How great was the harm the German nation caused to mankind under Hitler and the Nazi purges of non–Aryan races!

At first, I was not able to comprehend the Korean-nation-first principle of Juche. How could a nation achieve dignity and pride merely by having its people think that their own nation is a leader of the world? But then I learned that it really meant that the Korean people, a wise and brave race from ancient times to the present, must strive to regain confidence in their own ability to live as comfortably and happily as any other national society. A fundamental part of Kim Il Sung's plan was to encourage Koreans to help themselves regain their freedom and build a new way of life in their homeland.

I have been told that an American journalist, after visiting both North and South Korea, commented that South Korea had no national philosophy but North Korea had one of its own. The journalist then summarized his observations with this statement: "A nation that has no philosophy is a nation deprived of its soul and its future."

Historically, Korea has always seemed to be susceptible to the influence of the great powers of Asia. This was usually said to have been the unavoidable geo-political fate of a little country that is surrounded by major powers, or even an inherent tendency to accept the inevitable. But such a tendency cannot be an inherited trait of the Korean people, Kim Il Sung contended. The proof, he suggested, has been evidenced clearly by the historical fact that North Korean and South Korean patriots fought courageously for more than forty years against the Japanese occupation armies and are still resisting the post–World War II military and political restraints that are blocking reunification and independence of all Korea.

I would like to believe that the Juche idea should be the basic philosophy of the entire Korean nation because it symbolizes patriotism and incorporates the spiritual values of independence under which every effort should be directed at ensuring that the prosperity of the country is enjoyed by all its citizens.

Kim Il Sung stated on more than one occasion that Koreans are "really intelligent, talented and brave," and should rely on their own strength and efforts to build a prosperous and powerful Korea which other nations of the world would respect. He also urged me not to forget the roots and the pride of being a Korean even though I was living in an alien land far away from the motherland.

I believe that the Juche idea is the highest form of humanitarianism because it holds that the people's welfare should be the most important concern of government. I would have to consider the Juche idea as the Scriptures of our nation, and the Gospels for all mankind.

18
Applying the Truth of Independence to Practice

I first heard the phrase, "The people are my God," in Pyongyang. It literally means to believe in the people as "heaven." In his memoirs, President Kim Il Sung wrote that his lifelong maxim had been: "The People are my God."

When I met him in Pyongyang the first time, his demeanor was more like that of an ordinary parent than head of state. Although he was renowned as "The Tiger of Mt. Paektu," the general who fought the Japanese invasion and occupation armies, I didn't notice an imposing air or posture; he might just as well have been any father concerned only with the affairs of his family. I was convinced then, and subsequently by witnessing his involvement in political affairs, that the often-heard phrase was indeed his life-guiding maxim.

The Christian, Buddhist, Islamic and Confucian philosophies all exhort rulers to administer their country's affairs fairly and with love for their people. I have read Tongmeng and Samjagyong books on Confucian views on morality. They said a king should be gentle at all times and his subjects should be faithful to him. Furthermore, they said that a government must regard the will of the people as the will of heaven which under no circumstances should be opposed. This might well be applied to advantage today by all governments, whether they be a monarchy, a republic, a democracy, or a communist/socialist state.

Presidents and rulers of all countries routinely, upon ascending to power, pledge to do their best to serve their people well. From a cynical viewpoint, this solemn oath may have less to do with sincerity than awareness on the part of the swearer that he or she has more to fear from historians of the future than one's immediate political opponents. A tragic exception may have been U.S. President Abraham Lincoln who, in his Gettysburg Address in November 1863, expressed a basic theme of Kim Il Sung's Juche philosophy when he emphasized that "government of the people, by the people, and for the people" was the constitutional strength of the United States. However, he paid with his life for attempting to carry out that policy during his term of office.

I am not well-versed in history but it appears to me that not every ruler who has professed an intention to promote national affairs in the best interests and welfare of all the people has been able to or actually was dedicated to honestly carry out that promise. After my reunion with President Kim Il Sung I became convinced that he was a true leader and father of the country to which he had devoted his lifetime of service under the strong belief that "The People are my God."

One Korean resident of the United States, after his first visit to Pyongyang, had told me that the many patriotic signs and beautiful floral plantings throughout the city had left a deep impression on his mind. He said the city was a veritable park, decorated with gorgeous flowers and green foliage. The streetcars displayed the slogan, "We Serve the People," not only promoting its function as a transportation vehicle but also patriotically bannering the national political philosophy.

My wife is a native of Pyongyang and she was dumbfounded to discover the changes that had been made since she had lived there as a child. The family's house had been located near the River Pothong in a neighborhood known as Thosongrang but it had been completely replatted and rebuilt. The only way Yoo Shin could determine where her house once stood was to look for the Pothong Gate which was still standing. Recalling how she and her playmates had walked to the gate's park to play, she still was unable to make more than a rough guess about where the house had been. Nothing except the Pothong Gate had remained the same as when she was growing up there.

We visited the Grand People's Study House in the city center. While enjoying a bird's-eye view of the city from a balcony of the study house after our tour had been completed, Yoo Shin suddenly exclaimed: "Why, this is where my father's church was standing!"

Our guide confirmed that she was correct: the church buildings had been destroyed by United States bombers during the Korean War. The site was part of the city center which had been reserved for important government buildings when housing was being built in totally destroyed areas during the post-war reconstruction of the city. This planning followed the practice in most countries to erect their imposing government buildings in the central part of their capital cities. However, President Kim Il Sung had insisted that a large educational and cultural facility, easily accessible for use by the entire population, should be built there instead.

The Grand People's Study House is not merely a library; its modern facilities occupy tens of thousands of square meters of space and provide an opportunity for comprehensive research as well as extra-curricular education. The majestic and original architectural beauty rises through its blue-tiled roof.

Suddenly the clock bell of the study chimed.

"In the long-ago past a church bell chimed here," Yoo Shin said pensively. "They are the same bells but somehow their sounds are different."

She was right, of course. They were bell sounds of different ages. Where a small church that preached the revelation of God once stood, a grand study house, incomparable in grandeur, size and educational purpose, now was standing in its place, graphic testimony to the changes in culture that had taken place with the passing of time.

In North Korea, the citizenry is referred to most commonly as "The People." The governmental power organ is called "The People's Committee," the defense department is "The People's Army," and a hospital is "The People's Hospital." Titles of honor reflect the same reverence with which the people as a whole hold their way of life, for example: People's Actor, People's Journalist, and People's Teacher. Exaltation of "The People" is central to all civilian political activity.

To be able to carry out political programs that will benefit the people, President Kim Il Sung believed that it was essential to understand their needs and to feel their pain if they were oppressed. From his mid-teens, he constantly had moved among the people, acquiring knowledge of their needs and, over the many years of working for Korean independence, gradually had formulated his policies for leadership. He traveled throughout the country, visiting with citizens of all walks of life: in small rural hamlets, in large urban cities and in remote fisherman's villages along the seashore. This search to find direction for leadership became known among North Koreans as "seeking field guidance."

While touring throughout North Korea, I saw many granite monuments, large and small, commemorating the fact that Kim Il Sung had visited with the people there on such and such a date. I found monuments of this kind on Mt. Paetku, on Mt. Kumgang, at a seaside village in Jungsan (where my father had been born), and in a rural village in Unryul (which I visited at the request of my in-laws).

After the Korean War, the people living in the Onchon area suggested to Kim Il Sung that if water were available they could grow rice for themselves on land that was suitable for farming. However, a mountain separated that land from the River Taedong which flowed nearby. The president soon afterward launched a huge reservoir construction project which utilized pumping stations at two levels to draw water up from the River Taedong to fill the reservoir. The project included construction of canals to bring water from the reservoir to rice paddies not only in Onchon but also in Nampho. Since then, the people in South Pyongyang Province have been able to plant and harvest enough rice to meet their needs and surplus quantities which are made available to other consumers.

This was merely one example of the popular political and economic policies which President Kim Il Sung carried out through his intensive efforts to obtain field guidance from the North Korean people. To achieve construction of needed projects such as the Onchon reservoir and canal system, the state rallied the necessary numbers of white and blue-collar workers to plan and complete the construction.

In the same way, modern dwellings are built to meet the housing needs of the people. I was able to visit the family of my wife's brother-in-law in their apartment. An office worker, he and his wife were enjoying living in a unit which included a kitchen, a bathroom, and three spacious living rooms, all with heated flooring. Both he and she were born after the liberation and were unfamiliar with such terminology as "paying the rent"; the cost of living in their apartment was minimal.

North Korea had abolished all forms of taxation about twenty years earlier. When I had learned about that during my first visit to Pyongyang, naturally I was amazed because I could not immediately understand how the country could be operated without that type of financing.

From ancient times in Korea and elsewhere in the world, taxes have been the source of financing government. In feudal as well as modern times, taxes of various types have tormented the citizenry and often were indicative of misrule that penalized the poor and well-to-do alike. On one occasion when I hurriedly began to make preparations to return home from Pyongyang in order to meet the deadline for filing, I was urged to stay longer. When I explained that I had to get back home in order to file my tax returns on time, my hosts seemed unable to comprehend what was involved.

For the abolition of the tax system alone, I am of the opinion that President Kim Il Sung's political ideology is the most advanced embodiment

President Kim Il Sung (right) and Dr. Won Tai Sohn, after completion of the agreement on a sister relationship between the Christian Association for Medical Missions and Pyongyang Third Hospital on November 6, 1992.

of mankind's dream of an ideal life. It even could be claimed that Kim Il Sung's political ideals are more credible than those of such pioneers of bourgeois enlightenment as Jean-Jacques Rousseau, Voltaire, Montesquieu, or Denis Diderot, because they have been unsuccessful. In this sense, I would be inclined to assert that Kim Il Sung is history's most laudable idealist, a great man who devoted his entire life to materializing his ideals.

It is the same with free medical care. Some developed countries have pursued social welfare policies to relieve the poor, eliminate epidemics and provide partially free medical care. Having been a medical practitioner all of my life, I feel positive that the programs of universal free medical care and preventive medicine practiced in North Korea, thanks to Kim Il Sung, are quite excellent humane programs indeed.

It is not easy for a state to bear the burden of medical assistance for its citizens. Even a rich country like the United States has been reluctant to introduce universal free medical care. A person without full-coverage of medical insurance in the United States encounters serious trouble if he becomes ill.

Both my wife and I underwent medical check-ups in one of the hospitals in Pyongyang under arrangements made by President Kim Il Sung. After a few days of examinations, we received a bundle of tonics indigenous to Korea to take with us on our return home to Nebraska. After accepting her package filled with prescribed medicines, Yoo Shin commented: "It's unbelievable to receive a comprehensive medical check-up and be given all of the prescribed medicines without charges." I explained to her that all North Koreans were given this same treatment under the country's universal medical care program.

Two other United States citizens, Dr. Ko Chan Song and his wife, once visited Pyongyang. Mrs. Ko suddenly became ill about dawn one day and was rushed to the hospital. She received treatment for the ensuing five days, recovered well, and was about to be released from care. Dr. Ko then asked the nurse where the "catch-all" office was located because he wished to pay for the costs of the treatment which had been provided for his wife. The nurse burst into laughter and then told Dr. Ko about North Korea's free medical care. He was astounded; before going to North Korea he had black clothing made to bring to his relatives because he was under the impression that the country was isolated and poor, thus black clothing would serve best where soap was not readily available!

From late October to November of 1992, I visited Pyongyang with five doctors in my capacity as advisor to the Christian Association for Medical Missions (CAMM). At that time, North Korea had been under strict

Applying the Truth of Independence to Practice 171

November 17, 1992: From left, Prof. Choe Sang Soon, Assistant Secretary Kim, Dr. Won Tai Sohn, Director Kang Sok Sung and Dr. Samuel Song, at Sunan (Pyongyang) Airport.

economic sanctions by the United States. Prior to this visit in 1992, CAMM programs had been presented for briefing in 1991 to the U.S. State Department by Dr. Samuel Song, representing CAMM. He was officially supported with encouragement by Spence Richardson and Charles Kartman, then directors of the Office of Korean Affairs. During three weeks of my stay with Dr. Samuel Song in Pyongyang, the purpose of our patriotic, humanitarian medical exchange and assistance programs was presented and discussed with President Kim, who was warmly welcoming. An official agreement was made for a sister relationship between CAMM and Pyongyang Third Hospital. It was signed on November 6, 1992, by Kim Yong Ik (Deputy Minister of Health of DPRK), Samuel Song, M.D., Ph.D., and myself (representing CAMM). I went to Pyongyang again in May the following year to discuss plans for completing the building of the Pyongyang Third Hospital. The Christian Association for Medical Missions is a charitable organization which supports efforts of Korean doctors to provide medical assistance to other countries. I had been asked to serve as advisor to help CAMM bring medical assistance to the northern part of the motherland and I headed the medical team in that capacity.

During our visits, President Kim Il Sung had praised our projects and encouraged us to assure that Pyongyang Third Hospital on Kwangbok Street be excellently equipped. He also suggested that we supervise the building of a new modern hospital on Thongil Street, lauding the initiation and promotion of that project by Korean doctors residing in the United States as an "outstanding example of Christian charity and patriotism."

All of the doctors who accompanied me were presbyters and had volunteered as a practice of Christian charity. They had assumed that medical equipment in North Korea would not be fully modern and therefore its patients might not be enjoying the best quality of medical treatment. However, their visits to Pyongyang proved to them that their beliefs were erroneous and they had been misled by propaganda.

After inspecting the modern facilities and equipment in Pyongyang Maternity Hospital and Kim Man Yu Hospital, their viewpoint was totally changed. They were expecting to find submarginal medical equipment and had assumed that adequate assistance would be to provide second-hand equipment from the United States. They rectified their recommendations, however, to provide the hospitals with new equipment of the latest technical design.

The history of Kim Il Sung's contributions to the welfare of North Korean people can be learned from a visit to International Friendship Exhibition in the Myohyang Mountains. This imposing building of Korean architecture is situated in a beautiful mountain valley. It contains tens of thousands of gifts that have been presented to Kim Il Sung by various countries of the world. Each gift from heads of state and other distinguished world personages represents the donor's sincere respect for Kim Il Sung and recognition of his achievements as North Korea's ideological leader. The artistic value of the exhibits could not be estimated easily but as I viewed them, I wondered if any other world leader had ever been accorded the high respect that these gifts represent.

In ancient times, Korea, a small country dwarfed by it neighbors, had paid tribute to strong dynasties but seldom received even respect in return. History records that Korean envoys sent to China to pay tribute were required to crawl on hands and knees to the Tiananmen to be properly humbled before appearing in the presence of the rulers. Some of Korea's gifts were of insignificant quality and value. On a visit to the Soviet Union, President Kim Il Sung was embarrassed to see on exhibit in the Kremlin Museum a shabby vase which had been presented to a Russian czar by the king of the Ri Dynasty of Korea.

The number of valuable gifts given to Kim Il Sung by noted persons of the world had increased to a point where additional space was required to display them and that led to construction of many underground rooms. North Koreans cherish this museum not only for its artistic value but because it also embodies another reason for national pride. All of these personal gifts to Kim Il Sung, a treasure worth a great fortune, were given by him to The People as permanent assets belonging to the nation.

What a contrast in honesty and integrity Kim Il Sung represented in the world of political affairs since the Korean War! Reflect for only a moment about the scandals that have arisen in South Korea, where two presidents diverted hundreds of millions of dollars of public money to their own accounts; in the Philippines, where Ferdinand Marcos did the same thing with billions of dollars of state money; in Iran, where the Shah Pahlavi used Swiss and other foreign banks as depositories to steal billions of dollars of his people's wealth.

Kim Il Sung's travels throughout North Korea are documented in a film on field guidance which I viewed in Pyongyang. I was impressed by his distinguished bearing although he always wore plain clothing wherever he went. In fact, he has led a plain and modest life. After his death, his personal safe was opened. Contrary to South Korean presidential safes in the Blue House, it contained no money, only letters from his compatriots and a photograph in which he was shown with his comrades-in-arms in the days of resistance against Japanese occupation. His office was not ornately furnished; even his television set was an old-style model.

Kim Il Sung served North Korea as president longer than any other person had headed a country during the twentieth century. His career as a world political figure spanned not only the turbulent years following World War II but also his lifetime of serving Korea as a freedom fighter during the Japanese occupation as the leader of a continuing effort to achieve independence and reunification of his country that had begun when he was about 14 or 15 years old in the mid–1920s.

He continued to represent The People in less demanding activities and as advisor to his son, Kim Jong Il, who succeeded him as president after his death at the age of 84. That dedication to Korea continued, symbolically, even as his body was borne to interment because it was draped in the folds of a red flag which carried the symbol he designed: the hammer, the sickle and the writing brush denoting Kim Il Sung's Juche philosophy that government must be of all The People, by all The People and for all The People of Korea!

19

Genuine Patriotism

It is my opinion that Kim Il Sung, during his Korean leadership since the close of World War II, has deserved and received recognition as a political leader of great stature in many parts of the world. There are various appraisals of his political ideology and his mode of leadership under a socialist-communist form government. Having been a medical doctor the greater part of my life, I have no intention of becoming involved in arguments contending this or that interpretation may be the correct evaluation of his political contributions. However, I do feel obligated to express my thoughts which reflect what I have seen, heard and sensed during my visits to North Korea.

I find an answer to many questions from my personal experiences in the Democratic People's Republic of Korea. Patriotism is a loyalty more easily claimed than performed. My father, the Reverend Sohn Jong Do, was a Methodist minister who had an intense love for Korea and his fellow Koreans. Despite persecution, that love and patriotism motivated him to oppose the Japanese occupation of Korea and to work for its freedom although it eventually cost him his life. This motivation was the same as that of Ahn Chang Ho, one of my father's close friends and an independence fighter also. Mr. Ahn was one of the leaders of the Korean Provisional Government in Shanghai, as was Syngman Rhee. All of them, including Kim Il Sung, demonstrated their patriotism with their actions, not political bombast.

President Kim Il Sung dedicated his life to his version of communism and he steadfastly adhered to it while making it work for the benefit of the people. He maintained that the interests of the country and the people should be placed above communist idealism and their revolution was a just and righteous movement only if carried on for the sake of the people. My view of communism is quite simple: if it is designed to benefit the poor and provide equal and happy lives for all citizens, then it is not greatly different from the pure doctrine of early Christianity. However, the extreme doctrines, which call for the abolishment of private property and expropriation of the assets of the wealthy, appall me. The theory that workers have no motherland similarly seems absurd to me.

In North Korea, I learned that a different doctrine of communism was being followed. Just off the expressway from Sunan to Pyongyang, near the International Airport, there is the Patriotic Martyrs Cemetery. Buried there are patriots who dedicated their lives to the liberation and independence of Korea. I found there the tombstones of Mr. Choe Tong O, whom I had known since my youth in Jilin; An Jae Hong; Jo So Ang; Jo Wan Gu; and Om Hang Sop. They were dedicated nationalists and important figures in the Korean Provisional Government at Shanghai. All of them are alleged by South Korea to have been "abducted" by North Korea. Kim Il Sung had told me that he also had wanted to have the remains of my father buried in that cemetery but they could not be found.

Some critics have alleged that because Kim Il Sung was a communist, he recognized for meritorious remembrance only dedicated communist Koreans who had participated in the struggle against Japanese armed occupation forces, and no others.

It is true that there is also a large cemetery on Mt. Taesong in Pyongyang that honors the veterans of anti–Japanese guerrilla resistance.

The popularity of the provisional government's early accomplishments are historically recorded. Those patriotic Koreans held fast to their principles for freedom and independence but, despite the efforts of such martyrs as Ri Pong Chang and Yun Pong Gil, the government in exile eventually fell under the influence of Chiang Kai-shek in Chongqing. In contrast, Kim Il Sung continued armed resistance to achieve liberation of Korea from Japanese imperialism with a patriotic fervor that perhaps explains his efforts to pay tribute to all Korean patriots who bore arms or continued to work for Korean independence and unification in writings and in other ways.

I could not but admire the sensitivity of President Kim Il Sung. He was a nation-loving, people-loving man who placed the welfare of his country above all other goals or ideals. I could recognize his patriotism in every aspect of the structuring of the socialist government of North Korea.

After visiting the mausoleums of Tangun, the founder-king of our nation, King Tongmyong, the founder of Koguryo, and Wang Kon, the founder of Koryo, I have given a good deal of thought to the differences of many communist ideologies from that of Kim Il Sung. Many communists have made feudal kings and their enemies the primary target of their revolutionary aims to eliminate all exploitation and oppression of the people. The objective was to exorcise the past and build a new society in which everyone would enjoy equal rights and live a life free from the "evils of feudalism."

But under the initiatives of President Kim Il Sung, North Korea has recognized that the cultural history handed down in legends is a treasure to be cherished by posterity as a key to a clear understanding of a Korean's roots. This program has led to rebuilding and expanding of the grand mausoleums of its founder-kings. Although Tangun and Tongmyong had been feudal kings, Kim Il Sung paid due respect to their contributions to Korea as a nation by having their mausoleums rebuilt on a grander scale than those kings ever might have dreamed possible.

Tangun's mausoleum, built of white granite, is a magnificent structure situated in beautiful natural terrain. The Pharaohs of ancient Egypt had majestic pyramids built for their own interment and to serve as symbols of their mighty power over their enslaved civilizations. Kim Il Sung wanted to assure that the magnificence of the mausoleums of the nation's ancient kings would enhance the pride with which Koreans might view their nation's history and to pass on to posterity a deeper appreciation of their roots.

When touring Pyongyang, one will certainly be guided to the site of what perhaps is one of the world's greatest reclamation projects. North Korea's West Sea Barrage embraces the lower Taedong River from a point about 100 kilometers from Pyongyang to the West Sea. The last eight kilometers of the river was once open sea but by walling off the sea, the project has created an artificial lake and a system of locks which permit inland and outbound passage by ships of capacities up to 50,000 tons. Inland, the project supports a vast acreage of land which formerly was not available for irrigation farming.

I have been told that the project would have required an investment of perhaps ten billion dollars if undertaken in a country operating under a different economic system. I discovered on my trips to North Korea that the people don't calculate income and expenditure in minute detail on such projects if they are designed to benefit the country. If it will improve the North Korean way of life, a project is carried out regardless of the cost in personal effort and investment or the challenge it represents to be accomplished.

It would be difficult to calculate the value of the labor involved in construction of the West Sea Barrage. Countless numbers of office workers, youths and housewives took part in the work, carrying loads of earth and rock on their backs, day after day, but claiming no compensation except the pleasure of patriotically contributing to their country's welfare. No estimate of construction costs could put an accurate dollar value on such labor of love for country and fellow man.

I am not an expert in economics yet I readily understand that this great project could not be justified on the basis of immediate return of profits on the huge investment it entailed. The projections considered only the prospect of long-range benefits to North Korea. The barrage has no hydroelectric generating power facilities to provide immediate return of profits on investment. Its immediate goal was to expand control and use of water of the Taedong River and its tributaries by preventing flooding of Pyongyang and the lowlands and by channeling enough water to irrigate rice paddies and other agricultural fields in Kangso, Taedong, and Ryonggang, and even far-distant Hwanghae Province. I think the barrage represents an investment for both immediate benefits and, much more importantly, for the long-range future of North Korea.

I must comment that, whereas the Pharaohs of ancient Egypt are remembered for the pyramids they had slaves build to enhance their own glory, Kim Il Sung may be remembered for the West Sea Barrage, a Korean-style pyramid on the sea, which free North Koreans built for their fellow citizens.

Leaving the barrage after completing a tour of the entire complex, I left this acknowledgement as a tribute:

>A Beautiful and Noble Country,
>Land of Construction for the Well-Being
>Of the Generations to Come.
>Nothing is Impossible When Rallied Behind
>The Great and Benevolent President
>   May 16, 1991: Sohn Won Tai.

Early in the 1950s, during the Korean War, Kim Il Sung had visualized his plan to make greater use of the ample waters of the River Taedong by means of the sea wall. I learned this when I visited Paeksong-ri where Kim Il Sung had stayed during the period when the United States was randomly bombing North Korea. Despite the terrible wartime problems confronting him, Kim Il Sung was devoting thought to a project that would be able to hold off the turbulence of the West Sea and control all of the rivers of the Taedong waterway. Since the West Sea Barrage was completed, other barrages have also been constructed upstream at Mirim, Ponghwa, Songchon, and Sunchon. Those projects were part of the original development which Kim Il Sung had envisioned.

"After the tape-cutting ceremony when the West Sea Barrage was completed, the president went to Mt. Paektu where the River Taedong originates," Mr. Choe told me. "That summer the torrents of rain were three times heavier than in 1967 when the River Taedong had flooded the Pyongyang area. The president was very concerned, of course, so he was very pleased to learn when he called comrade Kim Jong Il, that the river did not overflow the promenade in Pyongyang."

Mr. Choe reported that when the president heard that the river had been controlled despite the record rainfall, he had exclaimed that "the country has been reimbursed in full for the cost of the barrage construction this first summer alone," and then had commented that he felt he was a very fortunate man to see that his plans had worked so well for the benefit of so many people.

I will write more about "walling up the sea." Reclaiming the tidal flats has added many hundreds of hectares of rich agricultural land, an area larger than most counties, to North Korea. Citizens call the project "widening the map of the country." The western coast of North Korea has been changed substantially by the scope of these reclamation projects. For instance, the Kumsong tidal flats, not far distant from the West Sea Barrage, also have been reclaimed by construction of walls which link its embankments and lock out the sea.

I had the pleasure of watching the spectacular closing of the last segment of the Kumsong sea wall during the few hours of ebb tide remaining. All of the workers were soldiers of the Korean People's Army. Suntanned, stripped to the waist, they were fighting a different enemy: the West Sea and its tide. They were led by an army general whose previous battles were along the military demarcation line in defense of his country. This was a different kind of campaign on behalf of North Korea.

The last caissons were submerged into place and the sea wall arms, reaching out from opposite points, were linked while the soldiers strained against the on-rushing power of returning tidal waves. It was a meaningful campaign for those soldiers but it was becoming even more emotion-packed as they struggled against the rising incoming currents that warned them that the West Sea's high tide was due to arrive momentarily. Then a loud cheer announced their job well done.

An official at the project told us that the land area reclaimed from the West Sea amounted to at least 5,000 square kilometers. This was inspiring information! In ancient times, the realms of Koguryo and Koryo had been large in territory and power but over the centuries Korea had lost land holdings until the country's territory had shrunk to the peninsula which it occupies, divided into North and South by peace partitioning after World War II.

People often say that President Kim Il Sung had resorted to a political strategy of increasing the military force to gain supremacy over South Korea militarily. However, here again at Kumsong I had been witnessing a new deployment of military power, not against the South but to push back the West Sea's invasion and lock out its destructive tides. Thus North Korea was expanding its territory by reclaiming rich agricultural land by peaceful means.

Historically, territorial expansion by aggression has been achieved only at a horrible cost in human lives and bloodshed on both sides. Korea, a nation downtrodden, robbed of its land and treasures and abused by its own rulers as well as its enemies, at last had found a leader who was expanding the country at the sacrifice of only the sweat of the citizens' labor. Kim Il Sung, I thought then, was a national leader who rightly could be eulogized by Korean posterity.

Although I was caught up in this emotional moment of triumph over the sea by the completion of the barrage before high tides could halt the construction work, there was an element of humor in the paradoxical situation that the army was invading the West Sea while halting its invasion of North Korea. So when I jocularly remarked: "You are invading the sea here," everyone in our group responded with a laugh and someone commented how good it would be if the sea could be walled up further to expand the land far enough to enable them to shake hands with the people on the Shandong peninsula yonder.

I was told, in response to my question as to what plans had been made for use of the reclaimed land, that a major part of the area would be developed into paddies and other agricultural fields and some areas would be mined as salt fields. When I said it also appeared to be a good place for housing because it offers an ocean view and fresh air, someone replied that I should submit an application for a residential permit quickly before "the rush was on." I picked up the spirit of banter and told him, "If I would be allowed to build a big house and could become a magistrate of the county, then I would settle here."

As our group was leaving the construction area, I recited a poem that came to mind:

> Ye people of other lands,
> Don't laugh at my divided country.
> When reunified by the will of the universe and air,
> The world will envy it.

20

A Noble and Clean Country

Pyongyang was a city of greenery and flowers, a city of fresh air and fragrance. I could not but admire the beauty of the city as I moved throughout its streets; it not only is modern and gigantic but clean and well-designed. It is dear to my heart because of its refined, noble and tidy appearance which is characteristic of Korea. That was the impression I gained merely from the outer appearance of Pyongyang.

Like someone whose personality increasingly charms you the more you see him, Pyongyang grows on one. The more I saw of it, the more I was attracted to it. In essence, Pyongyang, the capital city, is the face of North Korea; its appearance is the appearance of the country; its character is the character of the country.

On my trips to North Korea, I visited factories, rural villages, schools, universities, hospitals, and even nurseries, not just in Pyongyang but in many of the provinces. I was most impressed during my inspections of the Pyongyang Maternity Hospital, the Kim Jong Suk Nursery and the Xangyongdae School Children's Palace.

The Pyongyang Maternity Hospital is situated on Munsu Street in the eastern part of the city and is reached by crossing the Okryu Bridge over the Taedong River. When I was a child, rice paddies and grassy fields were there and I remember those enchanting moments when I watched airplanes landing and taking off from the plains nearby. Now there are apartment houses, white, milky and varied-colored, on those fields; there are parks, bedecked with flowers and green trees, on those fields; there is the sound of laughter and high-pitched voices of children playing on slides and merry-go-rounds in those parks. It was like enjoying a pleasant piece of music in peaceful relaxation just to be standing there, letting my eyes and ears absorb the beauty.

"That is the Pyongyang Maternity Hospital," my guide pointed out, awakening me from my meditation. We were approaching a gigantic but architecturally refined building. Unlike high-rise structures of a metropolis like New York City, this was of modern design, neither Gothic nor Baroque in style, as gentle and pliant as a portrait of Mona Lisa, its lines artistically capturing the lovely portrayal of a mother reaching tenderly for her infant child. I didn't know who had designed it but I sensed that the architect had truly captured the aura of a maternity hospital.

We entered the central hall and, while passing by a softly spraying fountain, were pleasantly surprised to find ourselves walking on a jewel-inlaid floor which glittered in gorgeous reflection of the lighting from the chandeliers. Upon closer examination, I was amazed to discover that rubies, emeralds and other precious stones were inlaid as carpeting on the floor. These were the rare stones which wealthy women and girls hang around their necks and wrists or use as ear adornments to enhance their appearance. Here, however, pregnant women of humble upbringing walk quietly over this jewel-carpeted flooring without giving it much thought. Of more consequence than embellishing their natural beauty, these women are concerned only with delivering and rearing their progeny, the really priceless jewels of their country!

The benevolent politics for The People, the social philosophy of North Korea, was amply visible in this ornately carpeted hall.

The woman who served as director of the hospital guided us on our tour of the facilities. There were 2,000 rooms utilizing 60,000 square meters of space but size was only one facet of the hospital's distinctive qualities; it also served as a general hospital for women and all of the medical equipment and apparatuses were of modern technology; its operating rooms and delivery rooms were furnished with equipment necessary for sterilization; there were highly sophisticated incubators for prematurely-born infants; the X-ray and diagnostic facilities were excellent.

Maternity hospitals in developed countries usually are large but I have visited none that are equal in size or are better equipped. Here Korean women receive treatment for several days and obtain all medical benefits free of charge. I studied everything from a medical doctor's point of view to attempt to evaluate the true quality of the care that was being provided. I could find nothing to criticize about the hospital's exterior or interior functions; I was convinced that nothing more could be desired and I was satisfied with the cleanliness, the well-regulated work assignments and the preventative medical procedures. Of special interest was an opportunity to watch newly-become fathers talking with their wives by means of in-house television.

It was also impressive to notice that every person visiting the hospital wards was required to put on a white gown and slippers provided as part of the practice of preventive medicine. From this fact alone, it was apparent to me that the leaders of this country concern themselves with even trifling measures to ensure prevention of the spread of diseases. As we walked out of the hospital, I realized that women were being esteemed and especially blessed because they make the gift of man to this world. Any country that respects mothers, loves babies and doesn't spare colossal amounts of money, and even precious stones, for their womenfolk without doubt is an excellent country in which to live.

I became more firmly convinced about this impression while visiting the Kim Jong Suk Nursery. Mrs. Kim Jong Suk was the first wife of President Kim Il Sung. She had been his comrade-in-arms, fighting shoulder to shoulder with him, against the Japanese in Manchuria. I had heard rumors about her before the liberation. Even middle-school pupils whispered that General Kim's wife was a woman general and a crack shot while firing two Mausers, one in each hand. She was faithful to him not only as a comrade but a woman who devoted her life to him. She had experienced great hardship and died not long after liberation. North Korean people grieved over her death and genuinely have missed her. She dearly loved children and therefore the nursery was named in her memory.

In the obviously love-filled nursery, the children appeared healthy and optimistic, their eyes clear and bright, their laughter spontaneous and cheerful. The women caring for their development and education were gentle and warm people who appeared to be as devoted to the children as if they were their own. Some 20 children were singing to the accompaniment of an organ being played by their nurse when we entered the playroom. When I was introduced as a boyhood friend of Generalissimo (a title recently conferred on his 80th birthday) Kim Il Sung, the children rushed over to us, clapping their hands and cheering. They greeted us as family, calling me "Grandpa" and Yoo Shin "Grandma."

Tears welled up in my eyes in spite of myself as those innocent children so enthusiastically welcomed two old people from America. What, I wondered, was the invisible tie that made them feel so familiar to us? Just as the president had been very happy at my returning gray-haired to North Korea, so were these children of his national family, his grandsons and granddaughters, happy to welcome us. In this nursery I felt keenly aware once again that the country indeed was one large family and the president was its father.

The children sang, danced and played musical instruments for us and then asked us to sing a song. We modestly were unable to decline their request so my wife sang a little ditty that she had learned as a child:

> Quack, quack, quack, quack…
> A flock of ducks waddle to water
> Through the front yard and back yard,
> Keeping their steps…
> One, two, three, four.

Laughing merrily, they clapped their hands and then indicated that it was my turn to entertain them. I hesitated for a bit, not knowing what to sing for them. Then I recalled from my early childhood the Methodist church on Namsan Hill which had a kindergarten annex attached to it. We used to sing the "Song of Thanksgiving Day" but I thought that was too commonplace to be sung for these clean and elegant children. Fortunately, memory brought back another ditty I used to sing in Beishan Park in Jilin:

> Animals held a party in Beishan Park
> On the birthday of Tiger, the mountain king.
> Roe Deer leaps with delight
> And Hare hops with joy.

When I finished, the children cheered and applauded and asked for an encore so appealingly that I couldn't decline. So I sang a little verse that runs:

> Bow-wow-wow!
> Whose Bow-Wow is it?
> It is Su Nam's puppy.
> Bow-wow-wow!

We became children again, not noticing the passage of time, and ended up in a circle, going around and around playing the reunification train game. As we were leaving the nursery I was aware that a long-gone bounce had returned to my stride and I felt young again!

Yoo Shin sighed: "It was like visiting heaven." She is a devout Christian, pious and sincere in her belief, and never misses a weekly prayer meeting. Indeed, neither of us have experienced being in heaven but we could find no other word to describe the nursery in which we had spent those few hours.

We had that same feeling when we visited the School Children's Palace on Kwangbok Street. There are many palaces in the world which were built to honor various men of authority in ages past: kings, emperors, presidents and other leaders. However, no country has ever built a world-class palace for its rising generation like this one.

Children can spend after-school hours in this palace attending classes for vocal or instrumental training and other skills. For budding artists, there is a fine arts circle room, and there are facilities for practicing swimming, for learning gymnastics and for training in calligraphy. Each class has a specialist to guide them. We observed children participating in all of those pursuits, cultivating their special talents to the limit of their aptitudes and desires.

An educational system such as this, in which every child can follow his wishes limited only by his aptitude, cannot be established without expense. I have yet to hear about any country, said to be rich and fully democratic, that has established a comparable system. It certainly cannot be achieved in a short promotional period such as a presidential election campaign or by donations from benevolent billionaires.

The North Korean educational development is the fruit of the long and bloody struggle, the yield of a lifetime of work by President Kim Il Sung and his compatriots. As I viewed with great pleasure the children growing up in such a splendid environment, I thought to myself that people the world over might learn here how politics could and should be conducted for the benefit of all people.

Juvenile delinquency is a great problem in the Western world. Far too many boys and girls, the future of a country, become addicted to drugs and commit crimes that appall and frighten adults and other children. Much of this may be attributed to the violence depicted in films shown at movie houses and on television. I ask myself: Is this freedom?

In North Korea, I witnessed quite a contrasting phenomenon. Returning from Onchon after enjoying a hot-springs bath, we encountered a young girl walking along a rural road. The only sounds were the croaking of frogs in the fields and she seemed to be deeply engrossed in thought, but when she became aware of our automobile, she stopped and greeted us. This was a peaceful, bucolic scene. Isn't this the kind of freedom people aspire to enjoy?

Some people call North Korea a "closed" country. It does guard against allowing the evils of Western civilization to infiltrate the society of its clean and noble country. What strange logic leads to calling it a "closed" country? Such critics cannot bring to their knees a nation of people who believe in the righteousness of their cause. Those who denigrate do not understand the source of the great strength of the North Korean people.

The first house I visited in North Korea was that of my wife's other brother, Ri Yu Song, a musician. During the Korean War he relocated in the North, later remarrying and establishing a career as a musician in Pyongyang. We arrived shortly after he succumbed to a fatal illness. Had we reached Pyongyang only a few days earlier, Yoo Shin would have enjoyed a reunion with her brother and I would have had the pleasure of becoming acquainted with him. When we arrived at the house on Kwangbok Street, we found his widow distressed and in tears, having just completed the funeral rites. It was regrettable that we got there a few days too late.

I shed many tears in that house, not because of the grief and sorrow that accompanies the loss of a family member but because of the beauty and nobleness of the home itself. A house in mourning can be a place of desolation. The dwelling had lost its head but it was not desolated; people visited throughout every day. Yoo Shin's brother had been a well-known musician in the North and his wife was a teacher at the University of Music and Dance and had been a famous singer so many artists came to offer their condolences. Among the many friends of the deceased and his widow were teachers and schoolmates of their children, and apartment neighbors and their children. All brought special foods when they called to express their condolences.

Friendly people tried their best to console the widow; they sang songs that Yoo Shin's brother had enjoyed singing; they played tunes on the piano that he had liked to play; and they repeated prayers for his soul. The days were filled with their tributes to the memory of a man who had lived his life honestly, everyone helping with their displays of affection to heal the spiritual wounds and alleviating the mental emptiness of the bereaved family. Here I learned what the slogan "one for all and all for one" actually meant in the social life and the human relationships in North Korea.

In this society, people consider another's pain as their own and feel the sorrow of their neighbor as the sorrow of their own family. How exalted is the plane of social and human relations of the country!

Everything I saw and experienced in North Korea was refreshing and surprising for me ... girls volunteering to become life partners of honored disabled soldiers; young mothers raising children bereaved of their parents; families attending to the needs of childless old men and women as if they were their own parents. Anecdotes of devoting oneself to comrades and neighbors are as many as the stars in the sky and they reflect the plain beauty of flowers in the field.

Someone once said that Jesus Christ would not find anything to do in North Korea. I fully agree with that. Here the leader and his men form an integral whole, the former loving the latter and the latter trusting the former, and the people forming a great family through mutual love and self-sacrifice. What force in this world can ever break the solid unity of this bond of love and spirit?

I do not say that the North Koreans are rich but they do not envy those who idle away their lives in clover. This is because they are spiritually at ease and know that their social system, cemented by mutual affection, cannot be exchanged for anything of equal worth in this world. They are convinced that, while they might be hungry, tired and cold, they can build the spiritually and materially richest country on the planet although it might cost more in sweat or blood than others on the world are willing to endure.

This was the true picture of the social system I saw in North Korea. The country, its system and its social life are the fruit of the lifetime work of the late President Kim Il Sung, and I believe the "Great Cause Leader" Kim Jong Il is determined to safeguard the nation at any cost.

21

Unchanged Friendship

Upon realizing that my friendship with President Kim Il Sung was representative of the experiences and feelings of North Koreans generally in their relations with the president, some acquaintances among our group viewed this to be virtually a legendary tale. This has been especially true of those who find it strangely different from the society in which they live where love and friendship seem to be measured in terms of money and personal interests. Others might view it, with malicious intent, as being mere propaganda or balderdash.

After several visits with Kim Il Sung at Pyongyang, I realized that I was not the only person who, after visiting with him, was filled with admiration of his noble stature, his friendly affection and his fidelity. Many of his visitors were the sons and daughters of his mentors and his benefactors and their offspring. In his position as the head of state, he gave audience to innumerable people of various official capacities while performing governmental affairs. But he was most gracious and pleased when he could meet with old friends of the days before and when he was the general who struck terror into the hearts of Japanese militarists. With them he was just an ordinary man, an intimate friend who was the personification of a kind-hearted father of a family of many children.

When I met him on my first trip to Pyongyang, he had said he was very happy that so many of his old friends were able to come to visit him. On my return the following year for his 80th birthday observance, I was put up at a lodge in Onchon. I found that many other people were also there to pay respect to the president; they were not political dignitaries but old friends, some of whom had brought their offspring with them; others were descendents of former friends of the president.

I first met the daughters of Shang Yue and their children at the lodge. Shang Yue had been the literature teacher at Yuwen Middle School in Jilin when Kim Il Sung was a student there. Mr. Shang had participated in the northward advance in support of Sun Yat-sen. After coming to northeast Manchuria, he had propagated the "Three Principles of the People" and "The Five-Power Constitution" ideologies advanced by Sun Yat-sen. He also had introduced his students to classic Chinese novels, including *Three Warring Kingdoms* and *Dream of the Red Chamber*, and he implanted the theory of democracy and fueled a patriotic fervor against Japanese aggression by teaching Maxim Gorky's *Mother* and other progressive books in his classes.

I was in primary school when Shang Hue was teaching in Jilin Middle School but I knew him because he was Kim Il Sung's mentor. So it was an emotional event for me to meet the children of a man who was an important figure in Jilin in the 1920s, the place so dear to my father and me. I was much older than them but they appeared to be greatly pleased to be meeting an old friend of their father and grandfather, someone who had lived in Jilin at the same time as the president and had been involved with him in the Association of Korean Children.

I learned from them that their father had been very pleased that his former student had become a leader in the armed struggle against the Japanese and was building a new society in his liberated country. They said he had written and published an essay on "The Historical Relationship Between Marshall Kim Il Sung and Me in His Boyhood," among many of his works, while he was professor of history at he People's University in Beijing. Shortly prior to his death, Shang Hue had urged his daughters to make plans to visit Kim Il Sung as a courtesy to his old friend. His oldest daughter, Shang Jialan, had visited the president in Pyongyang in the late 1980s but now, on this occasion, both of his daughters and their children had come.

Among other foreigners on hand to extend their felicitations was Zhang Weihua's son and daughter and their children. Mr. Zhang was the intimate friend of Kim Il Sung during his days at Fusong, China. His father was a wealthy, prominent, and patriotic man who had embraced contemporary democratic ideologies. In his enthusiasm, he had named his sons at birth, respectively: Weizhong, Weihua, and Weimin. Had a fourth son been born, he would have been named Weiguo. Their second name characters were Zhong, Hua, Min and Guo (if a fourth son were born). That series denotes "Republic of China."

Zhang Weihua continued his relationship with Kim Il Sung in Fusong and later on as a teacher in a school the president had established near Jilin. Zhang then set up a photography business at Fusong while working for the revolutionary movement. Once when Kim Il Sung was about to board a train in Jilin to go to Hailyong, he was shadowed by police employed by a northeast China warlord. Zhang, who had reserved a first-class carriage for himself, noticed that Kim Il Sung was being followed and rushed him to his own carriage. His father then met them with a luxury carriage which was guarded by privately employed soldiers.

When Kim Il Sung was involved in the armed resistance against the Japanese, Zhang Weihua had sent him clothing and other goods for the guerrilla army. He had been caught and imprisoned by the Japanese and then released on parole. Fearing he might be tortured into revealing locations where General Kim and his guerrillas were staying if he were arrested and imprisoned again, Zhang Weihua committed suicide by drinking developing fluid. He had fathered one son, Zhang Jinquan, and a daughter, Zhang Jinlu, who was born after his death. I met them both and their children.

President Kim Il Sung always remembered Zhang Weihua as a courageous revolutionary hero who had given his life to save the lives of himself and his Korean freedom fighters. He asked North Koreans who were visiting in northeast China to attempt to locate Zhang's son and daughter because the cultural revolution was at its height and they were undergoing extreme hardship as punishment because their grandfather had been wealthy and therefore they should be targeted for retribution. When President Kim Il Sung finally located the family survivors he became a foster father, assuring them care in their father's stead.

Zhang Weihua's daughter regarded Kim Il Sung as her father but his son, Zhang Jinquan, referred to him as an elder uncle when he was talking with me, and I noticed that his sons were clinging to the president's sleeves and calling him "great-uncle." They were staying in the same guest house in Onchon so I was able to accompany them on several occasions to commemorative functions arranged to honor the president on his 80th birthday and so I was able to talk with them every day.

Zhang Jinquan came to my lodgings toward the end of the celebration period and I hugged him warmly. There is a proverb that states, "A friend's friend is my friend." He was the son of a martyr who had given his life to save the life of my dear friend, Kim Il Sung. That day we talked at great length about Kim Il Sung and those long-past days in Jilin and

Fusong. As he prepared to leave he gave me a scroll of calligraphy written by himself. I learned afterward that he was a well-known calligrapher in Fusong, and I treasure it more for its message: "The farther we are apart, the nearer we feel."

His words expressed what I was feeling but had not been able to express. How identical were the thoughts of the president's friends despite their different nationalities, their different ages and their different life experiences. He also gave me a book which he had written and was published by the Lining Provisional Publishing House. Entitled *The Traditional Friendship*, it told of the relationship between Kim Il Sung and Zhang over half a century.

Because Zhang Jinquan's book was written in Chinese, I had difficulty with some passages. I had learned the language when I was young but have forgotten some of it. However, what I was unable to understand inspired me to want to put into writing the many years of close relationship between the Sohn family and Kim Il Sung. The president gave me a copy of Zhang Jinquan's book that was translated into Korean. On my visits to Pyongyang I would learn that Mr. Zhang had either just returned home to Fusong or would not be coming until a later date. Fortunately, we did meet on other occasions and we became very close friends.

I also gained a friend from Russia; two Russians had been staying at the guest house in Onchon. One was a former soldier named Ya T. Novichenko; the other was an army surgeon, Dr. Shulman. Both had served in Pyongyang when the Soviet army was stationed there under the peace settlement after the end of World War II. Mr. Novichenko had played a heroic role in saving Kim Il Sung's life and I wanted to become acquainted with him. However, our conflicting schedules and my inability to speak Russian prevented this until one day by good fortune I met his group in Pyongyang. I rushed over and embraced him in a warm hug. An interpreter came to us so I was able to explain that my conduct was the result of my gratitude for his part in saving the president's life so many years earlier.

"But for you, neither you nor I would have come here to honor Kim Il Sung. As a boyhood friend of the president, I extend my gratitude from the bottom of my heart," I told him.

Mr. Novichenko, a tall, strongly-built man, patted me on the shoulder and thanked me through the interpreter. He was a hero of the DPRK. On March 1, 1946, at a mass meeting in Pyongyang (an event known in history as the March First Popular Uprising), President Kim Il Sung was standing on the platform along with Soviet army officers and a number of democratic figures of various social functions. Suddenly a hand grenade flew out of the crowd and landed on the platform. Novichenko threw his body over the missile and it exploded beneath him. The fact that he was an avid reader saved his own life too, because he had tucked a thick book firmly under his belt and it served as a bullet-proof shield for his stomach. He sustained terrible injuries and lost one arm but survived. The grenade thrower was one of a group of terrorists sent by pro–Japanese reactionaries to carry out a mass assassination.

After he had recovered and the Soviet army had withdrawn from North Korea, Novichenko had been demobilized and returned to his home in Siberia. In the 1980s, while planning a journey to the Soviet Union, Kim Il Sung wrote to Novichenko to let him know that he hadn't been forgotten and advised him when the train would be passing through his town. Novichenko was waiting at the railroad station to greet him. The president hugged him warmly and asked, "Why haven't you written to me even once?" Then he quickly added, "I have been very busy with affairs of state, but you could have found time to write. Please come to visit me in Pyongyang soon."

When I next met with Kim Il Sung I told him about meeting Zhang Weihua's son and daughter and that I also had had an opportunity to meet Novichenko. He said he would never forget them: two heroic foreigners who had risked their lives to save his. Then he added, "A man becomes indebted to many people during a lifetime but those who saved his life are not many and are unforgettable."

"The Rev. Sohn Jong Do was the first person to rescue me from imminent peril and that is why I remember him so well ... and why I treat you as I would treat him," Kim Il Sung said. "A man must not forget what he owes to others and must carry his gratitude beyond the grave and return favors to others. However I try, I cannot fully repay him for saving my life. I'm only showing that I have not forgotten him."

How could anyone not feel attached to such a man whose sense of honoring obligations to others extends from the past, to the present and beyond through generations to come? I became assured that my emotional visits to Pyongyang to honor Kim Il Sung were a normal response to his kind and considerate overtures of friendship. There were many hundreds of others on pilgrimages to pay him honor in addition to the offspring of Zhang Weihua and the daughters of Zhang Hue and their families from China; Ya T. Novichenko from Siberia; Dr. Shulman from Russia; the son and daughter of Lee Jang Chan; and me, from the United States.

I believe pilgrimages will be made for centuries to come to pay honor to Kim Il Sung, perhaps the greatest leader in the history of Korea.

22

On the River Taedong

In May of 1994 I visited Pyongyang for the fifth time. I was accompanied by five Korean doctors who were residents of the United States. I again was serving as advisor on behalf of the Christian Association for Medical Missions. After discussing plans for Pyongyang Third Hospital with officials in charge, the team returned to the United States, but I remained in Pyongyang.

Those were busy days for President Kim. He was constantly in the news, attending national conferences, sitting with various participants for souvenir photographs, and providing field guidance to cooperative farm operators. I became concerned that his activity might be injurious to his health so I suggested that he should try to take it easier if he could.

President Kim, however, expressed his own concern about my health. A few days later when I returned from Pyongyang, I discovered some strangers standing in my yard. Mr. Choe informed me that they were there on orders from President Kim Il Sung to lay out a tennis court. Only recently, President Kim had asked me what I did for exercise back in Omaha and I had told him that I occasionally played golf and tennis. He acknowledged that moderate exercise is good for a person and said that he also had played tennis until a few years earlier but now rode a bicycle and sometimes swam to keep in condition. In spite of his rigorous work schedule, he still had taken time to make arrangements to have a tennis court constructed for my exercise needs. It was a fine court with a smoothly compacted sand surface and high fencing which was painted green to conform to the surrounding foliage.

The day after the court was completed, two men and two women professional tennis players arrived to play with me. We formed two teams and had a pleasant time. When I stayed at the guest house in Onchon, tennis players were available to play with me. I always felt invigorated and refreshed following a good rest after playing a couple of sets of tennis.

Early on the morning of May 26, 1994, President Kim Il Sung called to let me know that he would pick me up at my house about nine o'clock. I joined him in his automobile and we drove to the well-known Maekjon Ferry in Pongwha-ri on the River Taedong. His father, Kim Hyong Jik, had been the leader of the independence movement when he was a teacher in Pongwha-ri. In those days, the young Kim Sung Ju would cross the River Taedong by ferry, going to and from Mangyongdae, his birthplace.

A large excursion boat was moored at the dock awaiting us. Because it was late in May, the river banks were luxuriantly dressed in the green foliage of trees and the gorgeous multi-colored array of flowers. As Pongwha-ri fell behind us and we moved downstream, the president fell silent and pensive, his thoughts totally absorbed with events long past. In field after field, rice transplanting was in full swing. We passed by neatly-platted villages and sometimes the sound of singing fieldworkers wafted across the waters to reach our ears. To the president, this was the paradise he had devoted his lifetime to make possible in North Korea.

My father, the Reverend Sohn Jong Do, had also been an idealist much in the pattern of President Kim Il Sung. Many of his compatriots had been abused, driven into penury and deprived of their own land before coming to live in an alien country in the vicinity of Jilin. My father had attempted to help them build an ideal rural community outside of Jilin city, similar to the Ryultoguk Utopia portrayed in "The Tale of Ho Saeng." He put all of the inheritance from his father into the project but it failed to succeed. On the other hand, President Kim Il Sung had built an ideal society on land regained at the cost of great hardship and the loss of many lives. As we moved down the river, evidence of success unfolded mile by mile on both sides, the achievement of a rural society in which all are free to learn, to work and to share quality lifestyles.

President Kim Il Sung was in deep meditation and seemed to be enraptured by a sky fluffy with white clouds. I hesitated to break into his thoughts but at last I did find a moment to thank him for the tennis court he had built for my use. After being assured that I was very satisfied with it, he advised me to adjust my exercising to moderation as I aged. He then

From left: Dr. Won Tai Sohn, Dr. Choe Sang Soon, Director Kang Sok Soong, and President Kim Il Sung on board a cruise ship in North Korea.

abruptly asked me if I still remembered the Chinese language; I had to confess that I had forgotten much of it. The president said that he was still fluent in the language and recently had found it very useful while participating in a meeting with Deng Xiaoping in China.

Then he gave an account of the problems concerning relations with the United States, terming them "strained at the moment." He seemed very composed as he explained that the confrontation had been exacerbated by the allegation that North Korea was developing nuclear weapons. At one point the situation had worsened, he said, to a choice between "war or negotiations." As the world watched in suspense, the United States finally dropped its threatening posture and agreed to continue negotiations; however, after two more rounds of discussion, the talks ended in a deadlock.

"The Americans annoyed us somewhat but then suggested that they were ready for a third round of talks," the president said. "But, frankly, we didn't feel in any immediate hurry because they were the ones feeling a pressing need. They suggested reopening talks either on a Sunday or

Monday with the United Nations and asked us to inform them as soon as our government cabled its approval. So we instructed them yesterday to reopen the talks and the third round of talks will soon be held in Geneva."

The president explained that the United States had been attempting to learn more about the position of the leadership of North Korea in a variety of ways. Recent visits to Pyongyang had been made by Maxwell Taylor and the evangelist Billy Graham. A proposed visit by Sam Nunn, the chairman of the U.S. Senate's Armed Services Committee also could be viewed in that same perspective, he said. He smiled a bit when he recalled that, on the evangelist's last visit with him, the Rev. Graham had said, "You are a fine gentleman, Mr. President."

"They all wanted to see this man, Kim Il Sung," he said, laughing heartily. Then soberly, he added, "The Americans have been mistaken about the Korean people."

I could sense the strength of North Korea in the way it maintained a firm attitude in the discussions with the United States as it made efforts to equalize initiatives in the diplomatic relations and resolutely resisted the strategic ploys being attempted by the opposing negotiators.

This historical event perhaps is an indicator of changes to come in world politics: when small nations can stand up to rich and powerful countries and protect their national rights! While listening to the president speak, I was reminded of what my father had told my older brother, Won Il, and me when I was only ten years old. He said the history of Korea was a sad one because, weak in power and sandwiched between great powers, it had always kowtowed meekly to them. He predicted that the time certainly would come when the "white" people would try to conquer the "yellow" people. He meant that the western powers would infiltrate Korea, contending against each other to gain influence and eventually control it.

He had reached that conclusion after watching developments over the many years of anti–Japanese resistance. Quite a number of Korean independence campaigners had sought support and protection from western powers. They were fascinated by the theory of national determination advanced by U.S. President Woodrow Wilson. However, Koreans who pinned their hopes on diplomatic activities saw them dashed at the Paris Peace Conference where their western "friends" turned their backs on them. My father had also predicted that western powers one day would loom as the new aggressive force threatening to dominate Korea.

History has proved his prophecy to be true. After the end of World War II Korea was divided, not by Japan, but by the western super-powers. Regrettably, the political and military confrontation they created has lasted more than half a century. In 1905, William Howard Taft had been sent by President Theodore Roosevelt to moderate peace negotiations between Russia and Japan. That settlement in 1905 gave Japan "rights" to Korea and the Maritime Territory off Siberia to Russia. Three years later Japan invaded Korea and established its military occupation and began its aggression against China as well.

President Kim Il Sung said he had been informed that the Rev. Billy Graham was bringing a message from President Clinton so he had agreed to meet with him.

"I told the Rev. Graham that the United States and we North Koreans should get along well together, leaving aside the past wrongs," Kim Il Sung said. "They seem to wish it, but they cannot gain anything by bringing pressure to bear on us. Such pressure doesn't make sense to us."

"Journalists who accompanied the Rev. Graham to North Korea asked me if I planned to visit the United States," the president went on. "When I answered that I would like to do that, they asked what I would do there and I said that I would go angling and hunting and make friends. And they were happy with what I said."

I visited Pyongyang a few months after former President Jimmy Carter had been to North Korea. The president and Mr. Carter had discussed state problems in a most friendly atmosphere. As he had done with me, Kim Il Sung had talked with Mr. Carter while on a tour of the West Sea Barrage and an excursion on the River Taedong. On the excursion, the conversation had turned to Korea's rainbow trout when Mr. Carter mentioned he had learned that North Korea had developed technology which enabled hatcheries to inseminate this species artificially and that fingerlings released into the River Taedong would make their way to the sea, live to maturity and then return upstream to the place of their release.

Kim Il Sung explained to Mr. Carter how a rainbow trout species indigenous to the United States had become acclimatized to North Korea. After liberation, he said that he had gone to a gold mine lake in Unsan and saw people catching what they called a Japanese fish. Kim Il Sung said he told the fishermen that it was an American fish that had been brought to the lake from the United States. The species grows to maturity quickly and is very palatable. The president had initiated the research procedures which enable North Korea to acclimatize the trout species.

Mr. Carter suggested that President Kim bring some of the Korean rainbow trout with him on a visit to the United States "so they could return to their native land." So much for Korean fish stories! Perhaps international politics would be better served if conferees discussed their problems on excursion boats.

The life of President Kim Il Sung had spanned a period comprising many confrontations between powerful countries and smaller nations: World War I, World War II, the Korean War, the Vietnam War, the Persian Gulf War, and many more. He was born in 1912, two years after the Japanese formally annexed Korea. The occupation would continue until Japan's defeat in World War II. Kim Il Sung took up arms while in his teens and for more than 25 years fought against Japanese imperialist armies occupying Korea and China. The hard-won victory for liberation of Korea was snatched away when the country was divided into north and south by the U.S.S.R. and the United States in a peace pact in which Korea had no voice despite a half-century of struggle by Korean people to regain a proud existence, neither enslaved nor dominated by a major power.

The country had been powerful in the days of the Koguryo, but that strength waned through the corruption and incompetence of its feudal rulers. It had become a vassal state of the Ming Dynasty during the Koryo Period; its mountains and villages were destroyed by fire as warring countries fought over its territory during the Ri Dynasty; in the end, it was occupied by Japan and kept under colonial status. Against that sorry past, the pride of Koreans was being restored under the leadership of Kim Il Sung, healing the historical wounds of the Korean nation.

When the people undertake a building project in North Korea, it is designed to be a source of public pride. They build a barrage and it becomes a world-class control and reclamation project; they build an apartment complex and it compares with any such development anywhere in the world. The Kwangbok and Thongil street redevelopments in bomb-destroyed residential areas were accomplished in record time. Pyongyang is a modern city of beautiful boulevards, skyscrapers and massive housing apartments. All of this has been accomplished while its military strength has been increased to a defensive level that has enabled it to refuse to bow down servilely to threats from even a superpower. As a native of Korea and a naturalized American citizen, I am very proud of what President Kim Il Sung has accomplished for the North Korean people.

When the United States played "hard ball" with North Korea and eventually yielded to talks instead of violence to clear up the so-called nuclear problem, North Koreans were delighted. Some expressed the general attitude of the people in this way: "Though we may have to skip a meal, we don't feel hungry; though we're not clothed warmly we don't feel cold. What does it matter if we forgo rich foods and opulence? We feel proud of leader Kim Il Sung's policies to build our economy and strengthen our defense capabilities even though we've had to tighten our belts."

The president told me that the people didn't worry about food scarcity or not being able to live in luxury as people may in other countries. "A small country has to build its economy and its defensive capability on its own efforts. One day our people will understand me," he said.

I believe that the North Korean people have understood him, place absolute trust in him and are grateful for his leadership. This understanding and trust have made North Korea strong. The sharp confrontation with the United States appeared to be coming to an amicable settlement in his last days.

But back to our excursion down the River Taedoing! Our boat dropped anchor at an islet near the Mirim barrage. A group of people were excited about a large fish one of them had brought in although there were a number of big fish flopping about in large crates. We had lunch in a restaurant on the islet, then reboarded the launch and proceeded upstream. The president returned our conversation to the issue of national reunification and asked about the leanings of Koreans living in the United States on the matter.

"The Koreans living in Japan are well-informed about the history of the anti–Japanese struggle and your activities," I told him, "but most Koreans living in the United States have been brain-washed by anti-communists and they don't have a correct understanding of North Korea."

"There aren't many who are knowledgeable about communism in North Korea," I continued. "Some of those opposed to reunification are afraid of communism and others are skeptical about how capitalists would be treated."

The president interjected: "We are building communism to provide for all the people. What is bad about that? People who are opposed to communism say that it is evil; they even claim that we have horns on our heads. When I met the Reverend Billy Graham I asked him, 'Excuse me, are there any horns on my head?' And he had a good laugh."

"Another problem is how to treat 'wicked capitalists,' as the Rev. Mun Ik Hwan expresses the term," Kim Il Sung continued. "I think that depends on how we view them. Capitalists should not be considered 'wicked' because they exploit others; the point is whether they sell out the interests of their country or nation. Those who earn for the nation are laudable; those with money should donate money for the sake of their country. That would decrease the number of wicked capitalists!

"What is the use of defining those to be eliminated among a large number? There is no need to do so: let them earn their food and style of living, for if they are not cruel to those who work for them they will be left to their own devices. Frankly speaking, wicked capitalists probably don't number more than one percent of their total numbers."

The president continued: "There is no point in building communism on an island if you're living there alone. I have written in my reminiscences that not many capitalists could be defined as being wicked. When I say this to others, many admit that communism is excellent."

Kim Il Sung said that that is the kind of communism being built in Korea, adding: "There is no purpose in going a long way to make enemies in large numbers. We are going to make as few people our enemies as possible. We insist that a person not be subjugated to others and must refrain from doing things that are harmful to the nation; then everyone can be our friend."

I have quoted Kim Il Sung at such length here because his words are full of the spirit of loving the country and can form the basis for reunification. He spoke always in plain, everyday language but I always felt that his words contained philosophical and political ideals more profound than those contained in the Bible.

That day on the boat, he suddenly asked, "Tell me, Won Tai, have you been to church this time?"

"No, I haven't."

"Why? You had time, I think."

I must confess that I did not feel the need to go to church on that trip. When I visited Pyongyang with my wife, Yoo Shin, we had gone to Pongsu Church to say prayers, but being alone on this trip I just didn't think of going there alone. It may seem illogical if I, the son of a devout Methodist minister, profess being atheist or opposed to church itself. Yet, in spite of myself, I could not but think that the church has been slipping away from its original mission. Then I asked the president if communism disavowed Christianity because it has become degenerate.

"You're right," he replied. "My mother went to church every Sunday and I went with her. When I asked her why she went there she said, 'Just to relax.' After that, at church services, I found that she wasn't listening to the service but was dozing off and she wouldn't wake up until the last amens. We can see from this that religious believers may attend church, not because there is God; they go to regulate their conscience. I maintain that if one had to believe in a God he should believe in the God of Korea. It is laudable to cherish the God of Korea in one's heart and not do things harmful to the state. Do you believe in heaven? Has anyone been there?"

It was time to head back to my lodging. When he dropped me off, we embraced in farewells. Kim Il Sung looked at me intensely and said, "I feel that it has been a blessing to be reunited with you at our advanced ages. As time goes on, please come to visit while you can still travel in comfort by air. And when you are too aged, please come to stay and be buried here. But be

The last farewell between President Kim Il Sung and Dr. Won Tai Sohn, on May 26, 1994.

sure to come next August because I will arrange a party for your 80th birthday; and be sure to bring all of your children, your in-laws and your friends with you."

"Take care of yourself," I urged, as he turned to leave.

He laughed and said, "Don't worry about me; I do pay attention to my health."

Referring to my palm reading prophecy that he would live well beyond a hundred years, he chuckled as he said, "That would be a miracle."

Then he got into his limousine and waved goodbye as he rode away. How could I know that this was our last meeting and that we had enjoyed our last talk about the old times of our youth! From 9:30 to 1:30 p.m. on May 26, 1994 … that brief span of time held the last four hours that the great President Kim Il Sung and I would spend together!

PART IV

President Kim Il Sung Is Immortal

23

Overcome with Shock by Unexpected News

I was working in my garden at midday on July 10, 1994, stretching to loosen strained muscles, when my wife, Yoo Shin, came rushing up to me weeping. My heart seemed stricken; instinctively I knew that something terrible had happened. As soon as she was able to speak, she sobbed, "President Kim Il Sung has passed away!"

"What are you talking about?" I almost shouted, not wanting to comprehend what my ears had heard.

"I've heard it on the radio," she insisted tearfully.

Suddenly I felt all of my strength sagging; I could not believe that he could have died so unexpectedly; he had been so hale and hearty and full of vigor just a month and a half earlier when I had returned home after spending some time with him. He was all smiles, then, as he waved goodbye and said he was looking forward to seeing me again soon. A picture of his dear face flashed across my mind's eye and his sonorous voice seemed to be echoing in my ears what he once had told me: "I do pay attention to how to live long."

No, this cannot be, I told myself; the news report must be erroneous! Hoping frenetically that the report was not true, I rushed into the house and telephoned the DPRK diplomatic mission office at the United Nations in New York City. The official who lifted the receiver was unable to speak;

he was sobbing! My hopes vanished in that instant without a word being spoken; I was so stunned that I could not bring tears to my eyes although my heart lay submerged in sorrow.

I immediately made preparations to go at once to Pyongyang, finalizing the arrangements I had been making to attend the grand party President Kim Il Sung had promised he would host for me on my 80th birthday. I had been spending my days happily busy with those plans that involved a group of well over 30 people, including our sons and daughter, our in-laws and many friends who wanted to go to Pyongyang with me. Although the president hadn't suggested a number, he had said that I should bring my family and "all" of my friends with me. I had been somewhat hesitant about overdoing this so a few days earlier I had sent an inquiry to Pyongyang. An immediate response informed me that the president has said that I should bring "even 50" if I desired.

A few days later my wife and I boarded an airplane and departed for Pyongyang. While planning the trip, we originally had been anticipating a merry and happy occasion but now, aboard our plane, Yoo Shin and I were solemnly and earnestly praying for Kim Il Sung's resurrection so that we could meet him again in Pyongyang. I always, unconsciously, had felt that he would enjoy immortality; I never gave thought to the possibility that he would die during my lifetime.

After arriving in Beijing, China, we went immediately to the North Korean embassy. It was a scene of tearful sadness; we expressed our condolences and without further delay went to the airport to board a plane that would take us to Pyongyang.

The sky had draped the landscape of North Korea in an atmosphere of mourning; rain was falling in a deluge of tearful condolence over the passing of a great man. Upon landing, I took transportation immediately to Mansu Hill where a bronze statue of President Kim Il Sung stood. The entire memorial park, even the stairway leading to the shrine, was jammed with weeping mourners. There were elderly people dressed in white clothing, young women wearing white ribbons on their heads, young men with black bands on their arms, young children carried in the arms of their parents, Koreans from Japan and China, and many other people who obviously were foreigners. They stood with heads bowed in reverence, oblivious to the cold, drizzling rain. The silence was broken only by intermittent swells of sobbing and wailing; the mourners were swaying back and forth in their sorrow, much like rising tidewaters of the West Sea might swirl and eddy against a barrage which impedes their yearning to reach out for the comfort of nature's sandy beach far beyond. Some were crying out, sadly: "No, you can't have gone like this, Leader. Please come back, Father."

Despite the incessant flurries of pelting rain, no one seemed impatient to leave the shrine.

I carefully made my way through the mourners and placed a wreath at the foot of the statue in memory of my departed friend. Then I collapsed to my knees, head bowed, and cried most bitterly, but the tears somehow did not relieve the ache that was crushing my heart.

The next day I went to the presidential palace, officially known as the Kumsusan Assembly Hall, where President Kim Il Sung had conducted his daily business affairs. It was located in a suburb not far from the center of the city. I had been to that building on several occasions, once when I called on the president to congratulate him on his 80th birthday.

Foreign delegations were officially received in a large hall on the second floor of the assembly hall. Kim Il Sung had received me there once, hugging me tightly and saying, "Hello, Won Tai, how are you?" His voice was still ringing in my ears as if he had just spoken to me although I could see him lying there, silent and immobile, his body draped in a red North Korean flag. I moved quickly to him, my mind calling out, "Mr. President" ... but, lying there as if in deep sleep, he did not answer me. I shuddered convulsively, sensing an irretrievable loss and trying to believe that all of this was only an absurd dream.

I looked for but could not see the sunny smile and dimpled cheeks that had brightened and warmed my heart when I was a child and in moments of memory over the succeeding years. I could not see them now and I wept, unabashedly. Mentally, I prayed for a miracle, wanting to say, "I've come. It's Won Tai ... of your days in Jilin ... I've come, Brother Song Ju!" In my mesmerized state, I hoped he would stand up and open his arms to greet me, saying: "Ah, you have come, Won Tai!" But, of course, such a miracle didn't happen.

When I visited his bier a second time, many leaders of the government hierarchy were there as I made my way, in turn, to pay my final respects to the president. As I moved away after my last viewing, I passed Leader Kim Jong Il who was standing nearby. He stopped over to me and I was distressed almost to the point of tears to see his face convulsed in grief.

Kim Il Sung not only had been the father of the people of his country but he was Kim Jong Il's real father. Whatever the depth of grief North Koreans were feeling, it could not compete with the pain being suffered by Kim Jong Il for the loss of his father. I clasped his hands in mine in silence; I understood his pain and, in tears, I couldn't express my sympathy except by pressing his hands more firmly because sorrow had clutched at my throat, throttling words that would have been inadequate in any event.

Kim Jong Il kindly rescued me from my embarrassment, saying, "I'm very sorry, Mr. Sohn Won Tai. The leader said he would arrange your 80th birthday party but, to everyone's regret, he has passed away." Hearing his voice, as sonorous as that of President Kim Il Sung, I felt a deep sense of gratitude that he could be so considerate of me at a time of such great grief in his own life. Of what importance was my birthday party when the nation was in mourning for the father he had lost! Yet Kim Jong Il, concealing his grief, magnanimously had placed his concern for me to the forefront to express regret over circumstances which most probably would cause cancellation of the plans for my birthday celebration which I felt was a matter of no consequence to anyone now.

I gathered myself together and told him, "How grieved you must feel being bereaved of your father, the great president! Take good care of your health, please. You must remain strong so that you can lead the country as well as the president would wish." Kim Jong Il gripped my hand firmly and intoned, "Thank you, Mr. Sohn."

Many people who saw this interchange between Kim Jong Il and me on television have asked me about what he had said as he moved closer to my ear to speak. They said the gesture seemed to be full of kindness, warmth and affection in sharp contrast to the circumstances in which people were weeping as they passed in front of the bier of President Kim Il Sung. When I responded that Kim Jong Il had expressed concern about the 80th birthday party Kim Il Sung had promised to host for me, people expressed surprise, because funerals and birthday parties are functions quite different in importance. Yet Kim Jong Il had remembered this trifling wish of his father although his great concern was for what lay ahead for North Korea and how he could ensure that the whole nation would remain firmly united when it emerged from the sea of grief in which it lay stricken by President Kim Il Sung's death.

Throughout the mourning period, I attended all of the functions along with leading cadres of the government. When the funeral cortege was departing from Kumsusan Assembly Hall, I was standing in the front row on the platform in the hall's plaza; during the funeral ceremony, I was on the platform in Kim Il Sung Square. On previous occasions, when President Kim Il Sung had stood on that platform in the Square, smiling broadly and waving in response to the cheers of the people, I had been standing at one side, enthralled by his refined manner, my heart swelling with pride that I could be a friend of that great man.

As I again stood on that platform, this time to bid him a last farewell, my heart was heavy with grief. Suddenly, the sound of weeping and wailing from a far-off multitude reached the square and when the coffin, draped in the flag of the Worker's Party of Korea, approached, the people waiting in the Square became convulsed in sobs. In front of the hearse was a limousine carrying a large portrait of the president on the rooftop. He was smiling broadly and seemed to be saying to me, "Good-bye, Won Tai ... I'm afraid I will not be available, but come to Pyongyang frequently."

Without shame, I gave way to my emotions and cried uncontrollably; the people in the Square wept, too, and some were stamping their feet and shouting, "No, no! You cannot go, Father!"

The image of Kim Il Sung's sunny smile began to fade from my mind as if I could hear him saying, "Good-bye, my children ... Be happy for generations to come."

The president had held the people of Korea close to his bosom throughout his lifetime, sharing the good and the bad with them; North Koreans, in turn, had entrusted their destiny with him and walked beside him into the future he had envisioned for their country. This was the last farewell to the leader who had been a father to them ... and they his children. I wonder if history has recorded a similar instance where an entire nation has parted from its leader with such a tearful display of their grief.

There perhaps have been other rulers who enjoyed wide popularity and honor for distinguished service to mankind as well as to their nation but I doubt that all of the people of any country have shared such regret and sorrow as North Koreans did over the loss of their leader. Both CNN of the United States and NHK of Japan, two reliable world news services, truthfully reported the solemn events of the mourning period, providing incontrovertible evidence of an historical occasion. Where else in the world have such multitudes of citizens stood day and night in cold rain, a voluntary honor guard paying tribute to the memory of a political leader, as North Koreans did in bidding farewell to their president, Kim Il Sung? Certainly, it has served to enlighten the world as to what a great leader and outstanding politician of the 20th century Kim Il Sung had been.

During his lifetime, President Kim Il Sung demonstrated that he was one of the outstanding political leaders of the present era and his death has left a large place to be filled in world leadership. Someone commented that a star which has been lighting the way for mankind on earth had been eclipsed by the demise of Kim Il Sung. As for me, I realized only after his death what a truly great man he was. Kim Sung Ju, the emotional and inspirational young teacher of those days in Jilin, had left a legacy for mankind to follow in governing for the benefit of the people in a democracy.

When I realize how many people's lives had been part of his life during the six decades following the beginning of our friendship in Jilin, I want to step to the forefront to acclaim proudly that I was a friend of the greatest and most benevolent man in the world. I do feel regret that I have not been able to reciprocate during his later years for the pleasure I have carried in my heart because of his early friendship and influence upon my life.

I am reminded of a poem which I learned in my boyhood, which comes to mind as I contemplate on our lives:

> Please attend to your father when he is alive;
> So sorrowful is your heart when he dies.
> This is the only thing
> That cannot be repeated in life.

I fail to recall who wrote that verse, but it is permeated with the sorrow of a man who had neglected his filial duties to his parents during their lifetime. I feel some of this sorrow because I regret not having gone to Pyongyang earlier to meet with him and spend more of our lives together. As it turned out, we enjoyed the pleasure of resuming our friendship for only three short years, after sixty years of separation. I can only hope to atone for failing to afford him greater pleasure by remembering him and cherishing dearly the friendship we shared until the last moment of my life.

24

My 80th Birthday Celebrated in Pyongyang

President Kim Il Sung arrived and left the world in this contrasting way: He was born, unnoticed except by family members, in a small straw-thatched house in Mangyondae; his departure, eighty-four years later, stirred the entire world.

I felt his absence in my heart. Pyongyang, which had been so beautiful and welcoming when he was there, now was a lonely place without him. The vivacity seemed to have dissipated from its streets although life flowed on as the North Korean people overcame their sorrow and moved ahead along the path that Kim Il Sung had pioneered for them.

It was scorching hot in August after July had drenched the country in continuous chilling rainfall. The minds of North Koreans had risen in unison to overcome their loss but, although the initial mourning period and funeral service had ended, Mansu Hill still held great masses of people standing as a voluntary honor guard in his memory. Places associated with his activities were being refurbished and workers and peasants were returning to their labors rededicated to implement Kim Il Sung's teachings. An undercurrent of the sorrow his death had brought upon North Korea continued to be evident in all walks of life … people walking in the streets seemed more grave in demeanor; there was less laughter and song among schoolchildren; large throngs were visiting his statue shrines at all hours;

families were postponing wedding and birthday parties and, in fact, many young men and women postponed their marriage ceremonies.

The fountain park in front of Mansudae Art Theater in Pyongyang is magnificently beautiful. It is remindful of the Kumgang Mountains. Young men and women of Pyongyang customarily have had their souvenir wedding day photographs taken there. An aura of happiness has always been associated with the park but in the days following the passing of President Kim Il Sung, even the fountains seemed to be spraying pathetically.

Yoo Shin and I were reluctant to hurry back to Omaha and decided to remain in Pyongyang after the mourning period ended. Then, one day, we were informed by government officials that the people who had planned to come to Pyongyang with us would be arriving from the United States very soon and would be able to celebrate my 80th birthday with us. As I mentioned earlier, President Kim Il Sung had urged me to bring my family and as many friends as I wished and DPRK officials had assured me that the number of people I had invited was not too large.

All of them had booked passage on flights to the Orient and packed their luggage in a happy mood; they were eager to visit my "fabulous" Pyongyang. Yoo Shin and I became very excited about their coming to join us. My sons and daughter were married and lived in places far distant from Omaha. We didn't get an opportunity to see them very often and they had little understanding of the historical significance of Kim Il Sung's thirty years of struggle against Japanese imperialism from his base of the Independence Army on Mt. Paektu. My eldest son, Carl (Jong Ho), had been born in the year of Korean liberation but none of my children had much knowledge about how the Japanese had exploited our nation and why the generations of their father and grandfather had to fight an endless struggle against enslavement. It would be correct to say that they had very little opportunity to learn about it while being educated in the United States; they were more familiar with Alaska and the Rocky Mountains than Mt. Paektu in North Korea; they were more familiar with stories about presidents George Washington and Abraham Lincoln than of President Kim Il Sung of North Korea; they were knowledgeable about how the American West was developed but knew nothing about the reunification of Korea during the Japanese occupation and the struggle for independence by freedom fighters who were dying in the effort to rescue the nation from slavery. Worse yet, I realized, they did not know how to read or speak the Korean language although all had been born and spent their early childhood in South Korea.

When I took the first of my series of trips to Pyongyang, all of my children began to take an interest in their motherland and, when the news media in the United States and South Korea publicized my meeting with President Kim Il Sung in May of 1991, they became aware of their father's role in the history of the country. This awakening interest was intensified when they learned that I, a retired pathologist who had practiced and taught in hospitals in Chicago and Omaha, had been a friend of the renowned President Kim Il Sung of North Korea. They wanted to meet him and were eagerly looking forward to going to Pyongyang for my 80th birthday party.

Dr. Kim Jong Hwan and Mrs. Kong Tal Hwa, my in-laws who were natives of North Korea, were also making preparations to visit Pyongyang. When we heard that the president had died, the plans for my birthday celebration were imperiled. Everyone put aside their hopes for a pleasant sightseeing journey to Pyongyang and a number of them asked me what to do about the plane tickets they had already purchased. The best course to follow, I decided, was to go to Pyongyang and discuss the problem with Mr. Kang Suk Sung.

When Kim Jong Il was told that the people who had planned to come already had purchased their air fare, he said that all of them should be assured they would be welcomed in Pyongyang even though the country would still be observing a period of mourning for President Kim Il Sung. Responding to that advice, most of them had arrived shortly afterward; they were followed a few days later by my in-laws and my sons and daughter. All received a cordial reception from North Korean officials.

Everyone in our party had expressed a desire to go on a sightseeing tour to the Myohyang and Kumgang mountains and to climb Mt. Paektu but, because I had enjoyed that tour previously and wanted to reminisce quietly on events of my friendship with the president, I decided that I wouldn't go along with them. However, the officials in charge of the tour insisted that Yoo Shin and I accompany them. Realizing that they were only trying to ease our sorrow, we were unable to refuse.

It was very foggy on the day we toured the Kumgang Mountains. After lunch, we climbed the slopes near our lodge to get an eagle's eye view of the Manmulsang valley. The rock formations are very interesting archaeological specimens and rewarded us for the climb but the fog was so dense we could only hear, but not see, the stream meandering on its course far below. Later, while we were climbing Samson Rocks, the fog began to clear off and we could see, illuminated by shafts of sunlight, some strangely-shaped rocks that resembled three fairies. Far below in the distance, we could see the East Sea of Korea.

As we began our decent, the fog moved in again, denser than before, and we experienced great difficulty finding stones to step down upon safely. Fortunately, we were able to make our way downward without mishap but

I had an eerie feeling that the deceased president had been guiding our footsteps.

We later toured the world-famous Myohyang Mountains and viewed Mt. Paektu from an aircraft placed at our disposal by Kim Jong Il. The weather enfolding Mt. Paektu is said to be at its most inclement and capricious during the rainy season. Some people have made the tour by airplane and returned from their tour without having been able to see Lake Chon (Heavenly Lake) because the weather hadn't cleared up even after they had waited a number of days for the sun to appear. Fortunately for us, on the day when our party climbed the mountain, the skies were so clear we could see for miles in every direction.

Despite the pleasures of the tour, I began to be concerned because my birthday was approaching nearer day by day. Without a doubt, a man's 80th birthday is one of the most important to be celebrated in his lifetime because he cannot be sure that he will be around for another. Nevertheless, I began to feel that my 80th birthday didn't merit a celebration under the present circumstances. I even made a point of emphasizing that perhaps I shouldn't be observing it with festivities at all on this visit. However, I soon discovered that preparations were already underway for a celebration of grand proportions.

I had explained to people in charge that because I hold Kim Sung Ju as my brother from our days in Jilin and was in mourning for him, it did not seem proper for me to celebrate my birthday.

"We understand you," they said. But I could not influence their planning.

Several days before my birthday, I told my hosts that I would like to visit Kangso, my father's native place, for a few days. One of them chuckled, saying, "Are you planning to escape somewhere else? Our country is not as large as the United States so there is no place you can hide. You can go to Kangso and return here in a single day."

"If you are determined to host my birthday party, please make it simple without much publicity," I said, finally realizing that my reticence was accomplishing little or nothing.

My 80th birthday occurred on August 11, 1994. I arose early and went for a stroll. The trees and grasses were verdant and the air was moist and fresh. I was deep in thought as I strolled through the calming coolness of the woods and my mind strayed back to those birthdays when my mother would prepare my favorite morsel: rice cakes stuffed with bean jam. Father had always been away from home so I have no memory of celebrating my birthdays with him. After our marriage, Yoo Shin always expressed her affection for me in some special way on my birthdays. On this morning,

My 80th Birthday Celebrated in Pyongyang

in far-away Pyongyang, she had followed me out of the lodge and handed me a freshly-cut flower. "Happy birthday, my dear," she said warmly.

We had just finished breakfast when a man came to our house and ushered us into the drawing room on the first floor. Yoo Shin and I were amazed to find a large basket, as tall as me, filled with varieties of rare fruits, piled one upon another. Around the basket were a number of gifts from the late President Kim Il Sung and Leader Kim Jong Il. Tied to the fruit basket with a ribbon was this note: "Congratulations on your 80th birthday, Sohn Won Tai." The messenger also delivered a jeweled picture entitled: "A Pine tree and Cranes." It portrayed seven cranes perched among the branches and an eighth, with its wings spread, soaring in to join them. Under the picture was a card which said, "On the 80th birthday of Comrade Sohn Won Tai, August 11, 1994, Kim Il Sung."

I was told that the president had prepared his gifts the day before he passed away and I shed tears, realizing anew the affection which he held for me.

Yoo Shin and I also were given platinum watches by Kim Il Sung. The basket of fruit was a gift from Kim Jong Il.

That evening we went to the Mokran House to attend my 80th birthday party. The Mokran House, situated in the city center of Pyongyang, is a world-class banquet hall which is famous for its splendid architectural design. The DPRK government arranges official banquets there for distinguished foreign guests perhaps several times a year. Nearly 500 guests, representing the various social levels of Pyongyang, had been invited to my birthday party. Included, of course, were all of the people from the United States and my near and distant relatives who were living in Pyongyang and other areas of North Korea.

Respecting the wishes of the late president, and authorized by Kim Jong Il, government officials in attendance included Vice President Ri Jong Ok, Chairman Yang Hyong Sop of the Standing Committee of the Supreme People's Assembly, Vice-Premier Jang Chol of the Administration Council, and others in high positions. Among special guests were Mrs. Yu Mi Yong, widow of the late Choe Tok Sin, and Mrs. Ryo Yon Gu, daughter of the late Mr. Ryo Un Hyong.

Amid warm congratulations from the high-ranking officials, I was ushered to the top seat as the host of the grand banquet. First Vice-President Ri Jong Ok, rising to introduce me, told the banqueters that my 80th birthday table had been prepared according to the wishes of President Kim Il Sung. He expressed his belief that I would always treasure my friendship with the late president and he hoped that I would enjoy a long life in good health.

August 11, 1994: my 80th birthday party given by the late President Kim Il Sung at Mokran House in Pyongyang. The General Secretary, Kim Jong Il, greeted my birthday with baskets of fruit, flowers, and birthday cake.

When I took the floor to make a formal reply, I was so moved that my throat choked up and I couldn't speak for a few moments. Then I was able to recreate for the audience my recollection of the president's affection for me in those early days in Jilin and his repeated care and concern for me since we were reunited after sixty years of separation. I expressed the grief I felt over the bereavement of "my brother" and then I pointed out that, thanks to the late President Kim Il Sung and to Leader Kim Jong Il, I was being accorded such a warm welcome and the great privilege of occupying the seat of honor. I said that I had done nothing for the nation to deserve such treatment but would dearly cherish my friendship with the president for the rest of my life and I promised to dedicate myself to do everything possible to benefit the nation in return for the gracious treatment extended to me on this occasion.

The audience, which had been listening to me in silence for the most part, applauded at this point. They had held back their tears for me as I faltered at emotional moments as I thought how good it would have been if the president were there to enjoy the party. It seemed that everyone wanted to congratulate me sincerely: high-ranking officials, some renowned scholars, writers and artists, and others from various walks of Korean life who had come to raise a toast to me. One poet rose to his feet to recite a congratulatory poem he had written for my 80th birthday and then, at the request of a large group at the party, I sang an old song that I used to sing with Kim Sung Ju back in those days in Jilin.

But for the current circumstances, the famous Pochonbo Electronic Ensemble or the Wangjaesan Light Music Band would have been brought in to provide professional artistic song and dance entertainment, but this was too solemn and grave an occasion.

I felt a sense of guilt along with my elation. How could I, knowing the concerns besetting the whole country, be flushing with pleasure and pride while receiving congratulations from all these people? How could I, who had not shed one drop of blood as a freedom fighter or handled a single brick in its reconstruction efforts, be entitled to this adulation?

Needless to point out, all of the plaudits came my way only because I was an old friend of the president and was the son of the Rev. Sohn Jong Do whom Kim Il Sung praised as the savior of his life. Therefore I was regarded as a close friend by all of the people who revered the president as their country's father.

His last wish that this be done was being carried out faithfully so that the affection he felt for me could be expressed for him through their kindness to me.

25

Leader Kim Jong Il

I heard the following story related to the birthday party: Toward the end of July, Kim Jong Il had asked an official of the History Institute of the Central Workers' Party of Korea what was being done about plans for Mr. Sohn's birthday party, even though President Kim Il Sung had passed away. He was told that the president had talked about hosting it a number of times but it had been presumed that it might be improper to go ahead with arrangements so soon after the national funeral observances.

Kim Jong Il replied that the matter should not be looked at from that point of view but rather they should go ahead with arrangements on an even grander scale because that would be how to properly carry out the president's last wishes. He said that the party should not be limited to a family affair but should be held in the Mokran House and be attended by people representing all social levels of Pyongyang in the manner of an important national function.

Newspapers of Pyongyang, including the *Rodong Sinmun*, radio and television stations reported that on August 11 a grand party had been held in the Mokran House to mark the 80th birthday of Sohn Won Tai, a lifetime friend of President Kim Il Sung. While a birthday party for an individual during the time of mourning for the national funeral might seem to be inappropriate, Kim Jong Il announced that it had been arranged on such a grand scale because that had been the wish of the late president.

They say that a drop of water mirrors the universe. I was deeply moved by Kim Jong Il's benevolence, especially because it revealed the ennobling filial respect he showed for his father by carrying out his last wishes in this manner. I was also moved by the realization that Kim Jong Il had inherited his father's ideological, spiritual and leadership qualities.

I think that going through with Kim Il Sung's wishes to host a grand party for me just a month after the national funeral was especially meaningful because it demonstrated to the world that the president's ideology, his sense of virtue in government conduct and his philosophical teachings would continue to serve as guidelines for the future of North Korea; it also might well have been an indication that no changes in the country's social and governmental structure could be expected to occur. In this sense, President Kim Il Sung had become immortal and continues to lead his people by the examples he has left as his memorial to them.

As I mentioned earlier in these memoirs, Kim Il Sung was the patriot who took up arms to lead independence fighters when the destiny of Korea was at stake; he fought in the forests of Mt. Paektu and the wilderness regions of Manchuria more than fifteen years, eating and sleeping in the open while braving almost insurmountable difficulties. His exploits brought him recognition as a legendary hero so it seemed logical and natural that the nation, newly liberated from the yoke of occupation, would turn to him for leadership when endeavoring to build a new and independent democratic society which would embrace the ideals and traditions those freedom forces fought to preserve. Those ideals and traditions formed the foundation for the independent and prosperous North Korea which Kim Il Sung fostered in the post-liberation period. Unfortunately, a quite different scenario was played out in South Korea where pro–Japanese collaborators and many outright traitors maintained control of the government and pursued different or ambiguous traditions as the basis for government policy.

I felt, after the death of Kim Il Sung, that Kim Jong Il would be best able or take charge of carrying on his father's policies; he had been groomed for that responsibility for many years in various responsible subordinate positions and, in North Korea, the procedures for succession of leadership have been the mainstay of governmental policy for half a century.

I went for a stroll with my wife on Chollima Street along the Pothong River one afternoon. Cryptomerias, growing on both sides of the street, provided cool shade on the warm days of summer. This tree has a sleek trunk and cone-shaped green leaves. It grows rapidly to a great height and its high-quality wood has high commercial value. The species became virtually extinct on the northern hemisphere of the world several thousand years ago and in most areas it is found only as fossil remains. I was very surprised, therefore, to see these trees growing verdantly along the streets of Pyongyang.

Mr. Choe, an official of the National History Institute, had provided the story of Cryptomeria trees of Pyongyang when I had expressed admiration for their scenic beauty and shade value as street plantings. He said this particular species is indigenous to the basin area of the Yangtze River in China. A potted Cryptomeria seedling had been brought as a gift to General Kim Il Sung by the commander of the Chinese People's Volunteers unit which was sent to the front during the Korea War.

When informed that this was a very rare species, General Kim Il Sung nurtured it with care, possibly sheltering it in his operations room of the Supreme Headquarters of the North Korean forces. Even while engaged in defending his country against opposing forces, Kim Il Sung had been looking to the future when the mountain forests, then being destroyed by enemy bombing and shelling, could be restored. He entrusted the potted seedling to forestry specialists along with instructions to nurture it and from its seeds produce seedlings for planting throughout the country. That single potted seedling parented thick new forests throughout North Korea, Mr. Choe said, adding that "This species of tree is another legacy left behind for The People by the President."

Just as Chryptomeria trees adorning the streets of Pyongyang are an example of the care President Kim Il Sung practiced for the people of North Korea, I don't feel it is necessary that I dwell at length on the country-wide evidence of his handiwork as a leader. That would have to include the reconstruction of urban and rural cities and villages, the monumental edifices, the factories and the farms; in fact, the restoration of North Korea, rising out of the debris left by the bombs of enemy warplanes and the shells of its ground forces, was an amazing accomplishment!

Everything in present-day North Korea — its independent industry, a revitalized rural economy, a strong defense capability, and the high level of national culture — was developed under the creative and painstaking leadership of the late President Kim Il Sung. The socialist country, the Party organization and the armed forces of North Korea are his creations.

The North Korean people treasure the spiritual and material developments brought into being during his lifetime; these are the things he had wished for his people; these are the fruits bettering everyone's life; these comprise the common property of the society which can be bequeathed to succeeding generations.

North Koreans desire, I have observed, that the gifts which Kim Il Sung laid at their feet be passed on to their posterity, unchanged. I also believe that Kim Jong Il can defend and add luster to those treasures. This belief is based on the evidence that he is a man of sincere filial piety and of unfailing loyalty and obligation to the late president's ideologies and virtues. In fact, to many North Koreans, Kim Jong Il appears to be a replica of President Kim Il Sung in remarkable ways.

I learned the truth of matters easily and quickly, not from long explanations nor through the experience of many years of life in North Korea. It seems to be a natural and logical conclusion to be reached if a man takes an unbiased view of the political life and social climate of North Korea as well as the spiritual world and attitudes of its people.

A few things that I observed have confirmed for me that Kim Jong Il's accession to the political helm in North Korea was, to a degree, preordained by recognition by the people of certain of his inborn traits which make outstanding political leadership possible. On my first visit to Pyongyang, I became aware that people respected Kim Jong Il almost as highly as Kim Il Sung, a feeling that was rooted deeply in their respect for the president. Some people might not understand this; they might deprecatingly refer to it as a form of hereditary succession typical of royal dynasties. However, it should be pointed out that North Korea had three more years during national mourning for Kim Il Sung in which to evaluate Kim Jong Il before choosing to elevate him to his new status as their president and chairman of the defense operations.

After World War II, Jawaharlal Nehru assumed power in India; later, his daughter, Indira Gandhi, succeeded him as prime minister. When she was assassinated, her son, Rajiv Gandhi, served as prime minister of India until he became the victim of a suicidal assassin's bomb. A similar political phenomenon occurred in Pakistan. Some time after the overthrow of Prime Minister Zulfikar Ali Bhutto, his wife became prime minister and, eventually, his daughter, Benazir Bhutto, also was chosen to serve as Pakistan's prime minister. No one has called India's political period a "Nehru dynasty" or the Bhutto family's dominance in Pakistan a "Bhutto dynasty"; nor has either coincidence been called an example of hereditary succession as was the situation in countries ruled by royal families in the historical past before the advent of present-day democracy. Yet, strangely enough, both India and Pakistan have enjoyed cordial diplomatic and economic relations with the United States despite their own continuing territorial conflicts.

Kim Il Sung was an outstanding man, as impartial historians will acknowledge, just as they have acknowledged that the Nehru and Gandhi descendents brought excellent leadership and progress to India and the members of the Bhutto family brought a high quality of leadership to Pakistan.

In Kim Jong Il, North Koreans exalt the high virtues and capabilities that his father's leadership brought to the country. He has gained the people's trust and great popularity by his loyalty to the independence movement's goals and the political qualifications he has displayed during his many years of responsible public service under the guidance of his father and other officials of North Korea.

Even before being chosen supreme political and military leader of North Korea in 1997, three years after his father's demise, Kim Jong Il had demonstrated in both domestic affairs and international diplomatic areas his capabilities to represent the interests of the Korean peninsular nation. I believe that Kim Jong Il holds fast to the Juche philosophy on which Kim Il Sung based the resurrection of North Korea from the devastation wrought by the Japanese occupation and the Korean War.

The political diplomacy involving high-level state relations with the United States, Japan, the Soviet Union and China has been exacting. North Korea has been alleged to be under the influence of the Soviet Union but it should be recorded with emphasis that North Korea was not a participant in the Warsaw Pact Alliance or in COMECON, the Communist economic alignment. It has pursued the long-held freedom movement policy of maintaining strict independence in its relations with all powers.

Had North Korea restricted itself to seeking minimal indemnification from Japan, relations with that country might have improved to some extent, but Kim Il Sung kept his focus on fundamental issues in all negotiations with the major powers. Fortunately, during the interim of three years before Kim Jong Il was elected as head of state, there was no vacuum in diplomacy because he held firmly to the policies covering fundamental national interests laid down by Kim Il Sung during his lifetime.

Kim Jong Il gained great power for the manner in which he functioned as leader of the Worker's Party of Korea through almost 30 years of the Korean revolution. Among his talents is knowledgeability in literature, the arts, engineering, architecture and political economy. He played a major role in planning the reconstruction of Pyongyang—for example, in the Kwangbok and Thongil projects, where his knowledge of architecture is reflected by the magnificent monuments, public buildings and housing complexes. He has been able to guide the people of North Korea into ideological and spiritual unity. Among other things, he is an acknowledged military strategist and has deployed the manpower of the defense department into many civilian tasks in the reconstruction and development of the country, including sea control barrages, river and land reclamation projects, all of them utilizing the military in a peacetime role to work with civilians in efforts to build a greater North Korea.

I have noticed during my visits from 1991 through 1994 that everything in North Korea is clean and pure. Water and air are fresh and clean and the people reflect this unstained purity in their dress, their manners and their ideology. Pyongyang displays this slogan everywhere: "Single-hearted Unity." There is no need to explain that slogan at great length; it is obvious to observe how much it has achieved merely by strolling through the streets of the city.

While visiting the International Friendship Exhibition on a tour in the Myohyang Mountains, I was drawn into introspection. The many highly valuable gifts that had been presented to Kim Il Sung over the years all have been given to the nation and are displayed there; so are the many presents that have been given to Kim Jong Il. Just as his father considered that gifts to him rightfully belonged to the North Korean people, so does his son believe that gifts to the nation's leader are national treasures to be shared by the people of the country. I have come to realize that Kim Jong Il has enjoyed high respect and popularity form his early years, not just in Korea but among distinguished figures throughout the world.

In some countries, presidents have been criticized and ridiculed for retaining gifts received during their term of office, considering them assets to be included in their estates. In some cases, parliaments have impeached officials or caused them to resign under such circumstances. How totally different is the morality displayed by Kim Il Sung and Kim Jong Il! That is another reason that the Korean people call Kim Jong Il a second General Kim Il Sung.

When I heard that President Kim Il Sung had died I felt that the heavens were falling down and I assumed that I could not go to Pyongyang any more. I had never thought of Pyongyang without Kim Il Sung to greet me and be my host. I overcame that initial reaction and criticized myself for having such a narrow-minded outlook. Then I realized that perhaps I knew too little about Kim Il Sung's son and wasn't giving him credit for recognizing the intimate relationship that had existed between his father and me. After the president's death in 1994, I did go to Pyongyang on several occasions and I plan to return again and again to visit Kim Jong Il to enjoy his friendship as long as my health permits.

26

For Eternal Friendship

When I went to Pyongyang on the second occasion, President Kim Il Sung arranged a luncheon party for me. He said: "Let's toast to our eternal friendship!" We clinked glasses and, in a gulp, I emptied my glass which was brimming over with affection and friendship. The wine warmed my heart. "To our eternal friendship!" How beautiful and moving, how meaningful that phrase is! Since that moment I have always cherished in my mind the profound and cordial meaning of those four words. As pleasant sounding as a silver bell, his expression continues to prompt me to remain true to his fine ideals. When Kim Il Sung passed away, those words filled my mind with special meaning and renewed my appreciation for the extraordinary friendship that existed between us.

Respecting a great man is a natural human response. I think it has been an unparalleled honor, as well as a source of great happiness, for me to have had a relationship with President Kim Il Sung over so many years of my lifetime. During periods of quiet meditation in evening or idle hours, I now think back on those early boyhood days when I was drawn to him, and our friendship took root strongly enough to bridge the separation until we met again. I still find myself seeking a deeper, more significant meaning that our friendship might have served in Korea's search for independence and reunification.

In Jilin, both of us were the offspring of freedom fighters who were exiled from their ruined and occupied country; both of us were miserable as boys who were being shuffled around in an alien land.

I am reminded of the empathy we shared for freedom fighters:

> Don't blow, ye wind.
> Our men, shivering with cold in Manchuria,
> Think about their motherland
> When ye blow hard.

That was one of the patriotic songs sung by Kim Sung Ju, Won Yil and me and all of the members of the Association of Korean Children of Jilin. It was filled with nostalgia, reflecting the mental torment of those freedom fighters who struggled at great sacrifice to win back their country. By singing that song we cultivated our spirit of patriotism while still youngsters, dedicating ourselves to defending the soul of the occupied Korean nation.

The friendship between us was nurtured by nostalgia and yearning for our native places in the motherland. Sons and daughters of a ruined nation, we joined together out of common resentment and our friendships became bonded by the mutual ardent love for our Korean heritage. It was a friendship that was born of and consolidated by our patriotism.

One establishes relationships with many people in a lifetime. In my case, I have enjoyed friendships with pupils in the middle school in Jilin, students at the Chinese universities that I attended in Beijing, Suzhou and Shanghai, and pre-med students and interns at Severance Medical College in Seoul. Many of my teachers have added their friendship to my life experience and I also have a considerable number of good friends in the United States. However, I can never forget those friends of my days in Jilin because our friendship there was fused together tightly by our burning patriotism.

The youth movement in Jilin was led by Kim Sung Ju, who later became commander of the Independence Army guerrillas and brought fear and trembling and defeat to Japanese imperialist armies in both Manchuria and Korea in his continuing fight for liberation of the motherland. Although I would not meet him again for a long time after our parting in Jilin, I followed his activities with an interest that grew more intense with each report that I read or heard about new successes in the battlefield. My feeling of friendship, born in Jilin, developed into veritable worship as Kim Sung Ju, now known as General Kim Il Sung, became a legendary hero in the struggle for Korea's freedom. How else could I describe the respect and admiration I felt for this man, destined to become President Kim Il Sung, who had dedicated his entire life from early boyhood with patriotic resolve to liberate his country from Japanese oppression and lead it to reunification.

When I learned that Kim Il Sung had become the leader of the northern half of the liberated nation and was building a new society based on his philosophical and ideological beliefs, my reverence for him grew more fervent. My observations had been beyond arm's length for more than six decades because I had no opportunity to see him during all of that time. Therefore, as I have mentioned previously, when I eventually did leave my home in Omaha to travel to Pyongyang, I was filled with anxiety. I never had expected to be accorded more than a respectful reception; in fact, I would have been satisfied just to learn that he had not forgotten me, even if that meant merely recalling me as "that small youngster in the yesterdays" of his memory.

I had no reason to be apprehensive, however. From the first moment of my arrival in Pyongyang, I was treated as if I was the closest friend of the president; in fact, as if I were as an important guest of the state. At the time, I did wonder how long such royal treatment would continue, but it grew warmer and more sincere as the days passed. When I left the United States, my understanding of what lay ahead for me had been unclear. Now, in retrospect, I feel that my arrival in Pyongyang was like entering a paradise!

This reception was the first experience of its kind in my life. People have been eager to know why President Kim Il Sung loved me and took care of me so lavishly. Some have asked if he had a covert political motive behind doing this for me. I assumed that such a question might arise from a lack of understanding about my relationship with him as well as from a complete ignorance about the character of President Kim Il Sung.

I am not a man who went to North Korea after serving in an important post in the army and government of South Korea, like Mr. Choe Tok Sin; nor am I a man who had been imprisoned for involvement in any of those so-called North-controlled organizations, like Mr. Yun Isang. I am an old man who is living his remaining years on pension and savings after working as an ordinary medical doctor. I have remained largely ignorant about politics, even in the United States. How then could I be of benefit, politically or otherwise, to President Kim Il Sung other than as a friend?

When meeting with me, the president never initiated talk about political issues nor did he dwell on his many struggles and achievements, although I believe his role in the anti–Japanese struggle and the rebuilding of North Korea certainly merits some prideful reminiscing. Standards of appraisal may vary but no one can demean his great achievement for the North Korean nation as its president. Yet, whenever I mentioned something outstanding that he had done, he would change the subject and turn our conversation to other affairs. For example: One time when I remarked that he must have endured some difficult times, he turned to other matters, after commenting, "Of course, I experienced hardships; if I say that I haven't, then it is a lie."

Kim Il Sung made no attempt to discuss political issues with me but I once told him that some politicians in the United States were interested in using my "influence" to enable them to visit Pyongyang and meet with President Kim Il Sung. To that, he had responded, "It will not be bad if you introduce good American people to me. Then I will have many friends in the United States."

The closest top political commentary the president made to me were his observations that North Korea's productivity could be strengthened substantially if more electricity could be generated where it now is in short supply; and where paddy and other food grain fields in the lowlands are flooded by heavy rainfall, much crop damage will be prevented when planned drainage projects are completed.

He was well-informed on world politics and was especially familiar with economic statistics. Having a deep insight into the political and economic realities of his country, he would respond with clear-cut answers to any questions put to him. One man who was present while I was talking with the president told me that he had been very impressed by Kim Il Sung's unusual memory and his ability to recall factual data. He said that he was equally amazed that the president could involve himself personally in so much of the on-going affairs of state. The president's ability to quote statistics in detail brought comments of admiration from others as well, such as: "He's a walking encyclopedia."

In our meetings, however, the president was just a kind-hearted big brother to me. Concerned about my health, he once advised me to have a general medical checkup. During one of our chats, he said that he believed a person should remain self-controlled and dignified during a discussion and always guard against becoming "loose-tongued." "People in ancient times said that calamity comes out of the mouth, much like an illness is spread through the mouth," he said.

Our relationship was not one between the leader of a country and a common-place medical doctor; it was like the human bonding that exists between brothers.

If a DPRK agency had entertained plans to use me as a "political card," how could I, or any man of my temperament, be permitted to visit Pyongyang so often? I am not worth the effort! I feel quite certain that I have done nothing helpful or beneficial to Kim Il Sung politically or economically prior to my decision to write my memoirs and portray the real character of my friend. On the other hand, I trust I have done nothing disadvantageous to him.

For many years, wherever I was living, I avidly followed developments in Korea's armed resistance against Japan, but even after the division of Korea into north and south by the foreign powers following the World War II defeat of Japan and the Korean War, I had done nothing of benefit for him.

I practiced pathology in hospitals in the United States some 36 years until I retired in 1986. My financial situation is a comfortable one but it doesn't permit me to travel abroad as much as I would desire. I also have not been in a position to build a residence in Pyongyang or anywhere else in North Korea.

Several of my trips to Pyongyang were in connection with "pro bono" inspection and counseling during the construction and equipping of Pyongyang Third Hospital. Someone spread a rumor that it was the "Sohn Won Tai Hospital" and was being built with funds donated by me. That was, of course, not a true story.

Is there anything that I have done that has been helpful to Kim Il Sung? No, there is nothing! As is well known, my brother Won Yil was the defense minister of South Korea during the Syngman Rhee regime. This undoubtedly could have given President Kim Il Sung a bad impression of me in view of the serious political and military confrontation that existed between the North and the South. How than could President Kim Il Sung show such affection for me?

A man who was assigned to escort me in some of my tours in North Korea told me this story: President Kim Il Sung had asked another official if he thought I was well-informed about politics.

"Sohn Won Tai doesn't appear to be ignorant of politics but he certainly doesn't have much interest in political matters," that official responded.

"You are right; he is not well-versed in politics but he is a man of integrity," the president had said, adding, "Although he has lived in America for many years, he hasn't been stained. He is as honest and simple as he was in his days in Jilin."

From that brief dialogue, one can understand completely why he loved me so. He treasured my unstained integrity and expected only friendship from me. My conjecture is that he showed such affection for me mainly because he knew that I treasured friendship of our days in Jilin and had returned to Pyongyang yearning to renew it, even though we were living in political systems that were contradictory. Our friendship in Jilin was not an ordinary one; it was generated by pure patriotism and our exceptional mutual love for the motherland.

I have met many people in my life but only President Kim Il Sung

Members of the Christian Association for Medical Missions after visiting Pyongyang Third Hospital, October 26, 1992. *Left to right:* Sai Rok Park, M.D., Myung Kyu Yoon, M.D., Samuel Song, M.D., Ph.D., Won Tai Sohn, M.D., and Choon Soo Rim, M.D.

recognized my unshakable integrity. Some people have viewed my simple honesty with scorn but Kim Il Sung treasured, more than gold or jewels, a man's integrity and spirit of patriotism in this turbulent world.

Every man reaches a time to sum up the worth of his life. Whether he lives at the North Pole or the South Pole, a man must be measured in judgment in front of the great mother of mankind, his motherland. I appraised the value of my life only after I had met with President Kim Il Sung again in Pyongyang.

I am convinced that my meetings with President Kim Il Sung, occurring late in our lifespans, were my greatest personal achievement and my most inspiring and exalting experience. It became the symbol of the human value of my own life. One who has been separated from his homeland doesn't expect to enjoy noble and beautiful love or friendship, nor can he expect his life to have true value or worthiness.

However, I want to try to interpret my thoughts on the true meaning of the President's words, "eternal friendship," in this way: It was a friendship linked directly with the motherland; it was an eternal love for the motherland and for its heritage. Since Kim Il Sung passed away, I frequently have thought about what I should do, how I should live and what

Dr. and Mrs. Won Tai Sohn at Yon Sei University College of Medicine Alumni Seminar — August, 1995.

I might do to honor our "eternal friendship." At such times, I am reminded of what he had said to me on another occasion: "I wish everyone would live in harmony; everything goes well only then. So I say to my son: 'Everything goes well only when families are full of harmony.'"

Characteristic of Kim Il Sung's political philosophy was his continuing effort to achieve such harmony by leading the people into a national family relationship with their president as its father. I fervently wish for harmony between the North and the South of my motherland. What prevents the realization of harmony is misunderstanding, distrust and narrow ways of thinking. Misunderstanding and distrust often result from ignorance about each other.

I have made up my mind to devote my remaining years to efforts to eliminate this misunderstanding and distrust. One man said that I have become the chief propagandist for Kim Il Sung. I will perform that duty with pleasure. I will say with my own voice, whether it be heard or unheard, what I have seen, heard and felt as the result of my friendly relations with President Kim Il Sung and, more recently, with his son, Kim Jong Il. Realizing that this is the final duty I can perform for my motherland, the country of my birth, I will conclude the portion of my memoirs that recalls my close friendship with Kim Il Sung (the Kim Sung Ju of those days in Jilin) at this point.

27
My Brother, Won Yil, Is Memorialized

I would like to conclude my memoirs with a report of the memorial honors conferred upon my elder brother, the late Admiral Sohn Won Yil, as well as a brief backward glance at the ancient historical relationship between Korea and Japan as revealed by the recent work of two Japanese scholars.

My wife and I flew to South Korea in November of 1997 to be present when a bronze statue of Admiral Sohn Won Yil was unveiled to commemorate his 52 years of service to his country and founder and leader of the Korean Navy.

The dedication ceremony and the unveiling of the statue was performed at the South Korean Navy Headquarters at Jinhae in the southeastern province of Kyung Sang Nam Do. Yoo Shin and I had flown to Seoul from the United States and then took a flight to Jinhae on October 11, 1997. The head of naval operations presided at the unveiling which took place at the site where Won Yil had founded the naval organization, beginning with the Coast Guard and then developing into the Navy and Marines as well. The bronze statue is 3.6 meters tall and stands on a base which is 3 meters high.

The memorial address noted that Admiral Sohn Won Yil's ancestors in Korea date back some 1500 years to the family of Prince Im in Paek Jae,

The statue of Admiral Won Yil Sohn, dedicated in October of 1997, at the Jinhae Naval Base, South Korea.

the southern part of modern Korea. The family became the Samurai who controlled Yamakuchi Ken province in Japan. The official plaudits read by the head of the admiralty noted that "the late Admiral Sohn Won Yil had established the South Korean Navy and Marines 55 years ago" and "all of his life he had dedicated himself to the country and the Navy." In order to inspire continuation of the high quality of his service, the admiral said, the statue was erected at Chin Hae Navy Headquarters in recognition of those great contributions to the Korean nation.

Additionally, a stone marker has been placed at the original naval base site with an appropriate memorial inscription to remind people about Admiral Sohn's legendary service to the country. Many retired navy personnel contributed to the memorial effort. I humbly ask the reader's indulgence for my feelings of pride and exultation that my elder brother has received such adulation and recognition as a national hero from the South Korean defense department and the South Korean government.

Admiral Sohn had served as defense minister during President Syngman Rhee's administration and for a time had been South Korea's ambassador to Germany. Earlier in my memoirs I have mentioned examples of his intense patriotic loyalty to South Korea.

I have read with great interest excerpts from reports on the works of two Japanese scholars in which a relationship between Korean and Japanese social structures is propounded. Professor Namio Egami of Tokyo University has been quoted in the *News Review* issue of December 3, 1977, as stating that he believes the equestrians of Korea conquered Japan in the fourth century. Yasushi Inoue, Japanese novelist and one-time chairman of the Japanese PEN Center, acknowledged in Tokyo, while promoting the sale of his book being published in Korea, that he believed that all Japanese cultures had been introduced from Korea.

Professor Egami, 71, lecturing about the ancient equestrian rulers of Korea and Japan at the first International Symposium sponsored by the Institute of Korean Studies at Yonsei University, said that the descendents of Chinwang, equestrian ruler of the Samhan Kingdom of remote ancient times in Korea, had played an essential role in the formation of the ancient Japanese kingdoms in the fourth and early fifth centuries.

Professor Egami is a specialist in archaeology, history and folklore of oriental countries. In 1948, he had shocked academic circles in Japan by stating that the forefathers of Japanese emperors were the Korean Horsemen of the Koguryo (37 B.C. to 668) and Paekje (18 B.C. to 660) kingdoms. Until Professor Egami had conjectured differently, most Japanese historians had believed that their nation's culture had originated uniquely within Japan.

Top: In the summer of 1952 my brother (second from the left) visited the United States Navy. Names of the other two officers are unknown. *Bottom:* Second from the left is my brother Adm. Won Yil Sohn, Chief of Staff of the South Korean Navy.

The professor's subsequent research covered the Huns of Mongolia, the history of Asian culture and the archaeology of the Orient. He told the International Symposium audience that he had learned that the nomadic people of the Mongolian region initially had emerged as a threat to the peace of neighboring kingdoms as early as 1,000 B.C. Because they could fight well on horseback, they earned the name of equestrians.

The nomads who reached the southern part of the Korean peninsula became the people of the Puyo and Koguryo Kingdoms and, he said, the equestrians of the Paekje Kingdom reached the northern area of Kyushu, Japan, by way of Tsushima Island. They conquered ancient Japan and ruled under Emperors Sujin and Ojin. After expanding their hold on the Nara area, they established the Yamamoto regime which became the most competent ancient state in Japan, Professor Egami has concluded.

Yasushi Inoue, 79, speaking in Tokyo on May 27, 1997, at a promotional meeting to mark the publication of his novel, *The Wind Waves*, said that because "nearly all Japanese culture was introduced from Korea" the Japanese people should rethink the cultural exchange between Korea and Japan. He called for efforts by both sides to recognize each other with open minds. His novel covers the period of the Mongolian invasion of the Koryo Kingdom, describing it from the viewpoint of the Korean people. It has been said that the historical novel is seen as Inoue's attempt to refute the allegations of Japanese historians about Korea's involvement in the Mongolian invasion of Japan.

The Japanese novelist, alluding to old Japanese "sins" against Korea, was quoted as saying: "Those who inflicted damage on others in past history should reflect on themselves." It is most important, he stressed, that the Japanese people "be in the other's shoes" and to step up cultural exchanges before attempting political and economic contacts so that "mutual introduction and research on each other can be expedited."

Chang Pyong-hye, a Korean professor residing in the United States, has spent half a decade translating Inoue's novel into the Korean language. The translation was reviewed by a team of competent linguists to minimize errors.

Index

Ahn, Chang Ho 1, 30, 32, 37, 44, 71, 72, 73, 75, 77, 78, 90, 102, 144, 157, 174
Ahn, Philip 78, 144
Ahn, Sin Ho 78
Albania, invasion of by Italy 89
Amnok River 23, 31, 44, 93, 126
An, Jae Hong 175
An, Jung Gun 61, 62
An, Pung 43
Appenzeller, H.G. 21
Art of War (Sun Tzu) 83
The Association of Korean Children in Jilin 49, 51, 53, 54, 61, 88, 225

Bhutto, Zulfikar Ali 221
Bishop Clarkson Memorial Hospital (Omaha, Nebraska) 146

Carter, President Jimmy 197
Cha, Kwang Su 43
Cha, Ri Sok 25
Chamui-bu independence fighters 73
Chang, Professor Pyong-hye 236
Chiang, Kai-Shek 44, 144, 175
Choe, Chang Gol 43
Choe, Il Chon 82, 83
Choe, Jin Hyok 30, 126, 148
Choe, Man Young 73, 74, 75

Choe, Pyong Hon 21
Choe, Sang Soon 195
Choe, Tok Sin 2, 123, 157, 215, 226
Choe, Tong O 35, 37, 44, 134, 175
Choe, Ye Sun 106
Choe, Youngho 22, 118
Chongqing (China) 175
Choy, Sun Hak 102
Christian Association for Medical Missions (CAMM) 17, 170–173, 193
Clinton, President Bill 197
COMECON (Council for Mutual Economic Cooperation) 162, 222

Dagongbao (newspaper) 86, 89–96
Deng, Xiaoping 195
Dong Bei University (Fengtian, present-day Shenyang) 92
Dongwu University (Suzhou, China) 89

East Sea of Korea 213
Egami, Professor Namio 234
Ewha Womans University 97, 102

field guidance 167, 173

Gandhi, Indira 221
Gandhi, Rajiv 221

Gettysburg Address 166
Graham, the Reverend Billy 196, 197, 199
Grand People's Study House (Pyongyang) 166, 167

Ha, Ran Sa 31, 73
Hainan Island 89
A History of the Korean Revolutionary Movement Overseas (Choe Il Chon) 82, 83
Hitler, Adolf 162
Hong, Pil Hun 102
Hong, Tong Gun 2, 94, 123
Hungsadan organization 37, 72
Hwang, Kwi Hon 57, 66, 67, 81, 88
Hwashin Department Store (Seoul) 105
Hwasong Uisuk School (Huadian, China) 48
Hyon, Ik Chol (Hyon Muk Kwan) 43, 77
Hyon, Jon Gyong 43
Hyon, Sun 21, 22

Imjin Patriotic War 59
Inove, Yahushi 234
International Friendship Exhibition 172
Ito, Hirobumi 83

Jang, Choi 215
Jang, Chol Ho 43, 45, 49, 54, 69
Japanese occupation, Nanjing, China 89
Jiangzi Guoje 68
Jinhae Navy Headquarters 232
Jo, Min Haeng 102
Jo, So Ang 175
Jo, Son Hwan 30
Jo, Wan Gu 175
Jong, I Hyong 49
Jong, Il Kwon 87
Jongdong Methodist Church (Seoul) 21
Jongui-bu 42, 43, 46, 49, 73, 82
Ju, Yo Han 72
Juche philosophy 8, 162–164, 173

Kang, Sok Sung (Soong) 133, 148, 195, 213
Kang, Xam Chan 59
Kang, Sun Ung 38, 121
Kartman, Charles 171
Katsura, Taro 30

Kim, Ho Mun 97, 98, 145
Kim, Hyong Jik 25, 48, 49, 53, 91, 94
Kim, Hyung Uk (director of Korean CIA) 117
Kim, Il Sung (Kim Sung Ju) 1, 2, 17, 25, 26, 33–35, 40, 41, 45, 47–50, 52–54, 57, 60, 65–70, 74, 77, 78, 81, 83, 86, 88–91, 93, 94, 96, 100, 102, 108, 112, 118, 129, 133, 134, 136, 138, 147, 149, 156, 157, 160–163, 168–170, 173, 175, 176, 178, 179, 185, 194, 196–201, 205–207, 209, 213, 215, 218, 220, 221, 225–229
Kim, Jong Yun 44
Kim, Jong Hwan 213
Kim, Jong Il 1, 136, 156, 207, 208, 213, 215, 218, 219–223
Kim, Kang 88
Kim, Ku (Baek Song) 43
Kim, Ku (Paek Pom) 2, 93, 94, 102
Kim, Kyu Sik 2, 102
Kim, Myong Son 112
Kim, Ri Dae 43, 77
Kim, Song Rak 123
Kim, Yong Ik 171
Kim Jong Suk Nursery 181, 183
Kim Man Yu Hospital (Pyongyang) 172
Kimsusan Assembly Hall 207
Kingjing Military School of Manchukuo 87
Ko, Chan Song 170
Ko, Hwal Sin (Ko Won Am) 37, 43, 44
Koguryo Kingdom 176, 236
Kong, Tal Hwa 213
Korean Democratic Women's Union 78
Korean Red Cross Society 71, 72
Koryo (Kingdom) 176, 179, 236
Kremlin Museum 172
Kumsong Sea Wall 178
Kumsusan Assembly Hall 207, 208
Kwang Kwi Hon 157
Kwangsong Middle School 24
Kye, Sun Hui 63
Kyongsong Ilbo (newspaper) 93
Kyushu 236

Lee, Hak Mo 125
Lee, Hak Sun (pianist) 125
Lee, Jang Chong 45, 49, 75, 90, 95, 96
Lee, Jun 157
Lee, Moo Sung 139
Lee, Myong Yong 114

Index

Lee, Yoo Shin (Mrs. Won Tai Sohn) 24, 106–109, 133, 147, 157, 166, 170, 205, 206, 212–214, 216, 230, 232, 233
Lincoln, President Abraham 166

Manmulsang Valley (North Korea) 213
Mansudae Art Theater (Pyongyang) 212
Mao, Zedong 144
March First Popular Uprising (1919) 22, 25, 31, 191, 192
Maternity Hospital (Pyongyang) 172, 181, 182
Mausoleums of Tangun 176
Methodist church (Jilin, China) 45, 46
Mills College (Berkeley, California) 113
Mitsuya Agreement (1925) 76
Mokran House (Pyongyang) 215, 218
Montesquieu, Denis Diderot 170
Mun, Ik Hwan 199
Myohyang Mountains 65, 149, 157, 172, 214

Nagasaki Prison 97, 98, 100, 146
Nanchang (China) 89
Nehru, Jawaharlal 221
Northwestern University Medical School (Chicago) 38, 113, 146
Novichenko, Ya T. 191, 192
Nunn, Sam (U.S. Senator) 196

Oh, In Hwa 35, 37, 43, 44, 55, 76
Oh, Tong Jin 2, 49, 77, 82, 102
Ojin, Emperor 236
Om, Hang Sop 175
Orini (Korean magazine) 60

Paektu, Mt. 214
Pak, Il Pha 54, 88
Paris Peace Conference 196
Park, Chung Hee 87, 114, 117
Park, Dr. Sai Rok 229
Park, Shin Yil (mother and Mrs. Sohn Jong Do) 23–27, 34, 46, 47, 49, 50, 69
Patriotic Martyrs Cemetery 78, 175
Pochonbo, Battle of 93, 94
Poland, invasion of by Germany 89
Pongsu Church (Pyongyang) 200
Pothong River 24
Price, Colonel 113
Provisional Government (Korean Provisional Government in Shanghai, China) 25, 31, 32
Puyo Kingdom 236
Pyongyang Third Hospital 17, 171, 172, 228, 229

Ra, Sok Ju 73
rainbow trout 197
Rhee, Syngman 2, 87, 112, 144, 174, 228, 234
Ri, Hui Gyong 71
Ri, Jong Ok 215
Ri, Jong Rak 43
Ri, Kang, Prince of Uichin 22
Ri, Kyong Un 46
Ri, Ok Chon 43
Ri, Phil Ju 31
Ri, Pong Chang 175
Ri, General Sun Sin 45, 59, 60
Ri, Tong Hun 43
Ri, Tong Hwa 46
Ri, Tong Son 46, 81, 133
Ri, Ung 43
Richardson, Spence 171
Rim, Dr. Choon Soo 229
Roosevelt, President Theodore 197
Rousseau, Jean-Jacques 170
Russo-Japanese War (1904–1905) 15
Ryang, So Bong (sister of Ahn, Chang Ho) 157
Ryo, Un Hyong 94, 215
Ryo, Yon Gu (daughter of Ryo Un Hyong) 94, 215
Ryu, Jae Myong 158
Ryu, Kum Chong 45
Ryu, Mi Yong (Mrs. General Choe, Tok Shin) 157
Ryugil Association in Jilin 61

Samson Rocks (Kumgang Mountains) 213
San Francisco 113
Sanfeng Inn (Jilin) 43, 46, 50
Severance Medical College 112, 146
Shanghai University 92
Shulman, Dr. 191, 192
Sihanouk, Samdech Norodom 157
Sin, Chae Ho 2, 30, 102
Sin, Il Yong 45
Sin, Kuk kwon 85, 86, 89, 91, 92, 93, 134

Sin, Kwang Son 102
Sin, Kyu Sik 31
Sin, Yong Gun 69
Sinhan Minbo (newspaper) 94
Sinhung Military School 30
Sinmin Association 72
Sinmin-bu independence fighters 73
Sino-Japanese War (1894–1895) 15
Skiakowski, Chester (pianist) 125, 139
So, Jung Sok 45
Sohn, In Sil (younger sister) 24, 27, 28, 32, 36, 39, 44, 46, 57, 66, 67, 69, 70, 86, 97, 101, 110, 114, 132 134, 135, 143
Sohn, Jin Sil (older sister, Mrs. Yun Chi Chang) 26, 36, 37, 39, 85, 97, 101, 104, 146
Sohn, the Rev. Jong Do (father) 1, 2, 16, 17, 21, 28, 29, 31, 33, 34, 35, 38–40, 44, 70, 71, 72, 73, 76, 123, 134, 139, 144, 174, 194
Sohn, Kyung Doh 38, 39
Sohn, Song Sil (older sister) 26, 36, 90, 92, 93
Sohn, Won Yil (older brother) 2, 22–30, 32, 33, 36, 39, 45, 48, 52, 60, 81, 85, 87, 88, 92, 102, 103, 121, 123, 134, 225, 228, 232–235
Sojaedong Guest House (Pyongyang) 126
Song, Samuel S. 15, 171, 229
"Song of the Association of Korean Children in Jilin" 56
Songjon beach 107
Sorok Island 102
Sujin, Emperor 236
Sun, Yat-sen 59, 189
Sungsil School 24, 25, 48
Sunoo, Hak Won 125

Taedong River 157, 176, 177, 178, 181, 193, 197, 199
Taefenghe Rice Mill 37, 46
Taft, William Howard (U.S. Defense Secretary and President) 197
Taft-Katsura Agreement (1905) 15
Tamodu Youth Party 49

Tangun (founder-king of Korea) 176
Taylor, Maxwell 196
Terauchi, Japanese Governor General 30
Tongdaemun Police Station (Seoul) 101
Tongmyong, King (founder of Koguryo) 176
Tower of Juche Idea (Pyongyang) 162
Tsushima Island 236

Ulji, Mun Dok 59

Vladivostok 30
Voltaire 170

Wall Street Journal 139
Wang, Dingnan 161
Wang, Kon (founder of Koryo) 176
Warsaw Pact Alliance 222
Waseda University (Tokyo) 104
West Sea Barrage 162, 176, 177, 178, 197
Wilson, President Woodrow 196

Xangyongdae School Children's Palace (Pyongyang) 181, 183, 185

Yalta Conference (1945) 15
Yamamoto Regime 236
Yang, Hyong Sop 215
Yang, Ki Thaek 49
Yonhui College (Seoul) 92
Yoon, Dr. Myung Kyu 229
Yu, Ok Kyom 101
Yun, Chi Chang 36, 101, 107, 108
Yun, Chi Ho 101
Yun, Isang 226
Yun, Pong Gil 175
Yun, Tong Ju 25

Zhang, Jinquan 190, 191, 192
Zhang, Weihua 190, 192
Zhang, Xueliang 76, 86, 92
Zhang, Xueming 92
Zhang, Zuolin 42, 78, 92, 144
Zhang, Zuoxiang 42, 43, 46, 76, 86
Zhuge Liang tactics 83

www.ingramcontent.com/pod-product-compliance
Ingram Content Group UK Ltd.
Pitfield, Milton Keynes, MK11 3LW, UK
UKHW041940140426
5217IPUK00014B/574